# MONSTER OF THE MIDWAY

Bronko Nagurski, the 1943 Chicago Bears,
and the Greatest Comeback Ever

## JIM DENT

THOMAS DUNNE BOOKS   **M**   ST. MARTIN'S GRIFFIN
NEW YORK

THOMAS DUNNE BOOKS.
An imprint of St. Martin's Press.

MONSTER OF THE MIDWAY. Copyright © 2003 by Jim Dent. Forword © 2003 by Dan Hampton. All rights reserved. Printed in the United States of America. For information. address St. Martin's Press, 175 Fifth Avenue, New York, N.Y. 10010.

www.stmartins.com

Library of Congress Cataloging-in-Publication Data

Dent, Jim.
    Monster of the midway / Jim Dent.
        p. cm.

    ISBN: 978-0-312-30868-1
    ISBN: 0-312-30868-X

    1. Nagurski, Bronko, 1908 -1990.   2. Football players—United States—Biography.
    I. Title.

GV939.N24D46 2003
796.332'092—dc22
[B]

                                                                2003049273

P 1

My father took me to my first football game when I was six years old. It changed my life forever. If not for the great influence my dad had on my life, I would not have written this book or the others before it. That is why this one is dedicated to Jimmy Dent Sr. (March 25, 1918, to August 26, 2002). This is the first one he will miss.

# Author's Note

The greatest source for any book is a living memory. It was an honor to have interviewed Stephanie Nagurski, the sister of Bronko, and Ookie Miller, the Bears All-Pro center from the glory days of the thirties. The reason I mention them first is that they both left this earth before the book was published. I just wish they were around to see it in print.

Stephanie Nagurski authored "The Mini-History of the Nagurski Family," twelve pages of rich information about the family that she passed along to me before her death. It was both a fabulous resource and a treasure. Stephanie once set out to write a book about Bronko but did not find her brother very cooperative. The Bronk simply did not like to talk about his accomplishments. For years, he managed to dodge the dogged writers who tried to pry information out of him. That is why *Monster of the Midway* required so many interviews from the people who knew him best. There are many to thank.

First, the Nagurski "kids"—Bronko Jr., Tony, Janice, Ron, Eugenia, and Kevin. Both Janice and Kevin live in the International Falls area and were quite generous with their time, memories, pictures, and scrapbooks.

Also providing great information from Minnesota were Francis Einar-

son, who was Bronko's pilot, and Lee Bonicatto, the son of Paul Bonicatto, a wrestling promoter and great longtime friend of the Bronk's.

The living Bears who supplied recollections of the era and its people
are Ken Kavanaugh, Al Matuza, Harry Clark, and Ed Sprinkle. Glenn
Presnell, the Hall of Famer from the Lions who played numerous games
against Bronko and the Bears, was a wonderful source. George Gibson,
who played with Nagurski and was his roommate at the University of
Minnesota, provided great depth and insight into the Bronk. The
Nagurski-Gibson Football Complex was named for the two men. Gibson,
at age ninety-seven, remains one of the university's biggest donors.

How could you ask for a greater source than one sitting in the stands
on that cold December day in 1943 when Nagurski went back to fullback,
especially when that person is two-time Academy Award–winning
screenwriter William Goldman? The longtime writer was twelve years
old on the afternoon that the Bears rallied to beat the Cardinals. It would
change his life forever. In 1976, he included that Nagurski passage in a
novel titled *Magic*. His screenplay for *Hearts in Atlantis* often played on
Nagurski's indomitable spirit. The movie is the story of a mysterious
older man, Ted Brautigan, who is played by Anthony Hopkins, and how
he affects the life of an eleven-year-old boy, Bobby Garfield, played by
Anton Yelchin. Ted tells Bobby about Nagurski's powerful thrusts into
the line against the Cardinals, and how he led the dramatic comeback. It
was that scene that inspired me to write *Monster of the Midway*. Thank
you, Bill Goldman.

I would also like to thank my friend Greg Aiello, the vice president for
communications of the National Football League, for opening numerous
doors. He led me to Chris Willis of NFL Films. Willis mailed so much
information—newspaper and magazine clips, books, interviews, films,
statistics, and other material—that the U.S. Postal Service almost buckled
under its weight. Willis knows more football history than anyone I know.

Of course, Peter J. Wolverton, the associate publisher of Thomas
Dunne Books, deserves all of the credit for reading the proposal and lov-
ing it (thank goodness, Pete). Wolverton and my literary agent, Jim Donovan, provided tremendous editing as usual. I delivered the manuscript late
and that meant that Pete had to jump through hoops to make it happen on
time. Thanks to Donovan for his bulldog support. This was a complex
book that required more than one strong back. Thanks, guys.

AUTHOR'S NOTE

In Chicago, Hermann Schamberger III, Joey Schamberger, and John Schoenfeld were friends and supporters who kept the fires burning. They showed me what the North Side is all about. Don Pierson of the *Tribune*, my longtime friend and colleague, was always available. For about six months, he knew that every time the phone rang it was probably me on the other end. Pierson is the ultimate authority on Chicago and the Bears. Richard Whittingham, the poet laureate of the Bears, brought insight and plenty of valuable books to the project.

Ed Oerichbauer at the Bronko Nagurski Museum in International Falls came through with pictures and tons of information on Nagurski. The museum is well worth the trip to International Falls and is open Monday through Friday. Make sure you watch the thirty-minute video on Bronko's life. Oerichbauer provided information on International Falls, along with the oral history of Nagurski that was done by Hiram Drache and Mary Lou Pearson.

The Pro Football Researchers of America (PFRA.com) is a great nonprofit organization where the writers work for the love of the game. The Web site contains countless stories about the rich past of pro football. (Do not forget to make a contribution.) Special thanks to Bob Carroll, the founder of PFRA, who has written several outstanding books on sports. Pete Fierle at the Pro Football Hall of Fame provided priceless information, including newspaper and magazine stories on Nagurski that would have been impossible to find otherwise.

Thanks to the research librarians at the Harold Jackson Library who kept the microfilm coming for over a week.

A complete bibliography appears later in the book. But the following books were indispensable: *Total Football II* (Bob Carroll); *Halas* (George Halas, Gwen Morgan, and Arthur Veysey); *Chicago Days* (edited Stevenson Swanson); *Mudbaths and Bloodbaths* (Gary D'Amato and Cliff Christl); *Red Grange* (John M. Carroll); *Notre Dame, Chicago Bears, and "Hunk"* (Emil Klosinski); *The Bears—A 75-Year History* (Richard Whittingham); *What a Game They Played* (Richard Whittingham); *The Chicago Bears* (Howard Roberts); *The Game That Was* (Myron Cope); and the *Pro Football Chronicles* (Dan Daly and Bob O'Donnell).

Other writers, and their periodicals, who provided outstanding work on Nagurski and the era: Paul Zimmerman of *Sports Illustrated;* Bob Oates of the *Los Angeles Times;* Frank Graham, Norman Katkov, and Ed

Fitzgerald of *Sport Magazine;* Jim Dzuik of the *St. Paul Pioneer Press;* Patrick Reusse of the *Minneapolis Star-Tribune;* Frank Luksa of the *Dallas Morning News;* Loel Schrader of the *Tampa Tribune;* Shirley Povich of the *Washington Post;* Edward Prell, Arch Ward, Edward Burns, and Wilfrid Smith of the *Chicago Tribune;* Harry Sheer of the *Chicago Daily News;* Arthur Daley of the *New York Times;* Stanley Frank of *True Magazine;* Grantland Rice of the *New York World.*

Thanks to John Ancell, Paula and Mark Wright, Bruce Deckard, Debbie Brawley, Tom Paprocki, and Peter Golenbok.

My mother, Leanna Dent, and sisters, Janice Dent and Annabelle Loeb, really came through when I needed them. And my niece, Anne Woodfin, was a great help in Chicago.

A special pat on the head once more for Rolly Dent, my cat, who kept the chair warm during the coffee breaks. We have an odd tradition when books are finished around the Dent household. Rolly sits on the manuscript to give it luck. This time, he lay on it for about an hour.

# Contents

# CONTENTS

# Foreword

It was Draft Day, 1979, and I was horrified.

How the hell did I get picked by Chicago? I'm from the South, and the idea of playing pro football on the frozen tundra of that northern city was frightening. Besides, I'd never heard the Chicago Bears and the Super Bowl mentioned in the same paragraph. But, like many things, my first reaction to playing my pro football career in the Windy City was to change drastically. What was it that changed my mind? Little did I know that I had come to the mecca of pro football. As most folks now know, George "Papa Bear" Halas had a vision in the Roaring Twenties, and his vision would become reality: The sport was to become the most popular sport in America, with the Super Bowl the most watched event in television history.

No other sports franchise has had the endless parade of "characters" that have made the Bears the most fascinating—and enduring—in NFL history. We all know of Butkus, Sayers, and Payton, but back before them, when the game was in its infancy and desperately trying to find its niche in the baseball-crazy American sports scene, a group of men forged a game and a legacy for all those who followed to aspire to—and this is where Bronko Nagurski made his mark.

Some historians say times make the man, but I believe that men define their times, and at no time has a handful of men made a more lasting impression on the sports world. It was an impression that was to capture the imagination of a country—and no player did more to capture that imagination than Bronko Nagurski. Alongside his teammate Red "The Galloping Ghost" Grange, he redefined the concept of sports heroes.

I have always identified with Nagurski's story for many reasons, but the way he played the game was a metamorphosis of sorts in how he overcame the obstacles he faced. He arrived with mighty talent and energy, and slowly the ability and skills would be beaten out of him, leaving only his soul and fiber to fall back on. Here was where his true greatness would shine most brilliantly.

I've been told that a football player's career is judged not by the bright flashes but by the long dull roar—that his true measure is based on the sum total of his contribution to his team every week regardless of injury, however severe. I have been called such a player. Well—this is the story of a football player's player, a story that is brilliantly told by Jim Dent in a way that brings the original Monsters of the Midway to life.

Dan Hampton

# MONSTER OF THE MIDWAY

# 1

# Old Man

The storm blasted off Lake Michigan and bucked into the Navy Pier, hoisting an icy spray over the bow of the USS *Wolverine*, then cut a swath through the Loop and angled southwest along the Chicago River, kicking up wrappers and scattering old newspapers as the sound of forty thousand voices echoed across the South Side. The second storm blew ashore minutes later at the Museum of Science and Industry, rolling across the neighborhoods of Hyde Park and Kenwood until it turned left and headed west on Thirty-fifth Street, ticketed for Comiskey Park.

The stadium at Thirty-fifth and Shields looked like an old warship. The upper decks were shrouded in a freezing mist, and the light standards swayed against the heavy winds. A low rumble rose from the grandstand and swelled into a thunder that could be heard from Bridgeport to Brighton Park: "Bronko! Bronko! Bronko!"

The first snowflakes glided over the rim of Comiskey Park just as Bronko Nagurski slid the full-length black cape from his shoulders and reached for his leather helmet. Just then, the two storms collided on the South Side. Eyes that had been riveted to the action on the field for three quarters studied the clouds that circled and churned like a riptide.

Nagurski had spent the first nine games of his final season toiling in the Chicago Bears line. Now the Bears desperately needed a victory against the crosstown Cardinals in this regular-season finale of 1943. Otherwise, they could forget about playing in the NFL championship game. To the dismay of all the fans that braced for the bitter winter storm, the Bears were losing 24–14. One quarter was left to play. All eyes were now on the old man.

Of course, Nagurski wasn't really old at thirty-five, but the crooked nose, the bent fingers, the arthritic joints, and a degenerating hip belonged to a man perhaps twice his age. He could no longer run very far. Surely, he could no longer play fullback. He was ancient for a football player.

The Bronk had missed five seasons. He left in 1937 as the greatest player in the history of the National Football League. His name itself suggested primal power. Here was the man who had single-handedly dragged the NFL out of the back alley and into the American consciousness. It was said that professional football was invented to keep coal miners off the street. That was before Nagurski came along and the world took notice. It had been a long, hard ride. There had been joy and pain and broken promises. There had been laughter and bitterness. There were days in pro football when he thought it would last forever, and still others when he longed for his quiet little hometown way up in northern Minnesota. The day he walked away from pro football in '37 was the hardest he could ever remember. Now he was back for one last hurrah, and he prayed his body could weather one more quarter.

The spring in his legs and the steel in his arms and torso had been diminished by age and by the pounding of two sports—football and wrestling. A wrecking ball had been taken to his powerful frame. He was not half the athlete that he'd been ten years ago. But he was still Bronko.

It seemed like an eternity since Nagurski had last lugged the football. In his farewell in that year, the Bears were defeated in the NFL title matchup by the Washington Redskins and rookie sensation Sammy Baugh. The next day, he caught the Illinois Central back to International Falls, Minnesota, and swore he would never come back.

No one was sure about his reasons for leaving. It had something to do with his contractual arrangement with the Bears. Promises had not been kept. He once said, "George Halas throws nickels around like manhole covers." Nagurski's patience with Halas, along with his shrinking salary and the numerous IOUs, had finally run out. He felt certain that big money awaited him in professional wrestling. The Bronk had his own problems back home, and those problems could only be solved by money, and lots of it.

After the last game that season, Halas and Nagurski had heated words. It was the final nail.

Now, as he removed the black cape and reached for his helmet, the fans at Comiskey Park saw the round stomach and the bowed legs. A man in the fifth row behind the Bears bench dropped his flask and shouted, "Omijesus, he's coming in!" A woman screamed. Then the rolling thunder returned: "Bronko! Bronko! Bronko!" Chi Town had not entertained such a racket since '06, when the White Sox took the World Series in six games from the crosstown Cubs.

The day still could be saved. The Bronk was going in at fullback.

• • •

The world was at war in 1943. Bears owner and coach George Halas, the father of the NFL, was cruising the South Pacific as a lieutenant commander with the Seventh Fleet. More than half of the Bears had been summoned to active duty, including stars like end Ken Kavanaugh, tackle Joe Stydahar, and halfback George McAfee. But the Cardinals' casualties were far more severe: fullback Motts Tonelli was a Japanese prisoner of war and end John Shirk was trying to survive a German POW camp. Forty-two ex-Cardinals were fighting somewhere.

The battles in Europe and the South Pacific grew bloodier by the day. Sixty thousand Americans were already dead. A headline in the *Chicago Tribune* read, "Nazis Dig Up, Burn Jewisn Bodies." American and British troops were making broad progress in Italy, penetrating the Winter Line. This movement had prompted a bold prediction from Gen. Dwight D. Eisenhower: "We will win the European war in 1944." It was Eisenhower's farewell press conference in Algiers before taking command of Operation Overlord, the heavily guarded code name for the Allied invasion of Normandy, scheduled for the following summer.

On the other side of the world, Formosa had been attacked for the first time. China-based U.S. Fourteenth Air Force bombers destroyed forty-two Japanese bombers on the ground. That same day, five U.S. destroyers had scored a one-sided victory over the Japanese, sinking three of their ships at the Battle of Cape St. George in the Solomon Islands.

For Halas, the trip from San Francisco to Milne Bay near New Guinea had required twenty-two days. Most folks around the Bears thought the forty-eight-year-old coach was crazy for reenlisting. But Halas was still frustrated that he had frittered away World War I at the Great Lakes Naval Training Station, playing ball for the base teams. He had promised himself that if another war ever broke out, he would find the action.

The navy had reactivated Halas halfway through the '42 season, presenting him with his sword at halftime of the Detroit game. Chicago won 16–0. After the game, Halas named Heartley "Hunk" Anderson and Luke Johnsos interim co-head coaches of the Bears. He was gone the next day.

Halas tried to stay in contact with the coaches through the navy wire. But weeks often passed without communications. After the Bears lost the '42 championship game to the Redskins by the score of 14–6, Johnsos could barely find the words to tell his boss. He sat down to write a letter and finally finished it a week later. Given the delay in its arrival, Halas thought Johnsos had dropped the letter into a bottle and the bottle into Lake Michigan. Then, after reading it, he swore he could smell Washington owner George Preston Marshall's victory cigar all the way to the South Pacific. Halas hated Marshall, a promoter, huckster, showman, and owner of the Washington Redskins, with every fiber in his soul.

Halas racked his brain for a way to get revenge. During the summer of '43, while pacing the deck of the ship, he was struck with the idea of bringing back the Bronk. The Monsters of the Midway needed new blood. But wait—maybe some old blood would do the trick. Why not Nagurski? A comeback by the aging warhorse might save the day. Halas sent a cable to Hunk Anderson three months before the start of the season: SIGN NAGURSKI AND PAY FIVE GRAND. STOP. Naval decoders analyzed the message for days, wondering if Nagurski was a Japanese spy.

Then it was Anderson's job to sell the notion of playing football again to a man who said he would never come back.

Anderson was a roughhewn but likable fellow who had been around the block in both college and pro football and had played on Knute Rockne's first two undefeated Notre Dame teams in 1919 and '20; Hunk was the second All-American in South Bend following George Gipp. He went to work for Rock straight out of college and was his only assistant coach through the decade.

From 1922 through '26, Anderson helped coach Notre Dame six days a week. Then, Saturday night, he would catch a train to Chicago to play guard for the Bears. He also worked sixty hours a week at Edwards Iron Works in South Bend. Of this tireless wonder, Halas said, "Hunk was a terror on offense and defense during those sixty-minute days. And he's the hardest-working sonofabitch that I've ever seen."

When Rockne's plane crashed in the Flint Hills of Kansas in 1931, Anderson was promoted to the single most pressurized job in college football. Remarkably, he lasted four years before failing to satisfy the spoiled alumni. He was fired. He knocked around the college and pro game for the next seven years until Halas brought him back into the fold in 1940. It was the right time for the Hunk's return. Halas needed a blood-and-guts man to whip his Bears into shape.

Hunk Anderson seemed the right guy to approach Nagurski about a comeback. It didn't hurt his chances that the Nagurski bank account was drained again. Pro wrestling had been a living, but not a road to riches.

In the summer of '43, the Bronk could barely rise from the bed in the morning. His ankles popped like seasoned firewood as he shuffled barefoot across the cool hardwood floor toward the hallway where the phone was ringing. He reached for the receiver and noticed a bruise the size of a baseball on his heavily muscled right forearm, a memento from Saturday Night Wrestling down in St. Paul. Pain shot through his lower back where a cracked vertebra had tormented him since his college football days.

"Bronk, this is Hunk Anderson calling from Chicago," came the voice over the crackling line.

"Yes sir, Hunk."

"The old man says we're desperate for your services. Says we gotta have you this season. Bronk, I got the cable right here in my hand."

"Where's the old man?"

"South Pacific, Bronk. On a battleship."

"I got no more use for football, Hunk. I couldn't run from here to the john if my bladder was bursting."

But Nagurski could use the money. Wrestling had never panned out. As America plunged deeper into the Depression in the thirties, the crowds thinned and so did the purses. The Bronk was embarrassed that he had fallen for a seedy sport in which the bouts were rigged and crooked promoters skimmed off the top. It had left him with barely enough money to support his wife, Eileen, and two kids, Bronko Jr. and Tony.

He was torn.

Nagurski rarely spoke about his terrific football career, or his past public life, to anyone. Folks in the Big North Country were certain he would never return to the mad bustle of Chicago. He was finished with football, and there was talk he would open a gas station. But the Bronk listened to Anderson's sales pitch anyway. He wanted to say no, but an inner voice kept saying yes. Anderson seemed sincere. The old man desperately needed him. Otherwise, the Bears' domination of the NFL would end at a time when they were considered the New York Yankees of pro football.

"The old man needs you, Bronk," Anderson said for the seventeenth time.

A pause.

"Look, Bronk," Anderson continued, "if you can't run, we'll put you at tackle. We gotta have bodies in the line, anyway."

A long silence. Anderson suspected the telephone line between Chicago and International Falls, a distance of six hundred miles, had gone dead. Then he heard the Bronk clearing his throat.

"I need five grand, *up front*," he said. Anderson could have jumped high enough to touch the sky. Nagurski had uttered the magical words— *five grand*. It was the exact amount that Halas had hoped to pay and prayed that Nagurski would accept.

"You got it, Bronk," Anderson said with a renewed enthusiasm. "I'll send you a train ticket. Camp opens pretty quick."

Two days later, Nagurski was on the train to Chicago, and he spent the next two weeks trying to limber up legs that he thought would no longer work.

The Monsters of the Midway opened the season with a tie against Green Bay and did not lose a game until the ninth week—to the hated Redskins. The season had gone relatively smoothly in spite of Halas's absence. The Bears were 7–1–1 with the final game of the season against the Chicago Cardinals coming up. Win or tie and they would represent the western division in the NFL title game. Bears fans hungered for a rematch with Washington. But a loss to the Cardinals would be the greatest embarrassment in the history of the storied franchise.

Nagurski had awakened that Sunday morning with the first light angling through the shutters. Pain gnawed at his lower back and his right hip. Standing over him, blocking out the light, was George Musso, the pie-faced 270-pound guard who was Bronko's roommate and best friend.

"Let me give you a boost up," Musso said, chuckling. "Looks like you could use it, old fella."

The simple act of getting out of bed was torture. Two vertebrae had been cracked in a game against Northwestern in '28 and a degenerative hip condition from '35 had almost crippled him. He rose into a sitting position. Then, with his legs dangling over the side of the bed, Nagurski pounded the side of his right knee with a meaty hand. *Click.* The cartilage popped back into place.

There was dried blood in his nostrils. Musso passed a roll of toilet tissue. The Bronk coughed and felt a hammer slam into his ribs.

That morning, they decided to catch the elevated train from the North Side through downtown Chicago and into the South Side, where Comiskey Park was located. They sat alone as the car roared and clacked. They peered at the swirling clouds, and as the train crossed Lake Street, they could see in the distance the giant neon marquee of the Granada Theatre. Lucille Ball and Harry James were starring in *Best Foot Forward*. The other big attraction in Chicago was *Thank Your Lucky Stars* with Humphrey Bogart, Bette Davis, Olivia de Havilland, and Errol Flynn.

An elegantly decorated forty-foot Christmas tree towered over the Walnut Room at Marshall Field's. Bing Crosby had lonely souls around the world singing, "I'll be home for Christmas."

Nagurski did not start the game but replaced Musso at left tackle in the second quarter. The Bears outclassed the Cardinals at virtually every position, but the game was not going according to form.

What should have been a Sunday drive through the regular-season finale against the Chicago Cardinals had backfired. Balls had slipped through the hands of receivers and between the legs of kick returners. Any hope of reaching the NFL title game a fourth straight year was slipping through their fingers.

That the winless Cardinals could be leading the fabled Monsters of the Midway by the score of 24–14 entering the fourth quarter was unthinkable. The Cardinals were the worst team in pro football, possessing barely enough healthy players to fill out a lineup. They had lost fifteen of their last sixteen league games. While the Bears had captured two of the last three world titles, the Cardinals had earned the reputation as football's equivalent of the French army.

As the fourth quarter began, Anderson sidled up to Nagurski on the sideline.

"Bronk, you ready?"

"Told you I was. But don't put me in there unless you're gonna give me the doggone ball."

"Told you I would."

He was going in.

As the Bronk snapped on his chinstrap, he thought about the old days. God, he missed the old days—the days of the helmetless Bill Hewitt, the best defensive end who ever played, and Bill Fleckenstein, the giant brawler. In those days, the Bears were real *men*. Nagurski had learned the game in the hardscrabble era of George "Brute" Trafton, the roughest, toughest, meanest hombre ever to lace on cleats. Big George, the Bears' All-Pro center, had been like a big brother. God, Nagurski missed those great years with Trafton. And Red Grange! The Galloping Ghost! He was the greatest man Bronko had ever known.

The Bears of '43 would never be like the old Bears. The Bronk knew that. But they still could win one more championship before he went back to the Big North Woods for good. This was an able lineup. The Bears had Sid Luckman, who had shattered two NFL records by throwing seven touchdown passes and compiling 433 yards just two weeks earlier against the Giants. The problem with Sid was that he was up and down like the Midway roller coaster. He seemed at times more interested in driving his shiny new cars around Chicago and wearing his $200 silk suits. In truth, life was no bowl of cherries for Luckman. Virtually every time the Bears broke the huddle, somebody yelled from the defensive side, "Hey, Jewboy!" Or "Hey, Luckman, you kike!" He sometimes joked his name was "That Jew" Luckman, not Sid Luckman. Even his own center, Bulldog Turner, constantly rode him about his clothes, cars, and fat bankroll.

"God, Sid, you're damn lucky to be a Jew," Turner would say in his Texas drawl. "Otherwise, son, you'd be plumb shit outta luck."

With one quarter to play, the winter storm raging, the Cardinals leading by ten points, and the dynasty on the line, something had to give. As Nagurski trotted slowly onto the field, and the blizzard descended upon the stadium, he could sense thousands of eyeballs tracking his every move. His heart accelerated and the adrenaline flowed. The old feeling was back.

Darkness was starting to settle over the South Side. Nagurski regarded the Cardinals' linemen. They were bloodied and bruised and nearing exhaustion. Blood was smeared on their shredded jerseys. Their faces were streaked with mud. They had never left the field.

"Hey, Bronk," came a loud voice from the Cardinals defense, "your Jewboy sure could use some help."

"Go home, old man," came another, "or we'll send you home in a box."

Nagurski marched into the huddle and studied the weary faces of his teammates.

"What the *hell* you think you're doing, you old fart?" Bulldog said.

Bronko stared a hole through the Bears center.

"Block or get out of my way," he growled, "or I will break your spine."

# 2

# International Falls

The prison gates swung open in Pennsylvania in March of 1930 and Alphonse Capone walked out a free man. On that same blustery spring Chicago afternoon, twenty-one-year-old Bronko Nagurski bounded off the train at Michigan Avenue. Attention was drawn to the bricklike jaw and the blue eyes riveted into a thick, square skull. Another hitman railing into Chi Town, they surmised. That opinion swiftly changed, though, when onlookers saw the eyes widen as he gazed upon the towers along the shoreline.

Nagurski wore blue jeans and a flannel shirt and toted a battered suitcase supported with twine. Stuffed deep into his left pants pocket was the sum of twenty dollars. He aimed his powerful frame into the wind and lumbered eight lanes across Michigan Avenue at Adams. *Only tourists and wheat farmers look up.* But he couldn't stop; his massive neck rotated mechanically like a construction crane, his head tilting to the side. He ogled the Tribune Tower and the Wrigley Building. Then his eyes slid along Michigan Avenue where the bronze lions flanked the wide entrance to the Art Institute of Chicago.

People with wild eyes jostled each other along the sidewalks; they seemed to be rushing in all directions. Then he saw a black, lurid headline glaring at him from the news rack. CAPONE FREE. Down the street, more Chi papers: SCARFACE RETURNS: CHICAGO BRACES.

The underworld was primed for a celebration. Their mobster chieftain had come home. From dawn till dusk, a hard-fisted city would raise its glass, brimming with illegal booze, to the greatest outlaw since Jesse James. Chicagoans loved a winner, even the cheating kind.

Bronko Nagurski didn't know what he was walking into, and nothing could have prepared him for this mad bustle. His life's experiences had been limited to hunting, fishing, lumberjacking, sledding, plowing, and playing college football the last four years at the University of Minnesota.

Now, as he trekked westward through the downtown business district known as the Loop, his hands fumbled with a crude map that had been drawn for him by George Halas, the owner of the Chicago Bears. It was Halas who had insisted that Nagurski forgo all the other teams to play for the Bears, sealing the deal with a first-year salary of $5,000, the largest amount ever paid a professional football player at a time when the best in the game made only $200 per contest.

At the moment, the Bronk was feeling neither rich nor powerful. The first payment on his contract was not due for three months. Halas was a miser, paying the bulk of contracts at the end of the season. Professional football in 1930 was a redheaded stepchild compared to baseball. Players were regarded as hoodlums, owners and coaches as mere hustlers. Most pro teams struggled day to day just to survive.

So the big All-American from Minnesota was now just another face on the crowded and frenetic streets of the Windy City. While Capone and his gang reveled in the headlines, drank champagne straight from the bottle, flashed thousand-dollar bills, and pampered themselves in the most expensive and luxurious hotel in Chicago, Nagurski planned to rent a room on the North Side for five bucks a week. Capone had thundered west on the elegant Broadway Limited. The Bronk had endured the milk train that waddled and clacked for six hundred miles.

Actually, his new anonymity pleased him. His life the last two years had been a carnival ride in full public view. Football fans in the Midwest fawned over him. Women at the U. threw themselves at his feet. He became a folk hero during his senior season at Minnesota. It was no surprise that he was selected as the consensus All-America fullback. But though he had played only half of one game at tackle, the writers voted him All-America at that position, too. Grantland Rice, the preeminent sportswriter of the time, saw fit to choose only ten players to his All-America squad, noting that Nagurski was clearly the best at two jobs.

For the moment, though, Nagurski was just another wayward traveler, lost and alone in America's second largest city, already homesick for the frozen outpost known as International Falls, a tiny Minnesota hamlet that snuggled up to the Canadian border. He struggled to decipher a map that looked more like a worn jigsaw puzzle with missing pieces. Wandering through this canyon of tall buildings, his sense of direction now betrayed him.

The Bronk proceeded along Adams, and his nostrils were assaulted by the aroma of baking pizza that poured through the double doors of Sam Bellotti's. Through the plate glass, he could see men wearing tall, white hats kneading the dough and then spinning it on their index fingers until the pies were perfectly round. If not for the tightness in his throat, the Bronk would have marched straight into Bellotti's for a beer and a large pie. The baking cheeses, peppers, sausages, and dough, along with the garlic, sauce, and basil, played havoc with his olfactory system.

Down the street at the Palmer House, he peered through the glass to see the polished Carrera marble, the hand-woven Axminster carpets, the chandeliers, and the French candelabra. Across the street loomed the fortress of Marshall Field's, the grand marble palace with Corinthian columns built and nurtured by the ultimate entrepreneur, Marshall Field himself. The twelve-story department store on State Street housed a six-thousand-square-foot Tiffany glass mosaic dome, big enough to run pass patterns on.

The Bronk was now approaching Clark Street. According to the map, he was to climb the wooden column of stairs at Adams and Clark, keeping his eye peeled for the elevated train that rumbled along a forest of steel stilts. Even in his wildest dreams, the Bronk could have never foreseen this: a train on a wide rail above the city sidewalks, creating a cacophony heard for dozens of blocks. The Bronk climbed aboard the El and realized that he was now at eye level with second-story windows, where passengers often saw snippets of domestic life not visible below. As the train pulled away, heading north, his focus was suddenly drawn to an open bedroom window, curtains fluttering in the breeze. His eyeballs bracketed the lean but curvaceous woman, wearing nothing but panties, admiring herself in the full-length mirror.

• • •

Growing up in International Falls hardly prepared the Bronk for this rat race. His hometown now seemed as distant from Chicago as the snow-banks of the Ukraine. Situated on the muskeg swamp that comprises most of the North Country, the Falls' only claim to fame was its reputation as the "Icebox of America."

No wonder the place was so cold. A glacier standing ten thousand feet tall exerted tons of pressure for thousands of years on the land. The bog's only real stability came during the winter when it was frozen. At other times, it sufficed as the world's largest sponge.

Athletes who live by the sea and train each morning on damp sand will never forget the hot coals that burn inside their calves and thighs as the miles pile up. Running on the muskeg has the same effect.

Each afternoon young Nagurski would begin the trek across the swamp, tucked inside the Big North Woods, as dusk fell over the Falls. He really had no choice. The last mode of transportation available that after-noon was a horse-drawn schoolbus, and it had departed hours earlier from the tiny schoolhouse. The driver was Mike Nagurski, his father, who hap-pened to be the busiest man in the Borderland and had a grocery store to run. So Bronko, after a three-hour football practice, was left to hoof it alone four miles to the family farm. As the temperature plummeted, walk-ing no longer was an option. Only a brisk pace would serve to warm him.

The Bronk never considered taking to the roads, as they would merely add distance to the journey. So he struck out through the woods, the sweet smell of pine mixing with the musky scent of the moist ground. The twi-light flickered through the tall trees and, through the glare, he could barely make out the trail that had been forged by his own footfalls day by day through black spruce, aspen, balsam, white cedar, tamarack, jack pine, and balm of Gilead. One day the boy's heavy breathing frightened a large buck that whirled on its hind hoofs, its white tail expanding to cover the hindquarters as it sprinted through the low brush. The Bronk wished for his rifle.

After two miles the boy burst from the woods into a broad meadow as the day's final, golden light cast long shadows across the lawn of the Forest Hill Cemetery. But Bronko could still make out the names on each headstone—Bartkowski, Solobeski, Walkoviak, Skolsky, Ferruccio, Karsnia, Terebenetz, Pierarski, Tomczak, Lisowski, Agostinelli.

Darkness was settling over a flat stretch of farmland ahead, where the timberline peeled away. Nothing was more exhilarating than charging down that last steep hill at nightfall, pushing his body to its maximum speed, his pistonlike legs now burning, his chest heaving, his heart absent of fear. He could now see a black sky bursting with the constellations. His mind shifted to the big games on Friday night, to the field where the bodies scattered like bowling pins when his knees were pumping high. At night the big Ukrainian always felt faster. *I wonder why.* He homed in on a thin, naked bulb that dangled from the front porch of the Nagurski farmhouse. Past the sawmill he slowed to a trot, grabbing two plump logs with his meaty fingers. Inside, he thrust both into the potbellied stove, gaining an approving smile from his mother.

"Did you run all the way home?" Michelina asked in her native Ukrainian.

*"Ni."*

"No wonder you hardly seem winded."

Michelina Nagurski had birthed four children, two boys and two girls, in a period of six years. They were Bronko, Eugenia, Stephanie, and Marion, in that order. Bronko was born in 1908 in Rainy River, Ontario, and the family moved across the border to International Falls in 1912, shortly after the birth of Stephanie. Marion came along two years later.

Mike and Michelina never planned to call the oldest child Bronko. He was christened Bronislau and carried that name for six years until he entered the first grade in International Falls. His teacher noticed that the other first graders were having trouble pronouncing his name—*Brone-is-law.* One day she decided to change the name to Bronko. Oddly, there was no fuss around the Nagurski household when the boy returned home one afternoon and announced he had a new name; Bronko was fairly common in the Ukraine. Besides, the switch was far less radical than what his father had endured when the family crossed the border at Fort Frances, Canada. An immigration agent had scowled when informed that the man's name was Nicholas.

"That will not do," he snapped. "You will be called Mike."

Not once did Mike Nagurski protest. He was too happy to be in America.

Nicholas, armed with only a third-grade education, a small suitcase, and enough money for boat fare, had crossed the Atlantic at age nineteen, leaving his family behind in the tiny village of Walkowze, Poland. The only constant in Nicholas's life was war; the boundaries of northern Europe seem to shift with each sunrise.

American immigration laws stated that anyone without relatives in the United States would have to settle first in Canada. Nicholas Nagurski's dream from day one of the journey was to reach America. He was not a man of means, but he possessed an immense work ethic. He stood six foot two, weighed close to 220 pounds, and was strong as an ox compared to the others in Manitoba. He labored ten hours a day on a farm, worked six more at night at a country store, and built houses on weekends.

Driven by the same spirit was a determined young woman named Michelina Nagurski, who at the age of seventeen had already been married and widowed; her husband had died in battle. Oddly, her surname was the same as Nicholas's: They were fourth cousins. Before Nicholas departed the Ukraine, the two had been attracted to each other, and Michelina swore she would someday find the tall man with the high cheekbones, the large chest, and the powerful manner.

Michelina's trip required almost a year of traveling by boat, train, and stagecoach, but she got her man, and they were married in 1907. No one would ever question Michelina's spirit, for she awoke each morning with the feeling she could conquer the world. It seemed that a negative word never passed her lips. Of course, every word that she spoke was in Ukrainian. One of her favorite phrases was "You can make it"—*Ty moz'esz robyty tse.* She often expressed these words of encouragement to her oldest son, especially during the times when he seemed worn down by heavy work. Not a minute seemed to pass when Bronislau was not working at something—school, the farm, football, the family store, or his job at the lumber camps. *Ty moz'esz robyty tse, Bronislau.*

Michelina and Mike were happy as clams when the family crossed the long bridge at Fort Frances. At last, they had staked their claim to America. At first, the Nagurskis barely noticed that the Falls was a cold, gray place with harsh winters, a scarred land, and weather suited for Eskimos and grizzly bears. Temperatures dipped to sixty below, and no one had ever heard of a wind-chill factor.

One day young Stephanie Nagurski pleaded with her father, "Daddy, why do we have to live here? It is so *cold*."

"Because there are no tornadoes and no hurricanes," he said. "We can learn to tolerate the cold."

This rugged country that split the Mesabi Iron Range to the south and frozen lakes to the north had but two factors working in its favor—the gold rush of 1890 and its status as America's last frontier. Neither could be taken to the bank. The gnawing cold either drove away most of the hardy souls or cut them down at the knees.

Early settlers were met by insurmountable hardships--soil that could not be farmed, harsh winters, isolation, swamps, roads that were virtually impassable, and crude medical services. Most were pre–World War I immigrants from northern Europe, and their will to deny themselves was beyond human. It was estimated that only one in four homesteaders who stayed managed to survive, and most died in the wilderness when their food and kerosene ran out.

A tree carving in the muskeg swamp captured their plight: "Kick yourself for coming."

To the good fortune of the Nagurskis, Mike, their patriarch, was both diligent and creative. During the early years in America, he owned a thriving grocery store at 708 Fourth Avenue, and the family lived in a comfortable home just down the street on a corner lot.

Mike Nagurski was an enterprising man. When store customers asked for milk, he bought a cow. When they requested bread, he installed a huge oven inside the family's house; each morning, the children awoke to the mouthwatering smell of freshly baked bread. When the bohemian element of the Falls asked for Polish sausage, Mike built a smokehouse, concocted a recipe, and proceeded to make his own.

On the side, he built houses for a local contractor until he realized the banks were making loans. A real estate and construction business was born overnight. Instead of depending on the town's sawmill, he built his own on the Nagurski farm, where a dozen cows now grazed in the warm months.

All the while young Bronko was delivering groceries, herding cows, milking cows, working the family sawmill, chopping down trees, clearing fields, delivering groceries, toting logs, pulling stumps, and plowing. As a teenager, his upper body was chiseled, his legs marbled with muscle. Each autumn afternoon at dusk, Bronko would dash through the forest, frightening the deer, playing out the high school games, driving himself to new heights. And with each passing day it seemed another muscle sprouted from his rock-hard frame.

Bronko was working a plow behind the family's horse one day when a stranger stopped to ask for a drink of water.

"My God, son, if you don't stop growing you're going to be bigger than that danged horse," he said.

Life was good for the Nagurskis. Buttons bursting, Mike Nagurski drove a brand-new Ford sedan into the family's driveway one afternoon. It was the first of its kind in the Falls, and the family was quite proud of its owner. In spite of his broken English, Mike was both an entrepreneur and a business leader, and his hardworking little town was starting to burgeon. Most of the residents worked at the paper mill that had opened around the turn of the century. Several hundred more labored at the sawmill, opened in 1912. They lined up at the Nagurski store on Saturday mornings and cleaned out the shelves.

For a time the small town's economy boomed. Once the hardships were overcome, folks from the Old Country were glad they had come. They spoke many languages, but communication rarely seemed a problem. A smile or a wink often sufficed. Merchants were fair. Customers had money.

Edward Wellington Backus, a rich lumberman from back East, had converted the forgotten outpost into a town of commerce by spending millions on scouting the land and the waters, building a state-of-the-art paper mill, and enticing two railroads to lay tracks for the purpose of penetrating the vast wilderness. Before Backus, most citizens swung axes for a living. Now they were working for a decent wage.

Thousands upon thousands of logs were sluiced along Rainy Lake to the point where you could barely see through them to the water. Lumber not devoured by the paper mill was railed south to Bermidji, a town about ninety miles south of the Falls, where it met connecting trains to all parts of America.

But the town's economy tumbled in the early twenties, thanks to Backus's unpaid taxes and the influential environmentalists who campaigned and halted his plans for damming more water. Backus, who owed the IRS $2.5 million, filed for bankruptcy, and wholesale layoffs at the mill pushed the Falls toward financial doom.

Mike Nagurski felt the financial crash like a fist to the solar plexus. He was forced to sell the house on Fourth Street, and the family moved to the farm full time. There would be no more real estate deals, no more bank loans, no more marathon sawmill runs. The store on Fourth Avenue closed its doors.

Like other resourceful men pressed financially, Mike Nagurski's morals slipped: He was driven into the business of bootlegging. Given the troubling era and the fact he had four children to feed, Mike couldn't be blamed for seizing the opportunity. Canada, after all, was a half mile across the lake, and Canadians were known for distilling both an affordable and respected whiskey. During Prohibition boats ran night and day across waterways leading from Canada into the United States. From the day the Volstead Act went into effect on January 16, 1920, Canada was right and ready. Mike Nagurski had little choice but to grab a piece of that action.

Why not? Koochiching County was thirsty. The Falls was filled with saloons, brothels, and gambling halls. During one calendar year in the twenties, when the population of the region approached three thousand, 459 alcohol-related arrests were recorded. Lumberjacks freely spent their entire wages on whiskey, women, and dicing. Establishments that supposedly sold soft drinks but specialized in booze were called blind pigs, and the "piggers" were everywhere. Of course, it didn't hurt that people were generally depressed by the bitter weather and the endlessly rolling low, gray clouds.

The bootlegging trail was a dangerous one, and the whiskey runner felt the long arm of the law each day. In one series of raids federal agents arrested thirty bootleggers, who paid huge fines and were shipped off to Leavenworth. Mike Nagurski was living through troubled times. But he had to do something to make ends meet.

In these moments of depression Mike could still be proud of the way he had raised the strapping young man who possessed a great amount of horse sense along with a creative side. One day the Bronk decided he was going to build a sleigh that would provide transportation to the school in the morning. He yanked the backseat out of his dad's old Ford and attached two wood slats to the bottom. He hitched his newly concocted sleigh to the family's horse and, with Eugenia by his side, took off for school. They were the envy of all the kids as they glided through the deep snow, laughing all the way.

The Bronk was a natural at almost everything he tried. He mastered every position on the football field. He was smart, fast, agile, and strong, and a great student of the game. But there wasn't much he could do about the other ten players on his teams. International Falls High School lost every game during his junior season.

In the summer before his senior year, the coach at Bemidji sent a message: Move to Bemidji and play for a winner. Every year college recruiters flocked to Bemidji to find new talent, and they were far more likely to find Nagurski there than in the Falls.

For years it had been the boy's dream to play college ball, and he knew that Bemidji offered a better chance to get a scholarship. There were other factors that weighed in his decision to bolt the Falls. He disliked his coach and often told his father, "I learn more about football on the sandlot." Furthermore, the International Falls High principal had violated one of Bronko's principles when he canceled a trip for the basketball team the previous winter. He was trying to punish a few of the players for skipping school. Nagurski had not been one of them and felt he was being disciplined for no reason.

There was yet another reason that helped tip the scales. Bemidji had defeated International Falls 56–0 the previous season, and Nagurski wanted to avoid that kind of humiliation again.

So he left.

Naturally, folks back in the Falls were steaming mad when they learned that their star had been lured to its hated rival by its devious coach, Buck Robbins. Bronko's enrollment at Bemidji spurred school superintendent H. R. Jones to lodge a complaint with the Minnesota High School Athletic Association. This smelly kettle of fish had the entire state talking. The athletic association voted to suspend Bronko for the entire season, a decision that devastated him.

For days he walked aimlessly around Bemidji, homesick for his mother and father and three siblings. He was saved, however, by Robbins's plea to the athletic association that he be able to practice with the team. The fact he tore through the first-string line for large gains each day convinced him that college football was squarely in his future. The Bronk also learned a lot of football fundamentals from Robbins.

He worked as a janitor at the school and even slept inside the schoolhouse. At Christmas he returned home with a bundle of presents for his family. Six months later, though, the Bronk had nothing in his pocket but a few small-time offers—the most lucrative came from the University of South Dakota. Disappointed, he passed on them all.

That summer he was plowing behind the family horse on a sunny afternoon when a green Ford pulled onto the shoulder of Highway 53. Dr. Clarence "Fat" Spears, the coach at the University of Minnesota, was a large and gregarious man who told tall tales. He rarely did things by the book, and his scouting of Nagurski certainly followed no standard blueprint. He simply hopped into his old Ford one afternoon and drove up the crooked two-laner from Minneapolis to the Falls.

Doc Spears kicked up a low cloud of dust as his heavy feet traversed the tilled ground. From the road Spears had watched Nagurski working the plow, his skin shining in the sunlight. The coach was mesmerized by the large, square head, the broad shoulders, and the massive thighs and calves.

"Hey, boy, can you tell me where that ol' quarterback who plays for the Falls team lives?" Spears said.

This was the story that Spears would spin for years on the banquet circuit: Nagurski, who was plowing without a horse, managed to lift the eight-hundred-pound plow several feet into the air and point it in the direction of the quarterback's house. It really didn't happen. What Spears really said was, "Son, you look like you might be a prospect for the Minnesota Gophers." Bronko replied, "Well, why don't we go fishin' and talk about it?"

That afternoon they caught walleye after walleye at Rainy Lake. But communicating was a horse of a different color. The Bronk felt like toying with the big man who acted funny and was not like any man he had ever met.

Spears asked, "Who was your coach?"

Nagurski replied, "Well, you see, I really didn't have—"

"What do you mean you didn't have a coach?"

"We kind of coached ourselves," the Bronk answered.

"Tell me what position you play. And don't you tell me the stooped position."

"No," said Nagurski.

"No what?"

"I stood up," replied Bronko.

"Let's quit clowning. What position did you play?"

Nagurski said, "It didn't matter."

"Tell me exactly what you mean."

"Well, when the other team had the ball, I played where I thought I had the best chance to stop them. When our side had it, they generally gave me the ball," Bronko explained.

Spears gave up. This conversation was going nowhere. But one look at the Bronk was enough.

"How'd you like to play for the Golden Gophers?" he asked.

"Yes, sir."

Spears could not have been more pleased. He could not wait to get home. All the way back to Minneapolis he rehearsed the story about Bronko and the plow. It would not take long for Spears to revive one of the great legends of the Big North Country—the legend of one Paul Bunyan.

# 3

# Minnesota Gopher

Doc Spears found the boy's hot button on the first try that first day of fall practice in 1926. The Minnesota coach, standing in the middle of the practice field, ordered Nagurski to step forward and face his two hundred-odd new teammates.

"OK, boy, tell us what your name is."

"Bronko Nagurski," he said.

"Bronko, huh? Now that's a funny name. Where'd you get it?"

Nagurski glared at the coach they called the Fat Man. "Clarence ain't so hot, either," he said.

The players held their collective breath and tried not to laugh. It didn't work. Spears just smiled and winked when the laughter subsided.

"Now, Bronko, who was your coach in high school?"

"I kinda coached myself," Nagurski said.

"Well, then, let's just *see* what kind of job you did."

Spears wanted to test the Bronk in a drill called the nutcracker, a three-on-one testicle rattler that was relished by the coaches but reviled by the players. Two men would block against one while the running back tore through the hole paved between two blocking dummies. The defensive player's odds of winning this battle were equal to mighty Notre

Dame going winless for an entire season. When Spears wanted to rub a player's face in the mud—and he was often in the mood—he called for the nutcracker.

The blockers were all-conference linemen Ken Haycraft and Bob Tanner. The runner was fullback Herb Joesting, dubbed the "Owatonna Thunder" by the sporting press. He was six foot two and 220 pounds of cold steel. Bronko dropped into a three-point stance, aiming his headgear between the two giants across from him. On the snap he tore through the blockers and dumped Joesting on his back, pinning his knee to a blocking dummy and bending the joint. The big fullback cried out as trainers sprinted onto the field.

Spears couldn't have cared less. He blew his whistle and dispatched yet another running back into the fray. The ball was snapped and Bronko again split the blockers, driving his shoulder into the ball carrier's sternum for a three-yard loss. Yet another and another was handed the ball with the same result.

Spears finally sidled up to assistant coach Dutch Bergman and whispered, "I think we've seen enough." Spears had not expected this: Nagurski's football résumé spanned all of one season with a team that had not won a game. The coach expected Nagurski to be green and overmatched against the hardened boys from UM.

This day, Spears was anxious to unveil a new play he had designed on the chalkboard during the off-season, an off-tackle counter play from the single-wing formation. The tailback would take the deep snap, pivot and fake a pitch, then slide the ball into the belly of the fullback. "Fats" Spears loved smash-mouth football more than fried chicken, mashed potatoes, cream gravy, and corn dripping with butter. The second-year coach of the Golden Gophers was determined to forge a name for himself as football's tough guy. He would attack Michigan and Notre Dame with a hard-fisted running game. He would show Knute Rockne a thing or two.

The Minnesota program had suffered through some lean years in the early twenties, and three coaches had been fired in seven years. But Doc still had a firm foundation upon which to build. Minnesotans loved their Gophers. (They would not become known as the Golden Gophers until the thirties.) Northrop Field was filled to capacity each Saturday, regardless of the team's record, and the same could now be said of the fifty-five thousand-seat Memorial Stadium, unwrapped in 1924 for a game against

Red Grange and Illinois. Those who couldn't find a ticket were not deterred; they hung from tree limbs or climbed telephone poles to catch a glimpse of the Gophers. Some stood on car roofs. Others sat atop utility poles. That day they saw their own Clarence Schutte rush for 282 yards, a national collegiate record, as Minnesota upset Illinois 20–7.

Doc Spears thirsted for Minnesota's triumphant return to power. For now, though, Joesting, his ticket to glory, was sitting on the sideline with a swollen knee wrapped in a bag of ice. The Fat Man, though, was in no mood to wait. It was time to roll "thirty-two counter blast" off the show-room floor.

In 1926 freshmen were not eligible to play on the varsity, so they were regarded as blocking dummies and fodder for the first stringers.

"Get in there at tackle, Nagurski!" Spears spat. The other freshman followed, filling out the defensive eleven. Spears felt his heart quicken as the varsity broke the huddle for the first play of fall practice. Tailback Fred Hovde faked, pivoted, and handed off—it went nowhere. As the players unpiled, Nagurski was on the bottom, hugging the ball carrier.

"Run it again!" the Fat Man yelled.

They ran thirty-two counter-blast five straight times, for no gain. Nagurski made every tackle.

"Okay!" Spears bellowed. "Let's try something else. Let's switch. Freshmen to offense. Varsity to defense. Nagurski, you're at fullback."

Nagurski would be running behind a ragged line assembled just moments earlier. It didn't matter. On his first carry the Bronk powered his way through the arms of two tacklers, ran over a linebacker and the safety, and was thirty yards down the field before he heard Spears's whistle, followed by cursing. The Bronk gained ten yards on the next play, fifteen on the next. The first stringers knew he was coming but couldn't stop him.

"Goddammit," Spears snapped. "It's not the play. It's the players."

He stomped and ranted.

"Hell, Fats," Bergman said with a wink. "You knew how strong that Nagurski boy was. You're the one who saw him pick up the danged plow!"

• • •

The broad, grassy UM campus, situated along the high bluffs of the Mississippi River, counted a student body almost five times the population of

Bronko's hometown. Ten thousand were enrolled when the seventeen-year-old stepped off the train in Minneapolis that September evening with barely enough money to pay for his next meal.

For the next few days he worked his way through the maze of buildings, a painful and slow process, until he could at least find his way back to his own dormitory.

In November of his freshman year, when the leaves turned burgundy and gold and the bone-chilling wind rushed down from the Arctic, the Bronk peered across the campus through the yellow dusk to see the warm lights of the fraternity houses. Across the main campus, he could see students pouring into the cozy taverns, where shipments of illegal Canadian whiskey had just arrived. Kids his age were laughing, joking, and spending money. His eyes devoured the fresh-faced coeds in tight sweaters. *Those girls will never look at me.* The Bronk stuffed both hands into his pants pockets and turned them inside out. He was dead broke. He was homesick.

Oscar Munson, the Gophers' equipment manager, looked up from the pair of shoulder pads he was repairing to see a grim Nagurski standing over him.

"Gotta go back to the Falls," he said.

"Not until after finals," Munson said. "You gotta pass to keep yourself eligible for next season."

"I'm going home for good."

"Over my dead body."

The Bronk dropped his head. "I got no money. I'm hungry. My rent is overdue. I looked all over for a job. There are no jobs."

Football scholarships and training tables did not exist in those days. A football player was provided a job by the university, and normally the pay was good enough to cover both tuition and room and board. You worked, you studied, and somewhere in between you practiced and played football. When Nagurski's job petered out, he didn't know where to turn.

There was little glory in being a freshman football player at the University of Minnesota. Players like Nagurski did not ride around campus in convertibles bought and paid for by rich alumni. Other big-time football programs were offering cash under the table, and Bronk suspected that Joesting and a few others were getting cash. But a hick from the Big North Country? He was just out of luck.

Munson held up an open palm. "You wait," he said. "I will be back in five minutes."

It didn't take that long. Minutes later Nagurski was being escorted into the large and disheveled office belonging to Doc Spears.

"Why didn't you tell me?" Spears said.

"Didn't want to bother you."

"You don't think I like you."

No response.

The Fat Man cleared his throat. "Look, son, everything's going to be all right. You're the best goddamned freshman football player I've ever seen. I'm telling you straight. We've knocked your ass around a bit. But next season, well, the world's your oyster."

The Bronk was speechless.

Spears handed him a piece of paper. "Go see that man about a job. It's all yours."

The job paid fifty bucks a week—a handsome sum of money at the time—for firing the furnace at an office building on the edge of campus. The Bronk would have enough money left over to buy some bootleg beer and see a movie. Maybe he could make a date with one of those sexy sorority girls.

Though he had to stand on the sideline as a freshman during the '26 season, Nagurski learned a lot about football fundamentals and even managed to gain twenty pounds. He had made the tough adjustment from small-town boy to big-time collegiate player. Now they just needed to find Nagurski a position to play.

When fall practice began in September of 1927, he was tried at virtually every spot on the field, and it was clear that he could have replaced Joesting at a moment's notice. But Joesting was the preseason choice to become the Gophers' first back-to-back All-American. He had broken the collegiate rushing record the previous season with 926 yards in spite of playing on a fragile knee that was injured during preseason drills by a hard-boned freshman.

Under Spears, the Gophers were ready in '27 to challenge for the Big Ten championship. It had been twelve long years since Minnesota had won the conference title, and the alumni were getting antsy.

Spears, who was eccentric and unpredictable, was actually the right coach for the times. He possessed the kind of offensive creativity needed to make the Gophers a force in the Big Ten once more. There was no questioning his IQ. He had come a long way from the rice and soybean country of DeWitt, Arkansas, where he had worked the small family farm from dawn to dusk. Spears was accepted into Dartmouth, where he graduated magna cum laude, and then entered the University of Chicago and Rush Medical School. While attending medical school, he found time to play in the offensive line for the Canton Bulldogs, blocking for legendary halfback Jim Thorpe. Why not? Spears, a 255-pound guard, had been a two-time All-America at Dartmouth.

In 1916 Spears, along with Howard "Cub" Buck, Harold "Cap" Edwards, and Ed "Unk" Russell, helped make up the best line in pro football. Coach Jack Cusack won the services of all four, along with Thorpe, in a bidding war with other teams from the Ohio League, a forerunner of the NFL. While Spears rolled through medical school, the Bulldogs rumbled to an unbeaten season in '16 and were hailed as the greatest team in professional football to that point.

Spears managed to graduate from medical school while coaching his alma mater from 1918 to 1920. His medical practice continued at West Virginia in 1921, where he led the Mountaineers to their first unbeaten season in 1922. It was nothing for Spears to operate on patients in the morning and to coach football in the afternoon.

Four seasons at West Virginia produced a 30–6–3 record. Sportswriters on the East Coast believed his '24 team could have competed with Notre Dame the year the Four Horsemen rumbled across the landscape of college football. In what was unfolding as the Golden Era of sport, Harry Stuhldreyer, Elmer Layden, Jim Crowley, and Don Miller had ridden into the American consciousness on the typewriter of Grantland Rice.

Notre Dame now stood atop the mountain all others hoped to scale. Spears salivated at the thought of tackling the Notre Dame legend when he was hired at Minnesota in '25. He lost his first two games to the Fighting Irish. But the Fat Man had been building toward the 1927 season, thanks to a sophomore named Nagurski.

One chilly November morning, the Gophers packed their gear for the trip to South Bend. For most of the six-hundred-mile train ride from Minneapolis to Indiana, past Madison and Chicago and into the Corn Belt, Spears pondered the legend of one Knute Rockne. He barely noticed Chi Town when the train rolled through the bustling city. All he could think

27

about were the legends of the Four Horsemen and of George Gipp, the famous running back who had suffered a sudden and tragic death from pneumonia in 1920, dying in Rockne's arms. To compound the Notre Dame equation, the Fighting Irish had neither lost nor tied a game in South Bend in twenty-two years. The Gophers would be the decided underdogs.

As the train rumbled east into Indiana, Spears tried to imagine how the game would be played out. He allowed himself a brief smile because his strategy was solid. His team was better than average. He would lean on his powerful defense while praying that the short bursts of Joesting eventually added up to good field position. It was a common practice for a coach of that era to punt on third down, placing the onus squarely on the backs of his defense. That would be Spears's plan today.

Spears peered through the window at the brown and green quilt of idle farmland and pondered his secret weapon. Reporters had been asking about Nagurski for a year. But no one other than Nagurski's coaches and teammates knew about his Herculean feats on the practice field. When Nagurski lined up at tackle there was not a player on the Minnesota squad who could block him. His natural position was fullback, but with Joesting still on the roster, he would have to wait until the '28 season. So tackle had become his regular spot, and he'd started the first game of the season against North Dakota. He came off the bench the next three weeks. Then, during a week of practice leading to Notre Dame, with all-conference end Ken Hayworth suffering from yellow jaundice, Nagurski was moved to end.

What now excited Spears was the prospect of Nagurski attacking the famous Notre Dame line from the defensive side of the ball. This day, he would play sixty minutes, never leaving the playing field.

Cartier Field was filled to the brim. People had come to see the top-ranked and undefeated Fighting Irish play the Gophers, who had defeated North Dakota, Oklahoma A&M, Iowa, and Wisconsin by the combined score of 148–17. Only Indiana had taken Minnesota to the wire, the game ending in a 14–14 tie. Minnesota had never defeated Notre Dame, and few people expected it this time around; the betting money was squarely on the home team playing in the shadow of the Golden Dome, at odds of eight-to-one.

Oddly, the locker rooms below Cartier Field were situated next to each other. As Spears prepared to give his pregame pep talk, he heard a loud noise next door; it was the booming voice of Rockne penetrating the wall. Spears stopped his speech in midsentence and listened intently to the Notre Dame coach. He was quite curious as to what the Rock had to say:

"Boys, that Minnesota bunch over there thinks they are better than you. They have not lost a game this year. But they are not better. No sir. But you gotta go out there today and fight, fight, fight! Win it today for old Notre Dame!"

As Rockne paused, Spears looked around the Minnesota dressing room to make sure all of his players were listening. They were. Rockne continued: "Boys, we have not lost a game in this stadium in twenty-two years. That's right. Twenty-two years. And you're not going to lose today. Take the game to those fellas and you will come away winners today—Fight! Fight! Fight!"

When Rockne had finished, Spears stood, shrugged his shoulders and turned up his palms. "Boys, you heard what the man had to say. Now get out there and win one for *old* Minnesota."

Spears could never remember his players being so charged up. They tore through the locker room door and down the tunnel, their cleats scraping the concrete floor. They were whooping and hollering as if they were playing for the national championship.

In truth, the Gophers were too fired up. A nervous Fred Hovde fumbled the first snap of the game at the Notre Dame seventeen-yard line and the Irish recovered. They needed only three plays to push the ball into the end zone. The crowd of sixty thousand sensed a runaway victory.

But the next time Notre Dame had the ball, Nagurski's presence in the defensive line was felt immediately. They ran three plays and punted. In fact, the Notre Dame offense stalled for the rest of the first half as Bronko dominated the line of scrimmage. When the Irish tried Nagurski's side of the line, the ball carrier was stopped in his tracks. Running away from Nagurski didn't work, either. The Bronk roared into the Notre Dame backfield, making tackles from sideline to sideline. It was 7–0 at halftime.

Spears had a scheme during the intermission that he hoped would recharge his team. The strategy was risky and he could lose his job if he got caught. Without telling his players, he dumped two quarts of bootleg brandy into their coffee urn. In that era, the players drank coffee during the entire break to reenergize their minds and bodies. But this stuff was a hundred proof.

The Gophers roared down the tunnel at Cartier Field for the second half as if they had swallowed rocket fuel. Rockne peered across the field at the UM players, who were jumping and hollering, and wondered if his team could hold off this spirited bunch.

Neither team could move the ball in the third quarter, precipitating a dozen punts. The Minnesota offense was moving in inches and feet, not yards. Spears stuck with his plan of punting on third down, hoping to keep Notre Dame pinned deep. Both teams, in fact, were punting enough to shoo birds away from the stadium. Harold Barnett's booming spirals kept the Irish at the wrong end of the field most of the day.

A low, dark cloud hovered over the stadium as Notre Dame's Ed Wynne retreated to punt with three minutes left in the game. He was standing at the Irish nineteen-yard line when Nagurski crashed through three blockers and smothered the punt, then quickly recovered the ball at the sixteen. A pall fell over the stadium when the Bronk emerged from the bottom of the pile with the ball raised high in his right hand.

Joesting twice carried the ball behind Nagurski to the Notre Dame two-yard line. Rockne could never remember such a silence inside the home stadium. The Notre Dame forward wall succumbed on Joesting's third straight carry as Nagurski was like a snowplow clearing a six-foot drift. Joesting could have walked into the end zone. The extra point tied the score. Fifty-nine seconds later, Notre Dame fans took one last look at the scoreboard that read 7-7 and filed out of Cartier Field without a word spoken. For the first time since '05, they were without a home victory to celebrate.

After the game, Rockne told the *Chicago Tribune,* "Nagurski's defensive play was the single greatest performance in the history of our stadium. Minnesota has one of the best teams in the country. Hats off to them."

The triumphant ride back to Minneapolis was like a trainload of soldiers returning from war. A tie with Notre Dame equaled the greatest Minnesota victory in ten years. Spears frowned on drinking during the season, but the bootleg whiskey was abundant among the players. Spears just smiled, laughed, and shook his head.

More than twenty thousand fans, along with the Gopher band, met the train in Minneapolis. They partied as if the Volstead Act had been repealed. You would have thought Spears had brought home a national championship. The mad celebration lasted until dawn. For the first time, Nagurski was invited over to fraternity row where the booze flowed and the sorority girls flirted. His life was changing, his homesickness waning.

Joesting, a member of the Sigma Chi fraternity, invited both the Bronk and George Gibson over to the frat house for dinner. The hungry boys ate until the cooks ran them off.

Gibson and Nagurski were fast friends from the moment they met. They were of the same fabric, both having grown up in humble surroundings where hard work was part of life. Gibson hailed from Medford, a tiny town in the Oklahoma wheat country hugging the Kansas line. He worked the wheat harvest from Medford to Bismarck, North Dakota. During that time wheat shockers traveled mostly by covered wagon. The Wheat Belt included Oklahoma, Kansas, Iowa, and South and North Dakota.

Gibson was lucky in that his father worked for the Rock Island Railroad, meaning he had a free rail pass. In October of 1923, with the wheat harvested, Gibson was ready to catch a passenger train from Minneapolis back to Medford when his eyes focused upon a large and colorful poster replete with football players wearing helmets and funny garb. It included a 1923 Minnesota schedule. The Gophers were set to play the Haskell Indians that Saturday afternoon at Memorial Stadium, and since the station was a hop, skip, and jump from campus, George decided to forgo his travel plans for the chance to catch a glimpse of big-time football.

The experience would change his life. Brand-spanking-new Memorial-Stadium was filled with fifty-five thousand fans raising a ruckus that echoed for miles down the Mississippi River. Tailback Earl Martineau, a hero of World War I, scored a late touchdown in spite of a cast on his hand as the Gophers won a thriller 13–12.

George returned to Medford, where he had been a high school star, and announced that he would play football at the University of Minnesota. He would not even consider the University of Oklahoma, where Benny Owen was building a football powerhouse about ten rail stops away in Norman.

Until Nagurski came along, Gibson was the greatest raw talent Spears had ever laid eyes upon. In spite of spindly arms and skinny legs, he was deceptively strong. Spears stood over Gibson each afternoon during practice and bellowed, "I'm going to make a great guard out of you if it kills me." Spears succeeded and lived to tell about it.

In November of 1927, following the tie at Notre Dame, Gibson could boast of two distinctions: He was an all-conference guard and the room-mate of one Bronko Nagurski, now a rising star on the UM campus. More important, the boys were being served steaks, chops, chicken, ribs, and mashed potatoes each night at the Sigma Chi house.

"Life is getting good," said Nagurski one night.

"So why don't we join the frat?" Gibson asked. "What've we got to lose?"

The boys knew little about the requisites of joining a fraternity. They were ill informed about pledgeship, and neither had ever heard of "hell week."

Herb Joesting was a Sigma Chi upperclassman and knew about Nagurski's football reputation. But around the frat house, Bronko was easygoing and rarely seemed in a hurry. He ambled about the UM campus like an Ag major from Blue Earth, Minnesota.

The Bronk played football like a man boiling over with rage, but around campus he was like a big teddy bear. Until hell week arrived. At first Nagurski went along with the silly gags and macho drills—the push-ups, the sit-ups, and the broken eggs in his underwear. Then one of the Sigma Chi seniors told him to bend over the Ping-Pong table. As the paddle connected with his backside, the *whap* could be heard for several blocks. Nagurski, his face turning crimson, spun, grabbed the paddle and shoved the senior face down on the table. He busted him ten times squarely on the butt.

"Don't you ever hit me again, you sonofabitch," he growled with each swat.

Fortunately, Joesting was standing nearby and saved his Sigma Chi brother from further embarrassment. He also managed to convince the other members that Bronko should be excused from the rest of hell week. Without further incident, Nagurski was pledged into Sigma Chi. But Gibson had to stick around for more hell week humiliation as the frat brothers simply did not fear him nearly as much as they did the Bronk.

• • •

After the tie with Notre Dame, the Gophers closed out their undefeated season with wins over Drake and Michigan, taking the Little Brown Jug away from the Wolverines for the first time since 1919. As the Gophers celebrated in their locker room, a large right fist connected soundly with the jaw of Harold Hansen. He landed facedown in the shower room about fifteen feet away, and Nagurski landed atop him, swinging wildly. Bronko was still tearing at Hansen's head when his teammates pulled him out of the pile.

"Settle down, Nagurski," Hovde yelled. "Spears put him up to it. It's not Harold's fault!"

Hansen had been instructed by the Fat Man to verbally ride Bronko the entire game. It was Spears's opinion that Nagurski was not angry enough. He was confusing the boy's placidity between plays with a lack of inner fire.

Hansen, an All-America guard, had chided Nagurski throughout the game. Now he was sitting on the floor with a large lump over his right eye.

Across the locker room, Spears smiled. He had his reasons. For the first time since 1915, Minnesota had captured the Big Ten title, sharing it with Illinois. Then came the most disappointing and bizarre decision in the history of Minnesota football. The university president L. D. Coffman decided to withdraw any claim to the Big Ten title. Coffman never clearly stated his grounds for giving up the conference crown other than to say "the reputation established by the Gophers during the 1927 season was far more valued than any conference crown." Every fan, alumnus, player, coach, and cheerleader shook their head in disbelief. Spears threatened to quit, but realizing Nagurski would be around for two more seasons, he changed his mind.

The 1928 season found Nagurski moving to fullback, thanks to the graduation of Joesting, for the opening game against Creighton. He would still play tackle on defense.

Nagurski rushed for 111 yards that opening Saturday afternoon in September as Creighton fell 40–0. The Purdue Boilermakers put up a great defensive fight the next week, but still lost 15–0 as the Gophers controlled the ball and the clock with Nagurski powering the ball up the middle. The third week of the season brought the University of Chicago, one of the greatest powers in the history of the Big Ten, to Memorial Stadium. Led by the famous coach Amos Alonzo Stagg, Chicago had once won six straight conference titles; that string ended in 1924. Stagg, who would coach seventy-one seasons and retire at age ninety-eight, invented everything from the numbered jersey to reverses to tackling dummies to the forward pass. Before Stagg, college football was a provincial game taken seriously only on the East Coast. But now his dynasty was imploding as a new college president worked to deemphasize Chicago Maroon football and shift the university's focus to academics.

Nagurski and the Gophers had little trouble disposing of Stagg's Maroons. The Bronk rushed for ninety-eight yards and recorded twenty-two tackles as Minnesota won 33–7 before fifty-eight thousand fans at Memorial Stadium. The most interesting part of the afternoon was the postgame walk from the field. Stagg hustled over to Nagurski and grabbed his meaty right hand. This football purist had a message to deliver.

"Look, son, you're the best football player this game's ever had," he said. "And I know people are already filling your head with ideas about pro football. Football is not a game you should get paid for. I don't want to see you become the next Red Grange."

Nagurski could not believe his ears. Grange, now playing for the Chicago Bears, was his hero. The Bronk shook his head and said, "What do you mean, sir? Grange is one of the greatest players ever."

"But he shouldn't be taking money to play football," Stagg said. With that, he pivoted on his heel and strode away.

The 4–0 Gophers now faced the biggest game of the year against Big Ten coleader Iowa on the road. It was a grudge match for the Hawkeyes, who had lost 38–0 the previous season in Minneapolis. Iowa would have to figure a way to slow down the thrusts of Nagurski, while the Gophers' biggest challenge was stopping one of the nation's leading rushers in Willis Glasgow.

The defensive units controlled the game in the first half as the teams were content to punt on third down and play for field position. Iowa's running game was shut down by the one-man wrecking crew known as Nagurski.

Early in the third quarter, the Gopher coaches noticed that Nagurski was no longer lining up in his normal three-point stance. He was in a crouched position with hands on his knees. The Fat Man walked over to Dutch Bergman and asked, "What the hell is wrong with Nagurski?"

"I don't know," Bergman said. "Why don't you call time-out and ask him?"

There was no need to call a time-out as the Iowa offense had barely gained an inch against Nagurski and the Minnesota defensive wall. That was until Glasgow broke loose around right end midway in the third quarter and sprinted sixty-eight yards to the end zone for a 7–0 lead. Spears then decided to check on the Bronk.

"What's wrong?" Spears asked when Nagurski reached the sideline.

"Can hardly breathe," he said. "My ribs are sore. Can't bend over."

Spears had the trainers examine Nagurski, who pulled off his jersey and shoulder pads to reveal three ribs torn away from his sternum.

"He can't play any more today," the trainer said. "Those ribs are bouncing around like a xylophone. One of them could puncture a lung."

"The hell he can't," the Fat Man said. "Put some tape on him and get him back in the goddamned game."

Under the rules of the one-platoon system, Nagurski could not return to the game until the fourth quarter, and he was back on the field for the first play.

"Can he get down in a stance?" Spears asked the trainer.

"Hell, Fats, I doubt the boy can even breathe with that much tape around his gut," the trainer replied.

The Minnesota offense bogged down on the next series and was forced to punt back to Iowa. The pace of the game suggested that Minnesota's chances of springing a comeback were slim. But with slightly more than ten minutes to play, Glasgow was met at the line of scrimmage with a crushing tackle by Nagurski and the ball squirted high into the air. Gibson recovered it at midfield and the Gophers had their best field position of the day.

"You OK, Bronk?" Hovde asked in the huddle.

"Give me the ball, Fred," Nagurski said flatly.

The tape had been wrapped so tightly around his sternum that Nagurski could not bend at all. He stood in the backfield with hands on hips and waited for Hovde to slip the ball into his belly. Then he hammered the line for eight yards. Then he gained four more to the thirty-eight for a first down. The sellout crowd was suddenly on its feet in Iowa City, and the air was laced with tension. They exhorted the Hawkeye defense to stop this locomotive called Nagurski.

Bronko slammed into a hole at right guard opened by Gibson and suddenly there was daylight. His cleats tore divots out of the Iowa grass. He thundered over the thirty, the twenty-five, and the twenty as two

Hawkeyes jumped on his back. He carried them all the way to the twelve-yard line, where they crumpled to the ground. The two defenders landed on his damaged ribs with their full weight, and Nagurski's loud groan could be heard all the way to the Minnesota sideline. He lay on the ground as the trainers sprinted onto the field and rolled him over. They felt certain that he was finished for the day and were prepared to call for a stretcher. But the Bronk rose slowly and said with a grimace, "I'm staying in." Rules of the time would have prohibited him from returning to the game in the fourth quarter.

Nagurski limped into the huddle and said, "Look, guys, let's do it this play. I don't know how much longer I can go." Every face was now filled with a grim determination. Hovde took the deep snap from center, faked a pitch to the right, and handed the ball to Nagurski, who aimed his body between the center and right guard. Gibson went low and gained leverage on the Iowa tackle, pushing him to the outside. As Bronko powered into the line, the Gopher guard swore he could feel the earth moving around him. Nagurski ran over two Hawkeyes and was still moving at full speed when he burst into the end zone. With under four minutes to play the game should have been tied, and the Gophers should have been psyching themselves for one last push to win the game. But Jake Smith's dropkick slid wide right of the goalpost and the Hawkeyes still led 7–6.

Iowa then managed to run out the clock. It was one of the most heartbreaking losses in the history of Minnesota football.

Most players would have sat out the remainder of the season. However, the trainers fitted Bronko with a steel brace that hugged his rib cage. On the second play of the game against Northwestern, Nagurski attempted a cross-body block and hit the ground hard. He cracked two vertebrae in his lower back and would not be able to play the rest of the afternoon as Northwestern eked out a 10–9 victory that further reduced the Gophers' chances of winning the Big Ten title.

Nagurski would play about half of the game against both Indiana and the Haskell Indians over the next two weeks as the Gophers breezed to victories by the scores of 21–12 and 52–0.

The Gophers entered the final contest against Wisconsin with two losses and no chance of repeating as Big Ten champs. Regardless of the stakes, the idea of not suiting up never crossed Nagurski's mind. Not once had he asked out of a game, regardless of the pain.

En route to their undefeated season, Wisconsin had defeated Notre Dame 22–6, Iowa 13–0, and Chicago 25–0. All the Badgers needed against Minnesota was a tie to capture the conference title.

Bronk had a surprise visitor two days before the game. His mother, Michelina, had made one of her rare trips out of International Falls. She was toting a pint jar of potato whiskey when she walked into his dorm room on the UM campus. The moonshine had been brewed in Mike Nagurski's still.

"Drink this," she said to the Bronk in Ukrainian. "It will make you feel better."

Gibson, sitting across the room, had never tasted moonshine whiskey.

"Just dip your tongue in it," Nagurski said. "That's about all you'll need."

Gibson fanned his open mouth with his right hand, thinking his tongue was on fire. His intestines felt like hot coals.

"No wonder Indians call it firewater," George said. "God, I think it took the skin off."

Nagurski sipped the home brew the rest of the day. By the time the team boarded the train the next day for Madison, his ribs and aching back were feeling better.

That Saturday, the coaches moved Nagurski from tackle to linebacker. Play after play, he made the tackle at the line of scrimmage. He intercepted three Wisconsin passes. The game reflected the low-scoring, take-no-risks trend of the times. It was a scoreless tie when Nagurski recovered a Wisconsin fumble at midfield with two minutes to play.

"Block for me, Gibby," he said, leaning across the huddle. "I think we've still got a chance."

The Madison sky had threatened rain all afternoon. Thick clouds skimmed across the rim of the stadium, and a light fog hung along both sidelines. Passing was rarely an option in the Spears offense. Now the shrinking visibility completely ruled it out. The Gophers went to work with their steel-jacketed fullback, gaining four yards, six yards, eight yards, three yards. Nagurski plowed into the line from the standing position. Then he would dip his right shoulder and lean so close to the earth that he seemed to be scraping the grass. Tacklers experienced electric shocks throughout their bodies as they met him head-on.

Nagurski's face was streaked with mud. Blood leaked from a hole in his forehead. From the twenty-yard line, he burst through the line at right guard behind Gibson's block. He was hit at the sixteen and shook it off. He ripped through another tackler's arms at the ten. Two Badgers jumped on his back at the eight-yard line and another wrapped his arms around the Bronk's neck at the seven. Two more piled on at the four, and another leaped aboard at the two. While the Wisconsin fans stood and railed against this piston-legged madman, he carried six men on his back into the end zone. Then he shook them off like so many horseflies.

The 6–0 defeat cost Wisconsin the Big Ten title. The Gophers, having completed a 6–2 season, roared west on the silver bullet all the way back to the UM campus, where the party was on. The town was already talking about Nagurski's senior season.

• • •

The Big Ten title had eluded Minnesota in 1928 by a total of two points. So in making predictions for the 1929 season, the sporting press was behind the Gophers, picking them to win the conference title in a runaway. Most of the starters, including Nagurski, were returning, and the only meaningful loss was Gibson, who had been selected as an All-America his senior season.

Neither the public nor the press would be disappointed in the first five games of the season as the Gophers defeated their opponents by the combined score of 153–27. Nagurski, in spite of the lingering pain from his spinal injury, was virtually unstoppable in an offense that still spread the ball around to all four backs. When opposing defenses stacked the line of scrimmage, he bowled over tacklers, leaving them bloodied in his wake.

Against Northwestern the Bronk scored a late touchdown for the 26–14 win. He stumbled over the end line and rammed his shoulder into several hundred-pound bags of cement stacked at the retaining wall behind the end zone. Each one fell.

Sitting in the stands that day was none other than George Halas, who had made the short trek up from Chicago. He sneaked onto campus wearing a hat pulled down over his forehead and an overcoat with the collar turned up. If Tim Mara, owner of the New York Giants, had known how desperately Halas wanted Nagurski, he might have offered the Bronk the sun, the moon, and a racetrack to boot. Mara was a well-connected book-maker with more money than God.

What Halas saw that day was the toughest man in college football. After the game, Halas sneaked into the Gophers' dressing room. He stood in the corner, hat brim down, collar up, and watched Nagurski undress and then walk around the locker room in his underwear. Halas could never have imagined the sculpting of his body—the slabbing of leg mus-cles, the upper body powerfully developed from the plowing. He took note of the big man's grace and fluidity and the feet that seemed to glide across the floor.

Nagurski would not need the steel jacket again until the Iowa game in the sixth week of the season. Both teams were undefeated and shooting for the Big Ten title once more. Following a scoreless first half, the Bronk carried the ball eight straight times for forty-seven yards and scored on a three-yard plunge. The Gophers led 7–0. But Iowa would manage a touchdown and a field goal in the final two minutes of the game, and buzzard luck again bit the Gophers, who missed three short field goals. Iowa won the game 9–7, taking a one-game lead in the con-ference race.

Luck again failed the Gophers at home against Michigan the follow-ing week. The Bronk scored the go-ahead touchdown in the fourth quar-ter, but the extra-point kick failed. Michigan came from behind to win 7–6 on a late touchdown. Minnesota had played some of its greatest defense in Nagurski's three seasons on the varsity. Now the Gophers had lost four games by a total of five points. A break here and there and the Bronk could have finished with three conference titles under his belt.

The final game of his collegiate football career was going to be a party. More than two hundred fans railed from International Falls to Min-neapolis on the morning of the Wisconsin game at Memorial Stadium. In the entourage was Mike and Michelina Nagurski, who had not once seen their son play football. They hardly knew what to expect. Along on the trip were Bronko's siblings, Eugenia, Stephanie, and Marion.

A banquet was held honoring the Bronk at the Curtis Hotel. He wore his burgundy letter sweater with the large golden M, and a tie. This was not the same homesick boy who had shed tears when he left the Falls four years earlier. His heart was bursting with pride, his cheeks aglow, his smile ever-widening when the well-wishers formed a long line to greet their hero.

Near the end of the line was a bright-eyed, auburn-haired Irish girl, the daughter of the mayor. Bronko could not take his eyes off the sixteen-year-old. Finally, Stephanie Nagurski stepped forward and introduced Eileen Kane.

"So, you're from the Falls, are you?" the Bronk said. Then his mind could no longer find words. He simply smiled at the blushing girl. They stood silently and admired each other.

That afternoon Nagurski tore through the luckless Wisconsin defense for 137 yards, again scoring a late touchdown for a 13–12 victory. Fans at Memorial Stadium cheered wildly and pounded the back and shoulders of Mike Nagurski. But the proud father was still uncertain of what he had witnessed. Their Bronk had caused quite a fuss the last three years. But Mike and Michelina knew little about this quirky game that required men to sling each other into the mud. It was the first and final time they would see their son play, and that was something the Bronk would always regret.

A week later the Bronk was selected first-string fullback on every All-America team. He was the starting tackle on several others. He had led the entire nation in rushing with 737 yards, and no one could ever remember a better defensive performance—155 tackles, six interceptions, and four recovered fumbles. Even more significant is that opposing teams normally ran away from the Bronk and that a good percentage of his big plays were made on the other side of the field.

The Downtown Athletic Club of New York would not introduce their Heisman Trophy for another six years, which was unfortunate. Nagurski would have won the 1929 Heisman by a landslide. The Gophers were 18–4–2 during his three varsity seasons. He was clearly the best player of that era. Legendary sportswriter Grantland Rice would choose only ten players to his All-America team in 1929, naming Nagurski as a fullback and tackle. He later wrote, "Who would you pick to win a football game—eleven Jim Thorpes—eleven Glen Davises—eleven Red Granges—or eleven Bronko Nagurskis? The eleven Nagurskis would be a mop-up. It would be something close to murder and massacre. For the

Bronk could star at any position on the field—with 216 pounds of authority to back him up."

At the end of the season Doc Spears packed his bags and took off for the University of Oregon.

Nagurski's final act as a collegian would be the East-West All-Star game in San Francisco, where every scout, owner, and coach would be in attendance. First, the All-Stars traveled to Chicago, where they would be fitted for helmets, shoulder pads, and jerseys. Halas met Nagurski at the train station and offered a contract worth two thousand dollars for his first season. The Bronk balked.

"Let me tell you, son," Halas said. "We've got great players on our team making a hundred bucks a week."

Nagurski was not about to budge. He loved the idea of playing for the Chicago Bears, the closest pro team to his native state. But before boarding the train out of Minnesota, he had received a telegram from Mike Nagurski reminding him to stand by his principles. Only a few months after the stock market crash, a dollar was something you guarded with your life.

The offer was increased to $3,000 before the All-Stars left for San Francisco, and Halas came up empty again. He followed the team to the Bay Area and hung out in their hotel lobby, expecting to find Mara or some other rich owner ready to pounce on Nagurski. The Bears owner was dying to sign his man, but his bank account was running dry. The profits Halas had stashed away from the 1925 barnstorming tour with Red Grange had virtually vanished, thanks to the Wall Street disaster. Like many Americans, he had bought stocks on margin, believing it was the road to riches. Not only did Black Tuesday devour his stocks, it wrecked co-owner Ed "Dutch" Sternaman's once profitable real estate business. Halas was determined to sign Nagurski, even if it meant wearing sunglasses and begging on a street corner.

When Nagurski gained a total of 175 yards passing and receiving in the East-West Shrine game, Halas almost panicked. He sprinted onto the field after the game and shoved the contract under Nagurski's nose. "Sign it! It'll make you the richest player in the league!" The offer was $5,000 for the 1930 season. Nagurski scribbled his name on the bottom of the contract, and the deal was sealed.

A telegram awaited the Bronk when he returned to the UM campus the next day: OFFERING SEVENTY-FIVE HUNDRED FOR THE THIRTY SEASON. YOU'LL LOVE NEW YORK. TIM MARA.

Bronk was already a Bear. But at least he now knew his true value.

The Big Show awaited him. Soon he would catch the morning train to Chi Town.

# 4

# Chicago

George Trafton was the self-proclaimed greatest barroom brawler in Chicago, even though he rarely strayed into the rough-and-tumble South Side, where cowmen from the stockyards and railyard bulls were known for busting up tough guys with one hand while slugging down whiskey with the other. But as Big George put it, "Nobody's ever come to the North Side to whip me, and they're still not coming yet."

Several large and boisterous men were busy celebrating George's twenty-eighth birthday that winter of 1929 at a popular North Side tavern called the Cottage Lounge at the corner of Diversey and Clark. Around the table sat quarterback Joey Sternaman, ends Luke Johnsos and Bill Fleckenstein, and halfback Gardie Grange, the brother of Red Grange.

Trafton shouted to the bartender, "Send me another nurse!" The waitress, her perfume filling the room, her blouse unbuttoned halfway to Milwaukee, arrived in seconds flat. She leaned over the table, exposing healthy portions of her milky white breasts that Trafton lovingly called "gangsters." His eyes lighted up as her long, wet tongue probed his earlobe.

"Darlin', you make me harder than Chinese arithmetic. Bring us another round before I get too horny to think . . . I mean drink."

Of course, no one believed that George was only twenty-eight. There had been the army hitch in '17 and '18 after he left Notre Dame. He was around in 1920 when the hand pumps blew up the first NFL balls. Halas had tried to run him off the last two years, but Trafton kept coming back, cementing his reputation as the game's best center.

In spite of the drinking, the carousing, the fighting, the showboating, and the poor math, Nagurski would quickly come to idolize Trafton. The two were as different as Capone and Ness. Bronko rarely spoke, and George rarely stopped. Many of Nagurski's views of life and pro football would be shaped by the opinions and theories of the grizzled center.

Many men were faster, stronger, younger, and far less inclined to bootleg alcohol than Trafton. But there was something about this man with the steely eyes that caused physically superior men to think twice before risking a punch. Perhaps it was the fact that he was always looking for a fight. He was the dirtiest man in pro football. Trafton was everything that pro football stood for during the pioneer years. He was wild and spirited like a gunfighter. Noses had been broken, teeth shattered, by the right forearm that doubled as a billy club. No wonder they called him Brute Trafton.

He did not learn football in the conventional manner. Knute Rockne recruited him out of Oak Ridge High School in Chicago, and the legendary coach was convinced that Trafton would become Notre Dame's first All-America. But his collegiate career was terminated when Rockne caught him playing semipro football one Sunday afternoon under an alias. Not only did the Rock boot him off the team, he had the Brute expelled from school.

No other college program would take a chance on Trafton, so he knocked around the hardlots of semipro football. His hard-knuckle reputation spread like wildfire. By the time Halas signed him to play center for the Bears, Trafton, regardless of his age, was the most feared man in all of pro football.

George would fight anyone, any time, and he didn't care who he encountered. Before a 1926 West Coast exhibition game he was demoted to second string by the Bears' co-coach and co-owner Dutch Sternaman. He responded with a haymaker to his boss's jaw, sending him crashing through a plate-glass window.

Now, as the celebration rumbled deeper into the night, Trafton's audience hung on his every word, and the well-endowed waitress kept the beer flowing. Everyone at the table knew the conversation would inevitably turn to boxing. Chicago was a boxing town. A crowd of 104,943 had witnessed the most controversial fight of the decade on September 22, 1927, when Jack Dempsey knocked Gene Tunney off his feet in the seventh round. But Dempsey was late in moving to a neutral corner and delayed the referee's count. Tunney, thanks to the "long count," managed to rise one heartbeat before referee Dave Barry ruled it a knockout and racked up enough points in the late rounds to beat Dempsey by a judges' decision.

In truth, hard-fisted Chicagoans loved any kind of brawl, especially amateur night at White City Amusement Park, when local celebrities duked it out—normally for no more than three rounds—for a few extra dollars and minutes of fame.

Gardie Grange mentioned to Trafton that White Sox first baseman Arthur Shires, a big windbag from Texas, was angling for another fight. That night, before a full house at White City Amusement Park, Shires had disposed of Dan Daly in twenty-one seconds of the first round.

Shires, six-two and 190 pounds, was a loudmouth and a rounder. He had picked fights with practically every player in major league baseball and once whipped his own manager, forty-two-year-old Lena Blackburne, in the dugout.

He didn't scare the Brute. The big man belched and said, "I can whip him on the parking lot out back. Right now!"

Before George could say Jim Beam, Grange was on the phone. Grange smelled a potential payday. A packed house would mean a big purse. Gardie telephoned Jim Mullen, a local promoter, and within minutes the fight between Trafton and Shires was on.

"Shires said he'll fight you on any parking lot in town," Grange said.

"Well, get his big ass over here."

Grange studied George's face and wondered how much he would remember the next morning.

"You gonna do this, George?" Gardie probed.

"Does a bear fart, I mean shit, in the woods?"

Of course, the dawn found Trafton with a beastly hangover. The telephone rang six times at his North Side apartment before he finally answered. His head felt like a tumor.

"What the hell you doin' calling me in the middle of the night?" he barked.

"George, it's Jim Mullen. You ready to fight Shires?"

"Thought I already did."

"No, you big galoot. But if you show up next Monday night, I'll pay you a grand and give you a cut of the gate."

Trafton dropped the phone, and as it lay on the floor he yelled, "I'll be there with bells on." Seconds later, he was back in dreamland.

By noon the fight was the talk of the town. Grange and Trafton convened at the Cottage Lounge to share the hair of the dog. Two gangsters with bulges beneath their suit coats stopped by.

"Who's gonna win the fight?" one of them asked.

"Me!" Trafton said loudly.

Then the two men corrected him.

Grange could never remember seeing Trafton so nervous; it was a first that he was too frightened to speak. But Chicago gangsters were like three-hundred-pound gorillas with guns. When the goons departed, the two football stars sat at the bar, staring straight ahead into the mirror behind the bar, saying nothing for several minutes. The prospect of a fixed fight roiled their stomachs. They were ready to call it off. Trafton didn't want to lose, but he didn't want to wind up on the bottom of the very crowded Chicago River, either.

Just when it appeared that matters could get no worse, "Machine Gun" Jack McGurn walked through the door. McGurn inspired the kind of fear that strangles a man's heart. And McGurn wasn't smiling as he sat down on the barstool right next to Big George, who felt his throat grow to the size of a baseball.

"Okay, big boy, tell me who's gonna win this big fight?"

A more humble Trafton said, "Mr. McGurn, I think I'm gonna win."

"Good," McGurn said. "I'm glad everything's on the up-and-up. And if those bums come around wanting to fix things, just give me a jingle."

They could have kissed this gangster. If McGurn said the fight was not to be fixed, it was *not* to be fixed.

After McGurn left, Gardie raised a toast. "I know that George Trafton can whip any baseball player alive!"

That afternoon the phone started ringing in every bookie shop in town. Shires opened as a 3–1 favorite based on his easy win over Daly. But those odds were tumbling by nightfall. The owner of the saloon strolled into the room flashing a fistful of big bills.

"I haven't seen this kind of action since the Black Sox scandal," Mortie O'Brien said. "Traf, I hope you got the guts to pull this off. Every gangster in town is backing you. Hell, you're the biggest thing to hit Chicago since Shoeless Joe Jackson."

Trafton spent practically every waking moment at the gym that week, pounding the heavy and speed bags, sweating out the suds, even praying. Each day he ran the speech through his mind that he would deliver to George Halas. Trafton would have to carry his plea to Halas if he was going to skip the Giants game Sunday.

Given the gravity of his situation, Trafton desperately needed Sunday off. He needed to rest his weary legs, to psych himself for the big fight, so he strolled into Halas's office Friday afternoon with a sales pitch that would have melted a nun.

"Georgie, I'm sure you've heard about the big fight---"

"You're too old to fight," Halas snapped. "And you're too old to play football. But I got you under contract. You better show up Sunday. See!"

Play he did. Trafton made a vicious tackle of Giants fullback Tony Plansky and came away with a black eye. Before he climbed through the ropes Monday night, he wanted assurances that the crowd, the press, and the radio audience knew precisely how the shiner had come about; he didn't want Shires taking an ounce of credit.

Trafton was a bundle of nerves as he sat on the stool in his corner moments before the fight, mentally counting the gangster money now riding on his shoulders. Losing meant that he would have to leave Chicago. Then a drunk stumbled out of the crowd and wobbled toward Trafton's corner. The man had witnessed Shires's previous fight and had a few pointers for Big George.

"He's gonna come charging across the ring at you." The man slurred his speech as he gestured wildly with his hands. "Just hold out your left and he'll run right into it."

Mercifully, the fight began and Trafton's nervousness eased a bit. Shires kept running headlong into his left glove. Art kept charging, though. Trafton, suffering from boredom decided to engage Shires toe-to-toe in the middle of the ring. He knocked him down. Shires stood up for a few seconds and wilted to the mat without being touched. He rose on dead legs, but the bell rang, and he was revived by his cornermen.

In the second round Trafton tagged Shires with a hard right, but both of them were on the brink of exhaustion. In the third round the warriors sweated, panted, and barely had the energy to throw a single punch. Neither was in the kind of physical shape to continue much longer. They walked in circles, staring at each other, sucking air like spent racehorses. Now the crowd was getting bored. A few of the patrons decided to entertain themselves by throwing punches at photographers, who were irritating the crowd with their annoying flashes. Other thugs then attacked the thugs who were attacking the photographers.

Carroll "Pat" Flanagan, who was describing the chaotic mess to his listening audience, took offense at the entire affair. He was indignant that Trafton had spent the better part of the third round chatting with his Bears teammates—especially Grange and Fleckenstein—seated at ringside.

Fleckenstein, a brawler himself, overheard Flanagan's criticism. He threw the most lethal blow of the night, connecting with the announcer's jaw. Flanagan gargled, "I've been struck." He then prematurely signed off the broadcast.

Minutes later the referee raised Trafton's hand in victory. Most of the rioters failed to notice. But "Machine Gun" McGurn and Al Capone stood and cheered as if Trafton had won the heavyweight championship of the world. Two days later, McGurn would slide into the bar and deposit a thousand-dollar bill in Trafton's suit pocket. Big George didn't notice. He was too busy recounting the greatest fight ever to a bar filled with adoring fans.

At another time— maybe thirty or forty years down the road, when television was starting to turn pro football into America's number-one sport—Trafton would have been a media darling. He might have been the Joe Namath of centers. But Trafton wasn't just a lot of talk. He had the game to back it up. He made All-Pro eight of his thirteen seasons. Halas once said, "George's the toughest, meanest, most ornery critter alive."

Halas would know.

During their inaugural season of 1920, when they were known as the Decatur Staleys, Halas took his team by train to Rock Island for a rematch against the Independents. The Staleys had won the first game over Rock Island 7–0. Decatur gamblers had cleaned up on the action that day. So it was not surprising that Decatur fans wanted to line their pockets with big bills once more. Two thousand chartered a train from Decatur to Rock Island the day before the game, looking for action.

In spite of its infancy and ragged play, professional football was a lightning rod for gamblers, who were being shooed away from major league parks after the Black Sox scandal. Halas demanded that his players not bet on the games—either for or against the Staleys—but he couldn't be certain the fix was not in. Players made less than a hundred bucks a contest, and with bookmakers working every street corner, the lure of easy money rarely slept. Point spreads were still twenty years away. So if a game was to be fixed, the team taking the dive had to lose outright.

In the Roaring Twenties Americans played the stock market and gambled like there was no tomorrow. The postwar economy was booming, and high rollers like Arnold Rothstein, the man who fixed the 1919 World Series, enjoyed a celebrity normally reserved for politicians, entertainers, and baseball stars. He was the Babe Ruth of his industry. More than anything, he liked to hang around Chi Town, playing high-stakes poker with a southern hustler named Titanic Thompson.

Few people of the era knew that George Gipp, the Notre Dame star who had inspired the great Knute Rockne's "Win one for the Gipper" speech, was a pool hustler and high-stakes cardplayer and loved to bet on the games he played in.

Halas was one of the most worrywartish souls on earth. His gambling phobia bordered on an obsession. That is why the Staleys spent the night before the game against Rock Island across the Mississippi River in the small town of Davenport, Iowa. Halas planned to tuck his boys in early.

The bookies found them anyway. Several were already in the hotel lobby when the Staleys arrived, offering sizable odds against a Decatur win. They also served up an interesting proposition to Trafton: How much would he be willing to wager that the Independents *didn't* knock him out of Sunday's game? The bookies had a potful of money ready to back their side. They were certain that Trafton would fall before the end of the first quarter.

Word on the street was that a hired gun—some guy called Mr. Chicken—would take out Trafton. Mr. Chicken had been hired by the Rockford team specifically to maim or cripple the Brute. Naturally, when Trafton heard about Mr. Chicken, he quickly wagered every dollar in both pockets on himself at odds of 5–2.

Mr. Chicken turned out to be Harry Gunderson, the opposing center-linebacker, who was about Trafton's size. He gave Trafton all he could handle for most of the first quarter. On the final play of the quarter Gunderson burst past Trafton and tackled halfback Jimmy Conzelman for a loss. Trafton stood over Gunderson, waiting to see if the officials were watching. Then he dropped the full weight of his body on Gunderson. Both knees landed squarely on his forehead. The blow opened a six-inch gash that would require almost ninety stitches. Gunderson went to the hospital and didn't come back. Trafton's bet was won, or at least it seemed that way, until the side judge marked off a fifteen-yard penalty and threw Trafton out of the game. That is when Halas sprinted onto the field and started raising hell. After hearing the Bears' player-coach rant and rave for ten minutes, the referee finally overruled the side judge and reinstated Trafton in spite of the howls from the Rockford side.

From their fedoras to their spats, Rock Island fans hated Trafton. Their money was squarely against him making it past the first quarter. They had bet with the bookies until their hands bled. They were now madder than hell that those bets were down the drain.

In the second quarter Trafton really went to work. In a stretch of twelve plays the Decatur hitman knocked four Rock Island players out of the game. Each time a stretcher carried a player from the field, the crowd hurled rocks at Trafton. The officials considered calling off the game, but they also feared for their lives. With the contest locked in a scoreless tie, thousand of dollars were riding on the outcome.

"We're going to kill you, Trafton!" the Rock Island fans yelled. "You won't get out of this town alive!"

When the final gun sounded, and the scoreboard read 0–0, Trafton ran to the Bears bench, where trainer Andy Lotshaw handed him a gray sweatshirt.

"Put this over your jersey so they won't know who you are," Lotshaw yelled. "And run for your life, son." Trafton plucked two milk bottles from the ice bucket. He planned to use them for protection. Then Halas grabbed him by the sweatshirt and stuffed a large brown envelope into his pants.

"Don't lose that," Halas hollered as he pointed to a gate beyond the goal posts. "Run thataway!" Halas and the Bears took off running toward the bus. Trafton went the opposite direction. Hundreds of fans chased the big center, who dashed the length of the field, burst through an open gate, and hailed a taxicab. But before the driver could shift out of neutral, fans began bombing the windshield with huge rocks, shattering the glass. Trafton, still wearing a full uniform and helmet, slid across the backseat and through the other door, and hit the ground running again.

Three hundred yards up the highway, he was still huffing and chugging at full speed. A curious motorist, who had not attended the game, stopped, cranked down his window, and yelled, "Where are you headed, buddy?"

"Davenport—in a hurry. Gotta make a train."

"Hop in."

A few miles down the road Trafton remembered the thick envelope stuffed into the front of his pants. He opened it and counted seven thousand dollars in cash, the Bears' cut of the gate receipts. In the early years, when the pro league was nothing more than a drunken county fair, Halas made sure to get his money up front, in cash.

Trafton reached the station just as the Decatur team train was about to depart. He carried the money straight to Halas.

"Why'd you give it to me?" he asked.

"Because you were running for your life. I was only running for the cash."

• • •

Nagurski, under the tutelage of Trafton, was prepared for his rookie season of 1930 but felt a little nervous. His first training camp had gone so well that it seemed the Bears were counting on him for an NFL championship the first go-around. He knew it was asking too much.

The Bears had moved their training camp to the Notre Dame campus. A famous visitor came to practice that first day. His name was Knute Rockne, and he was looking for the Bronk.

After practice Rockne strolled up to Nagurski, who was cooling out with a bucket of water.

"Nagurski," the Rock said in his gruff voice. "You played the greatest game that I've ever seen a tackle play back in '27 against us. You remember that game. I'm sure you do. I was just starting to use the spinner series back then, and you were in my goddamned backfield all afternoon. At the half I asked our tackle why he wasn't blocking that big Nagurski and keeping him out of our backfield. He said, 'I am, coach. But the big guy just don't pay no attention to me.'"

Rockne threw back his head and laughed. "That's one of the funniest stories I've ever heard," he said.

"It sure is," said the Bronk. "But I remember your guys hittin' pretty hard that day."

"Not as hard as you, big fella," Rockne said as he turned to walk away.

The Bears coaching staff seemed enamored with watching Nagurski carry the ball that summer in South Bend. It took two, three, and sometimes four Bear defenders to bring him down. When the first offense scrimmaged against the defense, the other ball carriers were roundly ignored.

Rookie quarterback Carl "Brummy" Brumbaugh was so determined to win the starting quarterback job from Joey Sternaman that he arranged for the Bronk, his roommate, to pull a fast one on the coaches. As he was about to take the handoff from Brumbaugh, he would pretend to be tripping over his own feet. That allowed Brumbaugh to pull the ball away from Nagurski and to dash thirty-five yards up the middle. Ralph Jones, who had replaced Halas that season as the head coach, was so impressed with this improvisation that he handed Brumbaugh the starting job on the spot.

Though Brumbaugh and Nagurski were rookies, the offense came together rapidly that summer. Brumbaugh turned out to be the right man for the job. The Bears did not need a great passer in this era of the fat ball.

They needed a solid leader with the hands of a cardsharp. Jones's T-formation required that the quarterback fake, twist, twirl, and do everything but perform a back flip before handing the ball off.

Brumbaugh and Nagurski were not the only bright young stars. Ends Gardie Grange and Luke Johnsos became two of the best receivers in the league. Link Lyman was the first defensive lineman in the history of the game to move laterally along the defensive line before the ball was snapped. Lyman played havoc with blocking schemes. Bar none, Trafton and Bill Fleckenstein were the two toughest hombres playing end anywhere. Opposing teams now dreaded playing the bruising Bears.

Because the baseball season had yet to end in late September, the Bears were forced to move their home opener from Wrigley Field to Mills Field, where ten thousand showed up to see Chicago play the Brooklyn Dodgers—the football Dodgers, that is. Nagurski started the game at tackle but was soon moved to fullback.

Both teams moved the ball into scoring position without putting points on the board. Chicago's Sternaman missed two chip-shot field goals. In the fourth quarter Brooklyn drove inside the Bears' ten-yard line with less than three minutes to play, but fullback Izzy Yablock fumbled at the seven and Grange recovered.

With Grange and Nagurski tearing off big yardage, and Brumbaugh completing four passes on the drive, the Bears moved all the way to Brooklyn's one-yard line. Twenty seconds were left on the clock. Brumbaugh made the logical call—a straight dive to Nagurski. Brooklyn stacked the line as Nagurski took the handoff. The world was waiting for his first heroic moment as a pro. It didn't materialize. The Bronk fumbled, Brooklyn recovered, and the game ended in a scoreless tie.

Nagurski would rush for eighty-seven yards the next Sunday at Green Bay's City Stadium, but the Bears were helpless in the scoring department. Meanwhile, the district attorney of Brown County was gaining a lot of votes. The D.A., otherwise known as Verne Lewellen, gained forty-five yards on the only touchdown drive of the day and pushed the ball into the end zone on a one-yard plunge as Green Bay won 7–0.

Nagurski scored his first touchdown of the season in the first quarter against the Minneapolis Redjackets the following week. It was an eight-yard dive off right tackle. He would add another touchdown in the third quarter from two yards out as the Bears snapped their scoring drought with a 20–0 victory, their first of the season.

But their record would fall to 1–2 after the home opener of the season at Wrigley Field against the Giants. Dale Burnett returned a Brumbaugh interception forty yards to the two-yard line and scored the opening touchdown on the next play. Six minutes later he rumbled into the end zone and the Giants had a 12–0 lead. That was the end of the scoring for the day.

The Chicago Cardinals, however, could always be counted on for an easy victory. On October 19, Grange ran for touchdowns of thirty-eight and fifteen yards as the Bears won 32–6.

When Portsmouth sprang a 7–6 upset on October 22, Halas was beginning to wonder if his decision to leave coaching was the right one.

Nagurski scored his third touchdown on a four-yard run the next Sunday against the Frankfort Yellow Jackets for a 13–7 victory, and a week later the Bears moved their record above .500 for the first time all season by beating Minneapolis 20–7. Grange scored touchdowns on a twenty-five-yard pass from Laurie Walquist and a fourteen-yard run.

It seemed unlikely that the Bears, 4–3, could catch the Packers, 7–0, but at least they would be able to measure themselves against the defending NFL champions the following Sunday at Wrigley Field. The Pack was led by one of the best coaches, Curly Lambeau, and the wackiest player outside of Trafton, halfback Johnny Blood.

His real name was Johnny V. McNally, and as the thirties unfolded, he was a superb runner, excellent kicker and passer, good blocker, deadly tackler, and the best receiver in football. But he was no longer known as Johnny McNally. Now it was Johnny Blood.

He came from a wealthy family of newspaper publishers and paper-mill owners and he never needed football to make a living. But he was obsessed with the game. Like Trafton, he had been booted out of Notre Dame for playing semipro ball. He figured his final hope for football stardom lay with St. John's College in Collegeville, Minnesota, but the temptress known as pro football was forever flirting. One Sunday afternoon he decided to risk another shot at the pros, but he was determined this time to protect his college eligibility. He began toying with the idea of using an assumed name. He convinced his friend Ralph Hanson, another St. John's footballer, to join him on the new pro team in town— the East 26th Street Liberties.

They were riding past a movie marquee on Johnny's motorcycle when the boys spotted the title *Blood and Sand* on a movie marquee. The star of the movie was Rudolph Valentino. McNally decided to change his surname to Blood. Hanson became Ralph Sand. Neither went back to college or ever used their real names again.

Years later, after stints with the Milwaukee Badgers and Duluth Eskimos, Blood was discovered by Lambeau. He was the biggest reason that the Green Bay Packers were crowned league champions in 1929. Blood's football feats could not diminish the renegade side of his life. On the day the Packers completed their unbeaten season, edging the 13–1–1 New York Giants for the title, they were railing home and the bootleg booze was flowing when Blood ticked off one of his teammates, Lavvie Dilweg, who chased his screwball teammate from car to car until they reached the back of the train. Dilweg figured he had Blood trapped. That was before Blood leaped from the rear of the caboose, hitched on to a ladder, and hoisted himself atop the car. To the dismay of everyone, he ran toward the front of the train, leaping from car to car, defying death, screaming like a madman, until he slid down into the cabin of the locomotive, where he startled the hell out of the engineer and fireman. Blood rode the remainder of the trip up front, entertaining his two new friends with his zany sense of humor all the way to Green Bay.

Blood had hawkish features, deep-set eyes, and a thick tassel of black hair that fell across his forehead. Women loved everything about him, especially the devil-may-care attitude. Once, when a beautiful woman asked for an autograph, he opened a vein and signed in blood.

In November of 1930, the day before the Packers were to meet the Bears at Wrigley Field in one of the NFL's greatest showdowns, Blood was entertaining a voluptuous blonde and running a bit late to the station. The Packers' train was pulling away when Blood reached into his bag of stunts. He parked his Packard across the tracks. As the train bore down on them, the couple closed their eyes and prayed. The brakes squealed, and the engine finally stopped, the cowcatcher practically nuzzling the side of Blood's car.

As he leaped onto the train, Blood winked at the engineer and said, "I guess you stopped when you saw me."

"Nah," the engineer said. "It was the dame."

Blood had avoided yet another catastrophe. Now the Packers were two hundred miles from Chicago, where a locomotive named Nagurski was waiting.

# 5

# Wall Banger

It was spitting snow that November morning at the corner of Clark and Addison when the parade of Scarface Al and his hit men turned more heads than Greta Garbo waltzing to her window table at the Brown Derby. In the entourage that numbered more than a dozen burly gangsters were "Machine Gun" Jack McGurn and Jack Guzik, known as "Greasy Thumb." Conspicuously absent was Frank Nitti.

They were led to a reserved table beneath a wide plate-glass window that offered a view for blocks of any weasel, wise guy, or cop who might be passing by. You could wink at the dames on the sidewalk or gaze across the broad avenue at Wrigley Field, where the sign above the main entrance announced, BEARS VS. PACKERS—TODAY, 1 P.M.

Everyone was talking about the game of the year and the most exciting young player in pro football—Bronko Nagurski.

The Cubs Grille was aswing with football revelers. They had begun to pour in around dawn, when the late-night speakeasies closed up. The smoke-filled first floor was now bursting with politicians, gangsters, celebrities, bootleggers, and dreamers. Up the wooden stairwell they ordered highballs and danced to Louis Armstrong. In great demand were the local bookmakers, who scribbled down bets in black notebooks. The

Packers, boasting a six-game winning streak over Chicago, and starring the sensational Johnny Blood, were 7-5 favorites—for now, anyway. Capone and the boys were thirsty for some action.

Al Capone *was* Chicago and everything Chicago strove to be. He was a jowly Satan, a round man who wore a pinkie ring worth fifty grand and kissed old ladies on street corners, passed out large bills to strangers and twenties to hatcheck girls, and considered himself a latter-day Robin Hood. He wore custom-tailored suits of outrageous colors—purple, electric blue and yellow, along with the best fedoras money could buy. People on the street considered him a hero and federal agent Eliot Ness nothing more than a smelly beast. Clearly, he was the biggest game in town, much larger than the Cubs or the White Sox. The Chicago Bears, the fledgling professional football team, were not in his league, though Nagurski was raising the currency.

Capone's release from prison after ten months had landed him on the cover of *Time* magazine, an honor normally reserved for the tycoons adored by publisher Henry Luce. Capone, after all, was one of America's leading capitalists, a man with fifty million stashed away. He was the nation's leading purveyor of bootlegging and racketeering, and with every strand of hair slicked into place, his suit pressed, and his shirt starched, Capone looked the part of big business. For the *Time* photograph he turned the unscarred half of his face to the camera. A rose adorned his lapel. He was quite pleased with the portrait that emerged: "Capone is the No. 1 underworldling of the U.S.," the magazine reported.

Not long after the crowds cheered his Pullman car rolling into the Illinois Central Station, Capone and his lieutenants took command of the top three floors of the Lexington Hotel, his favorite roost in the heart of Chicago. He was photographed beneath the framed portraits of George Washington, Abe Lincoln, and "Big Bill" Thompson, the mayor and the master of the big wink. The morning after the all-night whiskey orgy that included gamblers, gangsters, politicians, and practically every prostitute in town, Capone was back at work. His racketeering throne reclaimed, and with Prohibition in full, ugly flower, the only limit to his empire was the broad, blue sky over Lake Michigan.

The Man had cemented his status as "Public Enemy Number One" on February 14, 1929, with the notorious St. Valentine's Day Massacre at 2122 North Clark Street, just about a mile from Wrigley Field. According to some reports, he wielded a machine gun that day; others placed him in Florida.

At ten o'clock that morning, when the mercury registered eighteen degrees, the Capone gang, led by "Machine Gun" Jack McGurn, arrived at the S.M.C. Cartage Company, a small garage on the North Side, dressed as Chicago cops and riding in a stolen police car. Their aim was to wipe out the O'Banion gang, which had made several attempts on Scarface's life. Their leader was "Bugs" Moran, who was obsessed with the idea of ending Capone's reign and thereby leapfrogging *Campansilo* to the top of the crime charts.

McGurn held an impeccable blueprint for death: Moran's boys would be lured into that grimy den with the promise that they could purchase a large shipment of Old Log Cabin, a reputable whiskey distilled in Canada, not in some South Side bathtub. On the evening of February 13 Moran received a phone call from a "hijacker" who claimed to have knocked over a load off the Saint Clair River, which separated Detroit from Canada. The two decided their transaction would take place at the nondescript garage that was the Moran hideout.

At ten sharp, the four button men, disguised as Chicago cops, stepped from the police car and rumbled into the garage, guns drawn, simulating an arrest for violating the laws of Prohibition. Their adversaries were quickly disarmed. Minutes later, four executioners opened fire on the helpless gang with two Thompson guns, a.k.a. "Chicago typewriters," along with a sawed-off shotgun. Seven gangsters slumped to the floor, dead. Two "cops" then herded two of Capone's men, now dressed in overcoats, into the squad car for the purpose of confusing possible witnesses. It was a clever plan. The Chicago police, it appeared, had made two arrests and now were hurtling back to the station, siren blaring.

The St. Valentine's Day Massacre not only defined Capone and his gang, it riveted worldwide attention on Chicago. Poet Carl Sandburg wrote of his hometown: "Here's the difference between us and Dante. He wrote a lot about hell and never saw the place. We're writing about Chicago after looking the place over."

Capone's fears of assassination had receded since his release from the Gray Bar Hotel. He was making regular public appearances again. The St. Valentine's Day Massacre was starting to fade from Chicagoans' memories. Capone's second love, outside of a brothel, was the swirl of sports fans. He was a semiregular at Chicago Cubs games, where he would sit in the front row close to the on-deck circle, often chatting with Cubs catcher Gabby Hartnett until a local newspaper photographer named Tony Berardi snapped a picture of the two. Kenesaw Mountain Landis, the fist-in-glove commissioner who had kicked Shoeless Joe Jackson and seven other White Sox players out of baseball for throwing the 1919 World Series, took one look at the Capone-Hartnett photograph and ruled that players could no longer fraternize with gangsters. That didn't stop Capone from making friends with whomever he pleased. Capone was drawn to the animal that lived inside Jack Dempsey, the Manassa Mauler. So tough was Dempsey that the man sloshed bull urine on his face because it made the skin harder to cut. He possessed a matchless dedication to the kill.

Before the famous second Dempsey-Tunney heavyweight title bout in 1927, Capone paid regular visits to the Dempsey fight camp. He also purchased a hundred ringside seats, at forty bucks apiece, and bet fifty Gs on his pal.

Scarface Al could not have chosen a greater era to fall in love with American sport: Bill Tilden smashing tennis balls, Babe Ruth swatting baseballs, Red Grange toting footballs from Chicago to New York and back—this was clearly the Golden Age of Sports. Grange was a per-durable drawing card. But the player Capone had come to see today was the bullish rookie from Minnesota, the man who turned tacklers into tomato cans.

The NFL had ridden into the 1930 season on the broad shoulders of Bronko Nagurski. It took less than half a season for Nagurski to forge a reputation as the toughest player in the game. The *Chicago Tribune* described his style as "smashing, driving and forever fighting." When the Bears and Packers had played back in September, he felled Hurdis McCrary with a knee to the chin. Also carried off the field that day with various broken bones was Cully Lidberg, a big fullback who was no slouch at hitting. But he had made the mistake of not avoiding a head-to-head collision with Nagurski at the line of scrimmage. Lidberg moaned in great pain as the stretcher removed him from City Stadium, the crowd booing Nagurski. The sight of a motionless Lidberg, another Minnesota native, shook the Bronk. It was not unusual for Nagurski to feel guilty after hurting a player. As Bronko and the Bears watched Lidberg leaving the field, he told quarterback Carl Brumbaugh, "I'm never going to hit a man like that again."

Lidberg had been eighteen-wheeled by a technique Nagurski had perfected back at the University of Minnesota. He folded both arms across his chest and leaned forward at a forty-five-degree angle, driving his right shoulder at full speed into the opponent's sternum. The player went down and often remained there. Some were left breathless, others unconscious. Still others heard birds singing.

"Brummy, I don't want 'em to think I'm a dirty player," Nagurski said. "No way."

George Trafton overheard those words. It still amazed him that a human tank like Nagurski could speak so softly in such a high tone.

"Look, Big Nag," he said to Nagurski. "Everybody in this league is gunnin' for your ass. Besides, with me around, nobody's ever gonna call you a dirty player."

"The Big Nag" was a college nickname that did not catch on with the pros until Big Bill Fleckenstein heard it.

"Big Nag!" the tackle bellowed. "Get out of the way and let the Big Nag gallop!"

Green Bay-Chicago on November 9, 1930, at sold-out Wrigley Field on the eighth Sunday of the NFL season was the Game of the Year.

The Bears, 4–3–1, had opened the season with a scoreless tie against Brooklyn and a 7–0 loss to Green Bay. The Packers, the defending league champions, stood unbeaten through seven games.

Chicago had won three of its last four games, and the biggest reason, at least in the mind of Trafton, was his own timely return to the starting lineup; some kid named Bert Pearson had swiped his job back in preseason camp when Halas had tried to run Trafton off. Halas leaked the news to six Chicago newspapers that Trafton was gone. The big center responded with his own one-sentence news release: "Although Messrs. Halas and Sternaman did not offer me a contract, I've joined the squad and am going to make them give me my old job back at center."

After the debacle in 1929, when the Bears finished 4–9–2, Halas was ready to try anything and finally relented to Trafton. Chicago had not won a game the final two months of that season, their final victory coming on October 27, two days before Black Tuesday. The Bears crashed just like the stock market. Meanwhile, the Packers reeled off seven straight wins, all on the road, and culminated their championship run with a 25–0 humiliation of the proud Bears on December 8, the date that George Halas hung up both his coaching whistle and his cleats and headed for the front office. He hired little-known offensive guru Ralph Jones to coach the team.

While the Bears licked their wounds in Chi Town after the final resounding defeat of the season, the Packers caught a train for Green Bay that arrived that night in a town gone mad. Some of the Packer players were concerned to see an eerie red light in the distance as the train approached the station. They speculated that an accident had occurred, prompting warning lights. Instead, it was thousand upon thousands of citizens lining the tracks waving red flares. On that bitterly cold night, an estimated twenty thousand fans, more than half the town's population, jammed the station, perching atop roofs and boxcars, even climbing telephone poles. The chief of police allowed the bars to stay open all night. Johnny Blood led the revelry straight into the dawn's early light.

Now on November 9, 1930, as Capone and the boys socked away pregame whiskey, more than a thousand Packer fans streamed down the long, wooden stairway from the El station onto Addison Boulevard. Green-and-gold fans were everywhere. They were liquored up and ready for action, having taken a rollicking train ride two hundred miles from Green Bay to Chicago. The railroads had converted baggage cars into bar cars. Naturally, a good portion of the green-and-gold contingency was headed straight for the Cubs Grille, where the bootleg whiskey never ran dry. To hell with the Great Depression!

Capone didn't like the looks of the mob descending on his turf. But two hours before kickoff, a delightful image crept into his head. "Nothing but a flock of pigeons," he said to himself. "Easy money."

Scarface Al summoned one of his lieutenants, Fred "Killer" Burke, to the table. Burke was as beefy and leathery-skinned as McGurn was sleek and handsome. Only a few bar patrons knew him or his reputation. Capone ordered the Killer to work the room, pumping the Packer Backers and taking their bets.

"Tell the suckers we'll give 'em even money instead of taking 7–5," Capone said. "I got twenty grand cash on me. Go out there and take candy from the babies."

Capone was a fan of Burke's work. The Killer was cold-blooded, mean-spirited, and efficient. He came from St. Louis, where he had worked for Egan's Rat Gang, which was affiliated with Capone's boot-legging operation. McGurn called him to Chicago to be a button man at the St. Valentine's Day Massacre. Burke's only known weakness was a penchant for cheating at golf; he liked to improve bad lies with a foot wedge.

As he collected the bets, Burke arranged for all of the money to be held in a safe inside the manager's office until the game ended. That way there would be no welshing—no need to hunt down a man and cut off his ear. It took the Killer less than a half hour to complete his rounds. He had tracked down every loudmouthed cheesehead and challenged him, and most coughed up a decent wager. Capone could not have been happier if the Killer had knocked off Bugs Moran.

The buzz inside the Cubs Grille since ten that morning had been about Capone and his boys. But catching a glimpse of the Mafia chieftain was another matter. Burly mobsters acted as human shields, surrounding him at the table and hiding him from the crowd. Thirty minutes before kick-off, though, the place started to thin out. Packer fans craned their necks to see Capone sitting in the corner. He wore a pearl-colored fedora with a black headband, a dark double-breasted suit with a diamond stickpin, and spats. The fans pointed at the kingpin. Then they spotted the bulky, stubble-faced man sitting next to him—Killer Burke!

"Oh, my God," one of them said. "We've bet our money with Al *Capone.*"

Snow was flying and the streets now teemed with foot traffic. Street-cars slowed to avoid the masses, brakes squealing. Vendors hawked ear-muffs and made a killing. Fans crowded through steel gates at Addison from the south, Waveland from the north, Sheffield on the east side, and Clark from the west.

George Halas managed a smile at the scene inside Wrigley Field. Every seat was filled, which was a rarity for the NFL, especially during the Depression. This would be one of Halas's rare opportunities to put some money in the bank. Hot dogs and peanuts were going fast. It was the kind of atmosphere you might expect for the Cubs and the Yankees in game seven of the World Series.

Not every Sunday in the fledgling football league was this exhilarating. Nor did the cash register always ring with such frequency. Green Bay versus Chicago was the rage of the NFL. Frankford or Portsmouth coming to Wrigley Field would draw a crowd that might fit into a soup kitchen. President Herbert Hoover kept saying, "Prosperity is just around the corner." But the NFL, like many other outfits, was slowly going bust.

Halas, believing the surest path to financial solvency was a smaller NFL, had led the charge to eliminate some of the bottom feeders— Racine, Hartford, Louisville, Hammond, and Akron. That was 1927. Now, with the onset of the Depression, a sharp axe was no longer required. The league, like the dollar, was shrinking—all the way from twenty-two teams to eleven in just three years.

As the Packers and Bears stormed onto the field, Halas's intestines coiled into a knot. He hated the Green Bay Packers and their coach, Curly Lambeau, with every fiber in his body. "Look at those Packer pricks," he yelled from his fifty-yard-line seats high in the stadium, "those bastards!" He scanned the west stands. His anger spilled over like a boiling pot at the ugly sight of Capone and his boys. Halas quickly surmised that the betting handle was astronomical. "Somebody oughtta put that bastard in jail," he said a little less loudly. "He better not be fixing *my* games."

Halas had far larger problems than Capone and his gangsters. The Bears had financial problems that ran deep. Anyone witnessing the events of this day—the large crowd, the fancy clothes, the willingness to spend—might suspect that Halas was sitting on a gold mine. Not so. Both Halas and co-owner Dutch Sternaman had gone broke during the stock market crash. Though Halas had recouped some of his money in a local real estate deal, Sternaman needed cash, and he needed it fast.

Halas left coaching for the purpose of putting the Bears and himself on the road to financial recovery. With Nagurski making five grand a season and Grange not far behind, he had the biggest payroll in the league. He needed every cent he could put his hands on. The day would come— and it would come soon —when Sternaman would demand that he buy out his fifty percent of the team. That is why Halas had stepped aside and hired Ralph Jones to coach.

Halas now gazed down upon the vast expanse of Wrigley Field, covered with Kentucky bluegrass, and regarded his prideful work: Nagurski at fullback and Grange at right halfback, along with one of the best lines in football, made the Bears contenders once more. Halas prayed the Bears could catch fire in the second half and somehow steal the championship from Green Bay. Of course, the unbeaten Packers weren't exactly cottage cheese: Johnny Blood happened to be the league's best runner-receiver, and big Cal Hubbard, all 250 pounds of him, was a man-mountain at tackle. Not only could Verne Lewellen pass and run, he happened to be the premier punter of the era.

Unlike most venues built for baseball, Wrigley Field was a football fan's paradise. Constructed in 1914, it became known as Cubs Park six years later. In 1926 it was renamed for William Wrigley Jr., the club's owner. The west grandstand stood parallel to what would have been the third-base line; the distance from railing to sideline was all of twelve feet. You could almost reach out and touch the players. Players frequently banged into the brick wall, and footballs sailed into the stands. Cops rode up and down the sideline on horseback to ensure that no brave souls toppled over the wall and onto the field.

The massive left-field wall, twelve feet tall, glowered over the north end of the field. Before a three-foot basket was added to the top of the wall, fans could lean over and dump beer or whiskey onto the players. The north end zone itself was only nine yards long—one short of NFL regulations—and it abutted the brick and mortar of the left-field wall.

The south end zone was a full ten yards in length. But if a player took one step beyond the end line, he was certain to land in the visiting team's dugout. Players often vanished after scoring a touchdown, tripping and tumbling down the dugout steps.

The smell of cigars filled the air. Not a soul in the house was without a lid—the men in fedoras, snap-brims, and Kangol caps, the women mostly in knit hairdresses.

With the game underway, all eyes were on Nagurski. He piled into the line for eight yards, then nine yards, then three more. Brumbaugh, playing without a helmet, was deadset on riding the Big Nag to victory. Before kickoff, the rookie quarterback from Ohio State had pulled Grange aside to set things straight.

"Look, I know a lot of people paid good money to see you run," Brummy said. "But I know you got the bad knee. What's up?"

"Give the ball to the Bronk," Grange said, smiling.

Brummy could have kissed the Galloping Ghost. He planned to feed Nagurski the ball all day, using Grange as a decoy.

Thanks to the conservative strategy of both teams, the game remained scoreless for most of the first half. Lewellen pinned the Bears deep time and again with his booming punts. As the teams lined up for yet another punt, tackle Link Lyman, one of the three helmetless Bears, shouted, "We're going to win this damned ball game. I guarantee it!"

Once again, Lewellen launched a rocket deep into Bears' territory.

As players hustled down the field, Packers center "Jug" Earpe wheeled on Lyman and said, "Are y'all ever gonna score?"

Lyman shot back, "You wouldn't be shit without Lewellen!"

"Maybe," Earpe said. "But we've got him. He's *ours*."

Minutes later, the Bears were lining up to punt the ball back to Green Bay. Big Cal Hubbard leaned over and whispered to Grange, "Hey, Ghost, let me through this time. I promise I won't block the punt. I just want a shot at that Nagurski. I want to see if the boy's as tough as everybody says."

Grange managed to hide his smile. Half a season with Nagurski was enough to see that this man was the toughest S.O.B. in the valley. So the Ghost was more than obliged to arrange this train wreck.

Hubbard rumbled untouched through the line and straight for Nagurski, who braced himself to protect his punter. Fans in the upper reaches of Wrigley Field could see the behemoth bearing down. Then a stiff right forearm, the size of a shoat, rose up and rocked Hubbard's jaw. The blow sounded like a baseball bat connecting with a melon. A long *oooooh* rolled through the stands as Hubbard crumpled. He staggered to his feet and stumbled groggily up the field until his eyes were able to focus on the number seventy-seven.

"Thanks, Ghost, my old pal," Hubbard slurred. "Please make sure that never happens again."

Just before halftime Lewellen managed to drag three tacklers into the end zone from the three-yard line, and the Packers led 6–0. But the Bears trotted confidently back to the locker room, knowing that Nagurski was getting the best of the Pack. Nagurski's run of thirty-five yards late in the second quarter had set up the Bears with a first down on the three-yard line. But Brummy bobbled the snap and Green Bay recovered.

Part of the halftime entertainment was an interview over the public address system with world welterweight boxing champion Mickey

Walker, who told the crowd, "After seeing these two teams play, I don't think my racket is very tough."

Early in the third quarter the Bronk tore through three tacklers, ran over Lewellen and Hubbard, and rumbled fifty-seven yards before the Packers caught him at the two-yard line. This time Brummy made a decoy out of Nagurski, pulling the ball from his midsection and pitching it to halfback Laurie Walquist, who darted around right end for the touchdown. The extra-point kick failed, and the score was tied at six.

That is when Blood got into the act. He carried the ball six straight times and caught two passes, moving Green Bay into Bears territory. And, of course, Lewellen would not go away. He caught a twenty-one-yard touchdown pass from Red Dunn, the fat ball wobbling like a wounded bird as it descended into Lewellen's thick fingers. The Packers led 13–6 with seven minutes to play.

A good many Packer fans were familiar with the scene about to unfold. Back in Madison in 1928 they had sat huddled in silence when Nagurski ruined Wisconsin's unbeaten season by carrying six tacklers into the end zone for a 6–0 victory.

As the final two minutes clicked away, Nagurski carried the ball eight straight times to the two. This time, Brummy forgot the trickery. With forty seconds to play, he slid the ball into the Bronk's gut. The Big Nag broke through the grip of two Packers like Tom Mix bursting through saloon doors and hurtled into the end zone. Head down, unable to halt his momentum, Nagurski plowed headfirst into the outfield wall. Thirty thousand fans were on their feet, cheering the touchdown. That was before his helmet struck the wall and his massive neck bent. A long groan rolled across the stadium.

Nagurski was punch-drunk. He staggered but managed to stay on his feet. His legs were like rubber. He managed to kick those legs back to life, and he trundled toward the sideline as the crowd roared. Trafton, who was by his side, yelled, "You all right, Bronk?"

"Yeah, Traf," Nagurski said. "But that last sonofabitch hit me pretty hard."

Trafton laughed. "Shit, Bronk, that wasn't no player. You just cracked a brick in that goddamned wall."

The cheering and the laughter died when Walter Homer's extra-point kick slid right of the goalpost. In the blink of an eye, the greatest day in the Bears' history was over. Green Bay 13, Chicago 12.

The final line on Bronko's day was 123 yards rushing, one touchdown, nineteen tackles, and a chipped brick.

Six rows up, on the fifty-yard line, the Capone gang braced for the inevitable explosion. The man was twenty thousand lighter. But Scarface Al rose slowly from his seat, crushed the cigar beneath his heel, and tugged at the brim of his fedora.

"Greatest fucking performance I've ever seen," he said.

Then, like thirty-eight thousand others, Capone buttoned up his overcoat and moved silently into the gathering darkness.

# 6

# The Ghost

Red Grange shuffled along the sidewalk that morning, the full-length raccoon coat shielding him against the swirling snow as a burst of wind tore down Clark Street and knocked him off balance. As he fell, Grange wrenched the left knee that had been nothing but torture since the Chicago–New York game three years earlier at Wrigley Field. The Galloping Ghost was a tragic story, that of a man who had climbed to the pinnacle, then fallen. He was the man who had saved pro football from the wrecking ball years ago. Now it would be a struggle just to save himself.

On December 7, 1930, the final Sunday of Bronko Nagurski's rookie season, Green Bay was back in town. The Packers needed a win over the Bears to clinch their second straight NFL championship. Chicago, in spite of four straight wins, was playing for pride alone; the Bears would finish third in the league standings regardless of the outcome. Christmas was around the corner. Bags were packed. It was little wonder that Green Bay was the 5–1 betting favorite.

Grange limped down the Wrigley Field steps into the tunnel that led to the locker-room door. Head down, raccoon coat soaked, the Ghost was on his way to see trainer Andy Lotshaw, the man he knew better than anyone in Chicago. The Ghost was the earliest arrival each Sunday because Lotshaw needed extra time to put his body back together. Thanks to the team's dwindling resources, though, the training room this morning was bereft of wrapping tape, rubbing liniment, even aspirin.

"Sorry, Ghost. The old man says that I got to wait for some ticket money before I can buy tape," Lotshaw said. "Times are tough."

Grange, a model of humility, merely smiled. He was good at hiding the pain.

The saddest commentary on the era was that the Bears did not have the pocket change to buy a roll of tape for the man once considered the greatest player ever to lace up cleats. The orders had come down from George Halas: Spend no money until customers slide some cash through the ticket window. Only then could Lotshaw dash across the street to Brandon's Drugstore for the medical supplies that should have been stacked high on the training room shelves.

Halas was not just financially strapped, he was a financially strapped penny-pincher. During a game against the now-defunct New York (football) Yankees, the Bears' Paddy Driscoll had drop-kicked an extra point into the stands. A fan stuffed the ball under his shirt and took off. Though Chicago was the home team, Halas refused to continue the game until the Yankees supplied another ball.

Still hours from kickoff, Grange grabbed the *Tribune* and sat down next to the locker where the drowned raccoon now hung. Five years earlier, when the Ghost had come spinning off the Illinois campus, the coat was a symbol of fame and affluence. The fashion item was purchased during the barnstorming tour of 1925, when fans were tearing through the turnstiles to see him play. The eighteen-game tour with Halas and the Chicago Bears netted him a quarter-million dollars, an astronomical figure for the times, when the average pay in pro football was a hundred bucks a game. Weeks after leaving the Illinois campus, the Ghost was making more money than Babe Ruth or Jack Dempsey. He was knocking down bigger headlines. He was twenty-one.

The Bears headed east at the end of the '25 regular season to start the barnstorming tour against the Giants, one of the NFL's newest franchises. So wild-eyed was New York City that the police chief assigned fifty cops to escort Grange to the dressing room. Sportswriter Damon Runyon described the scene: "Seventy thousand men, women, and children were in the stands, blocking the aisles and runways. Twenty thousand more were perched on Coogan's Bluff and the roofs of apartment houses over-looking the baseball home of McGraw's club, content with just an occasional glimpse of the whirling mass of players on the field far below and wondering which was Red Grange."

Sitting alongside Runyon in the press box was Grantland Rice, who had anointed Grange "the Galloping Ghost" because, in the mind's eye of the writer, the swift and elusive halfback left a vapor trail wherever he ran.

It didn't matter that Grange rushed for only fifty-three yards against the Giants on a muddy field that day or that the Bears prevailed 19–7 in a boring game. What registered in the public's collective mind was that the Ghost had dragged professional football out of the Dark Ages. Hundreds of thousands of fans sat next to their radios and absorbed every word of the broadcast. Millions of Americans in both urban and rural locales read newspaper accounts of the game.

They thirsted for more information about the man who had scored four touchdowns in the first twelve minutes of a 1924 game against Michigan. It was the showdown that America would never forget. Illinois versus Michigan had been hyped as Armageddon by the sporting press, for the Midwest in that era presided as the center of the college football universe. Illinois had not lost in ten straight games, Michigan in twenty. Sixty-seven thousand fans saw the Ghost whiz ninety-four yards for a touchdown on the second play of the game. Though Grange sat out the entire second quarter, he still rushed for five touchdowns, passed for another touchdown, and gained 402 yards on twenty-one carries against the second-ranked team in the entire country. Michigan boasted a defense once described as a machine. But the Illini never broke a sweat in the 39–14 victory.

Yet another powerful medium that illuminated the Ghost, especially during his pro years, was the ten-minute newsreel that served as standard fare with motion pictures. Sixty million people went to the movies each week in the mid-twenties. As the Golden Age of Sports unfolded, more and more football footage was fed into newsreels, a spicy forerunner to TV news. The grainy black-and-white images of Grange made him appear almost ghostly as he flickered across the screen, gliding through defenses from the Polo Grounds in New York to the Coliseum in Los Angeles. Moviegoers cheered the sight of their hero.

Grange and Halas were invited to the White House after the Giants game. Both men were filled with pride when they walked into the Oval Office and were introduced to President Calvin Coolidge as "members of the Chicago Bears." Coolidge gave both an admiring smile and said, "How are you, gentlemen? Welcome to the White House. You know, I've always been a great admirer of animal acts."

Not everyone was as misinformed as Coolidge. In fact, Babe Ruth could not wait to meet Grange and arranged for a dinner with America's newest idol when the Bears came to New York. Newspaper photographers swarmed the two as they strolled toward a steakhouse inside the Astor Hotel. The Bambino had this advice: "Keed, don't believe anything they write about you. Get the dough while the getting's good, but don't break your heart trying to get it. And don't pick up too many checks."

Timing is everything. It was an axiom perfectly suited for the twenties when urbanites let down their hair and unleashed their sexual appetites. They became a free-spending people who evolved with industrial expansion, the automobile boom, the birth of mass media, and the emergence of the motion picture. Hemlines rose and necklines dropped.

America was on the Nagurski muscle after World War I. Stadiums rose like steel temples across the country: Yankee Stadium was unveiled in 1923, and other massive structures—the Rose Bowl in Pasadena and Soldier Field in Chicago—were built for crowds exceeding one hundred thousand.

In America, no better model for adulation could have been constructed than Red Grange. A small-town boy from the Midwest, he was regarded as the rugged independent type who had risen by virtue of his own work ethic. Grange was known as the "Wheaton Iceman" because, as a teenager, he had delivered huge blocks of ice all over town. Before Wheaton was connected to Chicago by the electric railroad and swallowed by urban sprawl, it still possessed a small-town flavor, and Grange exuded that air of innocence. The eastern press would lionize Charles Lindbergh for his soft-spoken nature and absence of pretension. The same portrait of Grange emerged.

So stoked were Chicagoans with the news of Grange's signing back in 1925 that he was barely able to penetrate the gates of Cubs Park for a game he merely planned to watch. Three thousand fans mobbed him the moment he stepped from a taxicab. A squadron of cops ushered him to the Bears bench. He almost decided to forgo the second half and wait it out in the locker room, but midway through the third quarter he relented and was accompanied back to the field by what amounted to a military escort.

Four days later the Bears were scheduled to play the league-leading Chicago Cardinals on Thanksgiving at Cubs Park, and tickets were selling faster than they could be printed. Twenty thousand were gobbled up in one day. Nearly forty thousand fans were in their seats an hour before kickoff. But the crosstown Cardinals were not about to bow down to the rookie star. They were not amused that Grange had commanded all of the headlines in spite of their own Paddy Driscoll, clearly the best running back in the NFL. All afternoon Driscoll punted away from Grange, and the Bear faithful responded with boos and hisses. Grange did not break a single long run, and his rushing statistics were pedestrian: sixteen carries for thirty-six yards. His most noteworthy accomplishment was intercepting a pass in the end zone. The game ended in a scoreless tie.

Four weeks later the Bears railed east to begin their eighteen-game tour. A nation anxiously awaited the arrival of Grange, depot by depot. The only thing missing was the presence of Nagurski, who was still five years from bursting onto the pro football scene.

This should have been the best of times for the Redhead. Never in the history of professional football had there been such a clamor. Stadiums from St. Louis to Pittsburgh to Boston to New York to Philadelphia to Washington were sold out long before his arrival. Tall, bold headlines once reserved for the likes of Dempsey, Ruth, Tilden, and Bobby Jones were offered up to the feats of Grange. But the Ghost was not smiling. From town to town he was haunted by powerful men who opposed the very existence of the NFL. Grange was slammed from all four corners— from the pulpit to college presidents to his very own college coach, Bob Zuppke, who had virtually begged him not to play professional football. Zuppke flatly said, "Football is not a game to be played for money." Moralists questioned his values. Famous college coach Amos Alonzo Stagg, the leader of the anti-pro movement, released these biting words to the press: "To cooperate with Sunday professional football games is to cooperate with forces which are destructive of the finest elements of scholastic and intercollegiate football and to add to the heavy burden of the schools and colleges in preserving it in its ennobling worth."

Grange's face turned dark when he heard about Stagg's quote. "I guess I would've been better off if I'd signed on with the Capone gang instead of the Chicago Bears," he said.

As anticipated, though, the crowds were enormous, the hype unmatched, as the tour cranked up in early December. C.C. Pyle, the indefatigable promoter, rarely left Grange's side, and, unlike his star, he rarely stopped smiling. Pyle sat on the Bears bench next to his star during games. He always seemed to have Grange's ear. He became known as "Cash and Carry" Pyle by the sporting press. Before gaining a foothold in pro sports, though, he'd been nothing more than a bargain-basement entrepreneur.

To his credit, Pyle transformed Grange into a money machine. In promotions alone, the Ghost pocketed about forty grand on the eastern tour, hawking everything from meatloaf to ginger ale. Grange admired Pyle because he was suave and sophisticated. Most of all the Redhead appreciated his manager's hard-line negotiating tactics. When a company made an offer in the neighborhood of $5,000, Pyle always demanded twenty-five grand.

It seemed that everyone but Grange could see through Pyle, who floated the news to reporters during the tour that he had negotiated a $300,000 movie deal for the Redhead. Everyone laughed but Grange, who believed that a fledgling part-time actor really could command that kind of money in the mid-twenties.

Other problems arose. Pyle quickly proved that he was out of his league when it came to pro football. Eight games in twelve days—yes, eight sixty-minute games on the eastern swing against some of the best players the NFL had to offer—provided a grueling pace that would have worn down an entire roster of Bronko Nagurskis. Only eighteen Bears players made the trip, and substitutions were rare. Most of the games were played in wintry storms. Grange injured his arm against Philadelphia, and also suffered ankle, knee, and wrist sprains. Several times he was the victim of cheap shots, and he was knocked groggy by an illegal blow to the back of the head in New York. Little did the coaches or trainers know that Grange's body was already in the process of breaking down.

Believing that Grange was larger than the league itself, Pyle persuaded his star to break away from the NFL after the 1925 season and to start the American Football League. Pyle and Grange founded the New York Yankees. The league would consist of eight teams. Fans did flock to see the Ghost, but the other teams were financial busts. With the exception of Grange, the AFL was unable to lure any of the noteworthy names from the NFL.

When the AFL folded, Halas and the other owners were ecstatic. They quickly welcomed Grange and the Yankees into the NFL in 1927. Grange received top billing wherever he played, and the voices of the anti-NFL zealots were quieted. The Ghost performed miracles on the field, spinning on a dime and bursting through holes no larger than a block of ice. But during a game against the Bears in '27 at a place now called Wrigley Field, his world turned. A cleat caught in the mud as his knee locked up. Hurtling straight toward the Ghost was none other than George Trafton. His 230 pounds landed on Grange's left knee joint, creating a loud pop heard thirty rows up. Ligaments and cartilage were shredded. Grange, in spite of horrid pain, never blamed Trafton.

"There was nothing dirty about it," he said. So distraught was Big George at seeing the Redhead writhing in pain that he lifted him into his arms and carried him off the field.

Grange tried to play two weeks later on the bum knee, but it wobbled. Orthopedic surgeons often describe the knee joint as two broomsticks attached to a rubber ball, the entire contraption bound together by rubber bands. The Ghost was missing key rubber bands. Doctors knew little at the time about surgical procedures for the knee. They prescribed rest. One doctor stuck Grange's leg in a barrel of ice, another in a cast. Within days of the injury, the medial collateral and anterior cruciate ligaments, which are comparable to spaghetti strings, shriveled away. Grange could not walk down the street without the knee slipping out of place.

Football had known its share of balletic halfbacks, power runners, and speedburners. Grange was all three. He sliced between defenders as if on ice skates, and accelerated like a man shot from a cannon. If necessary, the Ghost ran over tacklers. Now, though, his graceful magic was dying. He was twenty-four.

Grange announced that he would skip the entire 1928 season, and the Yankees instantly went belly up.

The injury was really only the beginning of his troubles. His faith in Pyle and the promoter's outlandish schemes cost him a fortune. The fast lane no longer suited the Ghost. He told a reporter, "I will never marry until I meet a girl far more sensible than the flappers who have flocked around me since I became a headliner." Then, in Chicago, Grange was arrested in a paternity suit and forced to pay a huge out-of-court settlement. Lawsuits were coming from every direction. He lost cars and houses in civil judgments. The man who saved pro football was dead broke.

But at least one soul remained steadfast. George Halas picked up the telephone one day in the spring of 1929.

"Ghost, I want you to play for the Bears next season," Halas said.

"The Ghost is dead, George," Grange said. "I can't cut anymore."

"You can't gallop. But, by God, you can still play football."

Halas was on the money about Grange. Even a busted wheel could not diminish the sum of his football talents. Respect gained from teammates for being the consummate team player transcended the loss of his speed and torque. Concentrating on defense, he hammered ball carriers and became one of the league's biggest thieves in the secondary. When Nagurski arrived in 1930, the Ghost and the Bronk made a handsome backfield with Brumbaugh and Keith Molesworth. Thanks to the defensive prowess of Grange and Nagurski, Chicago allowed but twelve points in the final five games of the season.

Now, thirty minutes before kickoff against Green Bay, Andy Lotshaw dashed through the blowing snow across Clark Street to Brandon's Drugstore. With a few crumpled dollars in his pocket, he purchased several rolls of tape and rubbing liniment. He found Nagurski and Grange playing cards in the corner of the locker room. Lotshaw spent the next thirty minutes patching the Ghost from head to toe. First, he fitted him with the steel knee brace that he had built. Two rolls of tape were required to gird the joint. Then Lotshaw went to work on the battered right shoulder that was black and blue from the base of the neck to the quadrupeds. Lotshaw was certain that something was torn inside the joint, perhaps the rotator cuff, but no orthopedic surgeon had ever trained a scalpel upon this complex mix of tendons, muscle, tissue, cartilage, and ligaments.

The Ghost was so stiffly bound that he needed a hand-up from Lotshaw to get on his feet. As he waddled toward his locker, Halas popped through the door. He said, "Red, you look like a goddamn mummy." Grange just smiled and kept walking.

As Halas rolled up his sleeves and helped with the ankle taping, the Chicago Bears dressed for the last game of the season. Fans and the press expected a half-assed effort that afternoon. So did the gamblers. That is why Green Bay was heavily favored. A win would clinch the NFL title.

On the second play of the game, the ball was pitched to Packer half-back Red Dunn, who rolled right and searched for an open receiver through the blinding snow. He uncorked a wobbler that was snatched by the long, bony fingers of the Redhead. Grange flew across the snow-covered field like the Ghost of old, sixty-two yards to the end zone. Ten thousand fans who had braved the elements swore they saw the vapor trail once more.

Nagurski recovered a fumble two plays later. Brumbaugh tossed a quick strike to Luke Johnsos, and he, like the Ghost, vanished into the heavy flakes. Fans in the stands actually lost track of Johnsos for thirty yards. When he reappeared, he was standing in the end zone, having dashed sixty-three yards for the touchdown. That day Grange would intercept two more passes, Nagurski one. Johnsos scored another touchdown in the third quarter on a perfect twelve-yard sideline toss from Brumbaugh. After beating the Bears six straight times, the Packers were discombobulated from kickoff to final gun. Chicago 21, Green Bay 0.

An hour after the game the Bears gathered at the Cottage Lounge, where Brute Trafton bought the first round. "Bartender," he bellowed. "Send me that waitress, the one with the big gangsters."

Trafton stood and raised his glass. "Here's a toast to the Ghost. The sonofabitch we love the most." The room broke into applause.

Big George sat down next to Nagurski and put his arm around his wide shoulders. "Rook," he said. "You will drink 'em as fast as I buy 'em tonight." The Bronk could only laugh.

Thanks mostly to the play of Nagurski on both sides of the ball, the Bears had negotiated a U-turn in 1930, winning their last five games. This was the same team that had opened the season with a 1–3 record. In the second half of the season they had throttled Green Bay and New York, teams that would finish one-two in the league standings. Only two touchdowns were scored against the Chicago defense in those last six games.

The victorious players drank at the Cottage Lounge until Gardie

Grange managed to convince Trafton that his next fight would be against Primo Carnera, the Ambling Alp. Members of the Capone gang dropped by to congratulate the boys. A year after falling on their faces, their record was 9–4–1.

The Chicago Bears were back.

# 7

# Contenders

The toughest decision of George Halas's life was stepping aside and allowing somebody else to coach his beloved Bears. The grand experiment had somehow succeeded—at least for one season. The Bears had rebounded in 1930 under new coach Ralph Jones. By tinkering with the stodgy T-formation and adding a man in motion, the offense grew less predictable. Jones knew that if the linebacker followed Grange going in motion around end, a hole would open for Nagurski in the middle of the line. If the linebacker stayed put, Brumbaugh would pitch to Grange for a sizable gain.

Jones was a small, bald-headed man with a giant spirit, round Irish cheeks, a broad nose, and eyes that said, "Don't mess with me." He had been Halas's freshman football coach at Illinois back in 1915 at a time when the 140-pound end possessed far more desire than talent. Jones fanned the flame inside the little man. If not for Jones, Halas would have never played college football. So, yes, there was a debt to be paid.

Jones left Illinois in the mid-twenties to become the athletic director at Lake Forest Academy, a small but highly respected secondary school in Chicago's northern suburbs. The Chicago sporting press was astonished when Halas chose a high school man to lead the Bears. All six dailies slammed the decision. Halas couldn't have cared less about their criticism. It was by design that Halas had hired a man who did not boast a résumé that read like Knute Rockne's, or even Curly Lambeau's for that matter. A man with that kind of ego surely would have clashed with the Chicago Bears owner, and Halas wanted to let everyone know that he was still the boss, thank you.

Jones was not fazed by this new pressure, nor did he concern himself with the length and breadth of the Halas shadow. The job was not going to swallow him. On the day he was hired, he told Halas, "I will give you a championship in three years. But stay the hell out of my way."

All bets were against either proposition.

Furthermore, Halas made no promises that he would not meddle. But, in fact, he agreed with Jones that the T-formation was the best way to move the ball in the National Football League. Every NFL team at the time was running either the single-wing or the double-wing offense.

Jones subscribed to the tenets of T-formation that Halas had stood by steadfastly since the NFL was formed in 1920. Halas believed in having the quarterback under center. Of course, Nagurski was the model fullback for the power-oriented offense.

Jones's instructions to Carl Brumbaugh were simple: Either hand the ball to Nagurski off tackle or toss it to Grange around end. The two had combined for twelve touchdowns during the 1930 season, and if the Bears had not started slow, they might have unseated the Packers as the NFL champions.

In 1931, as the Great Depression brought the United States to the brink of revolution and gangland blood ran through the Chicago streets, the Bears were trying to win their first NFL championship in ten years. More important, they hoped to end the reign of the hated Green Bay Packers.

Brumbaugh spent most of the first game faking to Nagurski and pitching the ball to Grange. It was a night game played at Loyola Stadium in Chicago. Grange gained eighty yards and scored two touchdowns as the Bears defeated the Cleveland Indians, the NFL's newest entry, by the score of 21–0.

The game at City Stadium in Green Bay was a virtual rerun of the Bears-Packers in Green Bay the previous season. Verne Lewellen, the presiding district attorney, scored the only touchdown on a two-yard run. Again, the Packers won 7–0.

Grange provided the only scoring the next week as the Bears defense dominated in a 6–0 win over the Giants. The next game, at Wrigley Field between the Cardinals and the Bears, was one that would have the NFL talking for years.

The Cardinals surprised the Bears and scored first on a fifteen-yard pass from Ernie Nevers to Milan Creighton. Nevers, now in the final season of a great career, kept the game respectable in the first half as the Cardinals led at halftime 7–0.

Because the crowd sat so close to the sideline at Wrigley Field, several cops patrolled the area on horseback. They were often just a few feet from the boundary line. Drunks and rowdies thought twice about scaling the wall and charging onto the field. But on this beautiful sunlit October afternoon, when Lake Michigan fanned Wrigley Field with soft breezes, the paying customers were about half asleep.

The Chicago Mountie never saw the Bronk coming. Chased by three Cardinal players, Nagurski veered toward the sideline, his cleats tearing at the grass and his rock-hard frame hurtling straight toward the horse. He was going full steam when his left shoulder slammed into the animal's girth, lifting all four hooves off the ground. The snapshot taken by a lucky photographer was at once frightful and funny: the horse flying straight up, the cop suspended about two feet above the saddle, his mouth agape, his eyes like saucers, his hat flying out of the frame.

Fortunately, neither horse nor human was hammered into the brick retaining wall. Both landed on the soft grass without injury. As the cop was helped to his feet, Nagurski began to brush loose grass from the man's uniform.

"I'm sorry, officer," he said. "I didn't mean to hit you. But you really should get out of my way when I'm running."

Then, as the horse regained its footing, Bronko made a careful approach and gently patted the muzzle. "I'm sorry, horse," he said.

On the next play, Grange sprinted thirty-five yards round left end as the momentum of the game shifted dramatically. Brumbaugh then passed seventeen yards to Grange for a touchdown.

On the Bears' next possession the crowd was again treated to a grand display of brute strength by Nagurski. From the Bears' thirty-eight-yard line he bolted into the line off right guard and was met head-on by Nevers, one of the strongest players ever to suit up. Nagurski flattened Nevers like an asphalt grader rolling over a tin can. Nevers lay unconscious on the field for five minutes. The Cardinals safeties were also felled while trying to stop the Bronk. One suffered a broken collarbone and the other two cracked ribs. The sixty-two-yard touchdown run was the longest of Nagurski's career as the Bears rolled to a 26–13 win over their crosstown rivals.

The Bears would win four straight games during a stretch in the second half of the season, but two losses to the Packers and one to the Giants ruined their hopes for an NFL title. Nagurski finished the season with 401 rushing yards and two touchdowns; Grange with 599 and seven. Both would be selected to the All-Pro team. But the Bears' record of 8–5 left them in third place behind the Packers, who won their third straight title, and the Portsmouth Spartans, who finished second.

The Bears lost one of their biggest fans on October 24, 1931, the day before a one-point defeat to Frankford, when Al Capone retired to Alcatraz. Scarface Al had murdered, robbed, bribed, whored, gambled, and run Chicago with an iron fist for almost a decade. He paid off police chiefs and politicians. In the end, they got him for evading $182,000 in taxes in 1925, '26, and '27. It was noted during testimony that he lost that much betting the ponies in one weekend.

After his sentencing Capone said, "They blamed everything but the Chicago fire on me."

Much to the chagrin of Halas, Gardie Grange managed to cook up another fight for Brute Trafton, this time with a future heavyweight champ. Primo Carnera was on his first tour of the United States, knocking out one bus driver after another. So why not Brute?

Of the upcoming fight in Kansas City, New York Giants coach Ray Andrews said, "I believe Trafton won't deliberately quit. The big Italian will have to knock him out. But even that won't stop George from talking."

Andrews was dead wrong. Trafton hit the canvas three times in fifty-four seconds. The press and the eight thousand fans at the convention center swore that no punches ever landed. Trafton was suspended indefinitely by the Missouri boxing commission for "failing to offer any semblance of a fight in his 54-second swooning session." The *Kansas City Star* charged, "Trafton not only went into the tank, he must have bumped his head on the bottom."

With Capone off the street, no one was sure if the fight was fixed. It was Trafton's last trip into the ring.

Before there was a Bronko Nagurski, the NFL had Ernie Nevers, one of the roughest, toughest rawboned characters ever to play the game. His single-game achievements against the Bears back in 1929 will never be forgotten. That Thanksgiving Day at Comiskey Park, the Blond Blizzard scored all forty points against the crosstown rivals and set a single-game scoring mark in the process. He tallied six touchdowns and kicked four extra points to complete a 40–6 thumping of the Bears. Amid the wind gusts and the falling temperatures, Nevers did nothing fancy, hammering time and again between the tackles.

The Nevers legend actually dated to 1925, when he won the most valuable player award at the Rose Bowl by gaining 114 yards for Stanford University on thirty-four carries on what amounted to two broken ankles. He almost single-handedly defeated a Notre Dame Fighting Irish team that boasted the Four Horsemen. He would be inducted into the first class of the Pro Football Hall of Fame along with Nagurski and fifteen others in 1963.

Nevers also pitched for the St. Louis Browns in the late twenties and in 1927 gave up two home runs to Babe Ruth during his record-setting season of sixty.

Nevers's name will be forever linked to a more romantic time when men played for the love of the game. Nevers suited up for the Duluth Eskimos in 1926 a few weeks after the team was purchased for one dollar—that's right, a single buck. So financially strapped were the Eskimos that the owners offered to make a gift of the franchise, originally bought for $1,000, to the club's secretary-treasurer, Ole Haugsrud. To make the transaction legal, Haugsrud handed the owners a dollar. The four ex-owners quickly spent it buying nickel beers.

That season Duluth played one home game in Superior, just across the Wisconsin line. Four thousand paying customers were willing to fork over a buck apiece to catch a glimpse of Nevers and Johnny Blood. The playing field was located in the middle of a railyard. Rail workers managed to line up boxcars on both sides of the field so another four thousand rowdies could get a free view of the game. With the wind whipping off Lake Superior, they stood on the boxcars, chugged bootleg whiskey, shot off their pistols, and cheered wildly as Nevers and Blood ripped apart the Kansas City Cowboys.

The retirement of Nevers in 1931 would mark the end of an era. But with names like Nagurski, Grange, Blood, Shipwreck Kelly, Buckets Goldenberg, Mel Hein, Wildcat Wilson, and Benny Friedman on the marquee, the NFL was just getting warmed up.

# 8

# Stormy, Husky, Brawling

George Trafton seethed. He thought about wading into the sea of Green Bay fans that ringed the field at City Stadium as the Bears and Packers warmed up for the opening game of the 1932 season. As the tormentors pressed closer to the playing field, hurling profanities at Trafton, the target of their loathing for a dozen years, they were like mad dogs loose on the Green Bay streets.

Trafton's bad mood had kicked into gear at two o'clock that morning when a band of Packer Backers marched down the hallway of the Northland Hotel blowing trombones and trumpets and banging snare drums. They were either wildly intoxicated or knew nothing of musical harmony. Big George, wearing only his boxers, literally shoved each beefy musician through the backdoor, and threatened each a bloody nose if they ever returned.

Now Trafton marched in a circle in the middle of the field, throwing make-believe jabs and haymakers into the air, glowering at the antagonists.

"Cheesehead shitheads!" he yelled back at them. "You're a bunch of fairies!"

Trafton's love affair with opposing fans was legendary, dating to his great escape back in Rock Island when he'd saved his own life and a bankroll for Halas. But he could never remember being this mad. Halas had yanked his starting job days earlier and handed it over to a rookie named Charles "Ookie" Miller. Trafton's frustration was further fueled by the knowledge that Chicago had lost eight of the last ten games to Green Bay.

On a beautifully sunny September afternoon in Green Bay, with the temperature in the mid-seventies, the wind calm, and church bells ringing across the city, a hellfire storm was brewing.

Green Bay's Clarke Hinkle set the ball on the tee for the opening kick-off. Trafton lined up in the center of the front line. Chicago prepared to receive the ball with Red Grange as the deep man. Trafton stood ten yards from Hinkle.

"Hey, rook, you don't even know how to set the ball on the tee!" he hollered. "You got it all wrong. Let me show you."

Trafton ran straight for the ball. A hush suddenly fell over the twenty-one thousand fans. *He can't possibly be doing this.* Even George Halas was amazed. He saw Trafton apply foot to football and kick it the wrong way—all the way through the empty end zone at the other end of the field.

Trafton threw back his head and cackled. He pounded his chest.

Officials blew their whistles and ran in circles. Fans charged the field. Cops penetrated the mob and pulled nightsticks. Curly Lambeau ran to the center of the field. George Halas ran to the center of the field. Nose to nose, they peppered each other with flecks of spit.

"Trafton is a violation of everything that football stands for!" Lambeau yelled.

"You're a sonofabitch," Halas shot back.

"No, you're a bigger sonofabitch."

"No, you're the biggest sonofabitch in the world!"

The men quickly forgot what they were arguing about, but that didn't slow the flow of invective. Nothing ignited the pure flame of fire like the promise of a Chicago–Green Bay showdown.

As the fans poured onto the field, a few unfortunate Packer Backers managed to come within punching distance of Trafton. He slugged them with a fury once reserved for Art Shires. Bronko Nagurski waded into the fray and the crowd began to retreat. The sight of number three, with the rock-hard jaw and the steely body, inspired most of the rioters to turn and run.

"Better haul ass!" Trafton bellowed. "I taught Nagurski how to fight!"

Nagurski, now in his third pro season, was the most frightening man in the National Football League. Everyone by now had heard about his Paul Bunyan strength and the rage that drove him. The Bronk knocked players out of the game left and right. He ran into brick walls and knocked down horses. He was a banger who never let up. If Nagurski delivered a blow to the head, look out. Somebody was going to the hospital.

The most fearsome sight was the Bronk as a ball carrier. He normally stood straight up as the ball was slid into his belly. This allowed him to survey the field. Then he would dip the left shoulder. A common sight was to see the Bronk run straight over the first two defenders. Past the line of scrimmage, he tunneled low to the ground. He had speed—surprising speed for the biggest man on the field. A reporter once asked, "How fast are you?"

"Fast enough," he replied.

Defensive backs who weighed around 170 pounds had a hell of a time bringing him down in the open field. Normally, it took three or four players to push him toward the sideline and finally ride him over the boundary.

Red Grange knew the helpless feeling of having to tackle Nagurski alone. He dreaded midweek practice scrimmages when he lined up at defensive back and the Bronk was carrying the ball.

"When the Bronk hits you, it's like getting an electric shock," he told the press. "Better not hit above the ankles. He'll kill you."

The sight of Nagurski with his hands balled into fists inspired the Green Bay fans to haul ass back to the sideline. Then it took fifteen minutes to clear whiskey bottles from the field. Cops formed a human barricade around the sidelines to discourage further interaction. Officials sorted through the various infractions and decided to toss Trafton out of the contest. That was before Halas stomped and threw his hat on the ground and threatened to put his team on the first train back to Chicago.

"I've already got the gate receipts," Halas said to the referee. "Don't think for a minute that I won't take the goddamn money and run."

The officials huddled for ten minutes and decided to take Halas at his word. But the cops warned that if Trafton kicked the ball off Green Bay's tee again, everyone was going to jail.

As Hinkle propped up the game ball once more, all eyes were riveted on Trafton until the kick sailed in the proper direction. Then, and only then, did a football game manage to break out amid the riotous conditions.

Nothing cleansed the palate like a Chicago–Green Bay fracas at City Stadium. Knuckle sandwiches were exchanged from kickoff to final gun. Team trainers kept needle and thread handy. Minutes before kickoff, Halas delivered this pregame pep talk: "Go out there today and stomp those Packer pricks!"

Halas had allowed Ralph Jones to stick around and coach one more season. But Papa Bear had his hands firmly on the team now. He doted over practices, patrolled the sideline on game day, edited the playbook, and vetoed lineup decisions. He wanted to be closer to the action, to smell the sweat, to see the blood. It was little wonder this Green Bay–Chicago rivalry was so personal to Halas. He had suited up for the first sixteen games between the teams over a period of nine years and had scars to prove it. In that first encounter, back in 1921, he caught a long touchdown pass as the Bears won 20–0. That same afternoon, Halas was standing on the sideline, attending to his coaching duties, when a Packer pulverized one of the Bears right in front of the Chicago bench. Halas grabbed the opposing player by the jersey and shook him. It appeared he was taking exception to a cheap shot. In truth, he was yelling at Hunk Anderson, "Son, you're the toughest sonofabitch I've ever seen. Next year you will be playing for *me!*"

It just so happened that Anderson, a senior at Notre Dame and former teammate of Lambeau's back in South Bend, was moonlighting illegally as a Green Bay player. Lambeau had recruited several other current Notre Dame studs to play on Sundays under assumed names. This so angered Halas that he led a crusade to have the Packers kicked out of the league in 1922. Banishing the Pack would turn out to be more of a public relations gesture than anything else. Halas and other owners were concerned that the growing number of public scandals surrounding the illegal use of college players might trigger the demise of their new pro league.

Halas then turned around and campaigned for Green Bay's reinstatement. He encouraged Lambeau to find another packing company in Green Bay to bankroll the team. Lambeau raised the franchise fee through a cash loan from a friend who sold his automobile.

Lambeau was back in business with two stipulations: He would forfeit all rights to Hunk Anderson. Upon graduation the stout, hard-hitting All-American guard would sign with the Chicago Bears.

The Packers were forever getting a raw deal from Halas and the boys. The Bears were leading Green Bay 7–0 during a 1927 game when the Packers' Verne Lewellen scored on a one-yard run late in the game. Everett "Pid" Purdy, a dropkick specialist, entered the game to attempt the tying point. Trafton sidled up to the skinny kicker and said, "Boy, what a hero you'll be tonight, my lad! There will be free champagne at every bar in Green Bay, and they'll probably nominate you for mayor. But, brother, if you miss, what a bum you will be. They'll run your lousy ass out of town!"

Purdy, one of the best in the business, who once made ninety-two straight dropkicks in practice, missed the kick by a city block. Green Bay lost 7–6.

In another game, Trafton broke through the line and blocked a Green Bay punt. So discombobulated was kicker Verne Lewellen that he yelled, "Who the hell blocked that?" Trafton spoke up, "It was Fleckenstein." The next time the Packers lined up for a punt, Lewellen shifted the blocking formation to Bill Fleckenstein's side of the line. Trafton sailed through a gaping hole on the other side and blocked his second punt of the day. It was recovered for a touchdown. Chicago 14, Green Bay 6.

The Packers were an early success on the field, but that did not guarantee they would survive from one season until the next. Small-market teams faced additional pitfalls, not to mention the Great Depression. Teams like Dayton, Rock Island, and Toledo disappeared from the NFL landscape every year. The only hope for survival was to keep the turnstiles spinning. Columnists from the *Green Bay Press-Gazette* didn't mind preaching the need to support the Pack.

Packer fans responded in funny ways.

Thanks to a mayor's decree, saloons opened at seven in the morning on game days. Fans were normally lined up at Three Corners in the early morning light, waiting for the manager to unlock the doors. Three Corners represented the intersection of Main, Baird, and Cedar streets, where most of the taverns were located. Fans fortified themselves until kickoff approached, then walked, or wobbled, about a mile down to the rickety field known as City Stadium. It contained no rest rooms. Men seeking relief did their business along the fence. Women either went below the stands or talked their way past the security personnel who guarded the doors at nearby East High School.

City Stadium seated about ten thousand on its splintery wood bleachers. When Chicago came to town, another ten thousand would stand on the sidelines. Bear players learned to avoid the crowds along the sidelines; a foot to the solar plexus or a fist to the leather helmet was commonplace.

Because there were no locker rooms, the Bears dressed at the Northland Hotel and boarded the bus in their stocking feet. They entered the stadium through the north gate amid the flying pint bottles. At halftime they dodged more missiles as they gathered beneath the stands for a pep talk and second-half strategy session.

Everyone expected a low-scoring game for the 1932 season opener. The Bears and Packers were like two old pugs, jabbing and retreating, feeling each other out. Neither Jones nor Lambeau was above punting on third down, and the forward pass was virtually out of the question. Nagurski and Grange hit the Packer line for sizable gains, but the drives stalled inside the twenty-yard line and Tiny Engebretsen missed two fields. Green Bay also moved the ball consistently, with Hinkle, the powerful second-year fullback, carrying the bulk of the mail. But there was no score in the first half.

Hinkle was almost a mirror image of Nagurski as he plowed through the line and made thundering stops on the defensive side. Nagurski stood six-two, weighed 217 pounds, and Hinkle was five-eleven and weighed 205. Both were molded by the same blast furnace.

In the third quarter Nagurski made a rare request for the football. He seldom spoke in the huddle. Now he told Brumbaugh, "Give me the damn ball." To Trafton he said, "Don't block number twenty-seven [Hinkle]. I want a piece of his ass."

The Bronk bucked the line and aimed his massive right shoulder at Hinkle, who made the mistake of digging in. Nagurski flattened the Green Bay linebacker like a steamroller over fresh asphalt. A knee clocked his chin, and cleats were planted in his chest. Hinkle's final waking thought was, *He sounds like a train*. It took six Packers to pull Nagurski down forty yards later.

Hinkle awoke on the sideline several minutes later with the acrid odor of ammonia in his nostrils; the trainer had broken two capsules of smelling salts. Hinkle coughed as the pain of his shattered nose registered. A gash on his chin would require seven stitches. Then he had a little talk with himself: *You've got to be tougher than this if you're going to play this game.*

In spite of the crashing and the gashing, the game ended in a scoreless tie. The Packers and Bears missed two field goals apiece. But a game with no scoring was no reason to stop the presses. Almost two-thirds of the NFL games since 1920 were shutouts. Reasons abounded: the fat ball with thin laces, an across-the-board disaffection for the forward pass, and poor footing on rock-hard fields. Rules of the time didn't abet scoring. An incomplete pass in the end zone resulted in a loss of possession. Penalties were severe—twenty-five yards for clipping. There were no hash marks. When a player ran out of bounds, the ball was spotted just a foot or so from the sideline. Goalposts had been moved from the goal line to the end line in 1927.

Strategy of the time was to pin your opponent deep with towering punts and to play for field position. The quick kick on third down was especially effective because, with no deep man to field it, the round ball rolled and rolled.

But the foremost reason for the pitiful point production was a total lack of offensive imagination. Knute Rockne possessed the only fertile football mind of the time, and he had perished in a plane crash the preceding spring.

Still, all of these reasons could not explain what happened to the Chicago Bears in the first months of the 1932 season—four scoreless deadlocks. When Green Bay defeated the Bears 2–0 in the fifth week of the season, the game seemed like a shoot-out.

How was it possible that the only scoring in a five-game stretch would be a punt blocked through the end zone for a safety?

The upside was that the Bears were playing lights-out defense. Nagurski was a monster at fullback. But he was equally overpowering at linebacker, where his lethal lateral speed and nose for the ball, his blitzes and sledgehammer strikes stymied the run-oriented offenses of the thirties. It was rare that teams ran the ball to his side. But the Bronk was the master of backside pursuit. It took less than a heartbeat for him to figure the angle required to run down ball carriers from behind all the way across the field.

The Bears were being rebuilt around the Nagurski style, and Halas's blueprint called for balls-out toughness. The newest hit man added to the lineup was Bill Hewitt, who refused to wear a helmet. A few games into the season, he was dubbed the "Offsides Kid" because of his quick start from the end position. Hewitt was often in the backfield before the tailback got his hands on the deep snap from center.

Officials heard the same complaint each time Hewitt made a tackle: "Ref, that sonofabitch is offsides!" Individual statistics were finally introduced for the '32 season, and by the end of the twelve-game schedule, Hewitt had compiled more than three hundred yards in losses. And this was at a time when quarterbacks rarely dropped back to pass. Sacks were not yet part of the game. Hewitt was basically limited to throwing ball carriers for losses.

The incomparable Chicago defense managed to hold opponents to negative yards through the first four games. The fifth game finally revealed another side of the Chicago offense. Nagurski scored touchdowns on runs of fifty-six and twenty-three yards and tossed a touchdown pass to Grange for thirteen yards, and Johnsos hauled in a thirty-yard touchdown pass from Brumbaugh as the Bears defeated Staten Island 27–7. Chicago's record was a 1–1–3, hardly the stuff of champions.

What really disheartened Halas was that the crowds were staying away, and no one seemed to be talking about his Bears. After each home game Halas would type a newspaper account that he hand-delivered to the offices of the six Chicago dailies. One Sunday evening as he was delivering his game account to the *Daily News,* the sports editor stopped him.

"Hey, you're a pretty good writer," he said. "How would you like to cover some basketball for us?"

The sports editor did not even recognize the founder of the NFL and the owner of the Chicago Bears.

Chicago that year was again madly in love with the Cubs. The Cubbies were getting all of the ink. Led by strong pitching, Chicago had grabbed the pennant from Dizzy Dean and the St. Louis Gashouse Gang. The prospect of the New York Yankees coming to Wrigley Field for the World Series turned the town upside down. Buried alive that October in the avalanche of newspaper print, at the bottom of page ten, were the Chicago Bears.

The 1932 World Series was one of the most controversial and talked about in the history of major league baseball. It was fueled by the acrimony building between Cubs players and Babe Ruth. When the Yankees took the first two games of the series, the Ruth swagger was irrepressible.

In game three Ruth and Lou Gehrig hit home runs into the right-field seats. In the fifth inning the Cubs dugout was riding Ruth mercilessly when he strode to the plate. So foul was the language that baseball commissioner Kenesaw Mountain Landis stood up from his box seat behind the dugout and loudly commanded the Cubs to shut up. They did not. Fans along the third-base line wished for earplugs.

Chicago sidearmer Charlie Root quickly got two strikes on Ruth. Fans tossed cans and bottles onto the field. Ruth turned and said something to catcher Gabby Hartnett. Then he raised his right hand and pointed with two fingers in the direction of Root. The initial interpretation: "That's only two strikes, keed." On the next pitch Ruth smashed his famous shot far into the centerfield bleachers, a mere ten feet shy of the centerfield scoreboard, the longest home run in the history of Wrigley Field.

That night over cocktails Ruth gave the writers a scoop. "I called the home run shot," he said. Grantland Rice and Chicago columnist Westbrook Pegler bought the story. They had been seated that day in the press box behind home plate. There was no question that Ruth had gestured with his right hand. A home movie shot by spectator Matt Kandle showed Ruth with his arm outstretched, and it is possible that he was pointing over Root's head all the way to the centerfield seats. The Called Shot would be debated in every tavern, barbershop, and stockyard.

It made George Halas want to puke.

"Those goddamned Cubs get all of the publicity in this town," he grumped, long after the Yankees had swept the Series.

The entire Bears organization was axle-deep in prairie mud. Fans were simply not turned on by the plodding style of pro football. Furthermore, the entertainment dollar was becoming more and more scarce as the nation suffered through the Depression. Almost twenty-five percent of the workforce was jobless. Families were losing their homes, their savings, their lives. As the Bears sank into this financial quagmire, Franklin D. Roosevelt flew to Chicago to accept the Democratic presidential nomination. The Democratic convention was held at Chicago Stadium, a newly constructed indoor facility on the near west side. He pledged to deliver to the American people a New Deal, a federally funded, federally administered program of relief and recovery.

Now if Roosevelt could only fix the Bears.

After the seventh week of the '32 NFL season the Bears had two wins, one loss, and four ties. The Bears were trailing Portsmouth 13–6 in the fourth quarter, and if not for Halas's bag of tricks, another game would have gone into the loss column. Between plays Luke Johnsos, pretending to suffer from leg cramps, limped toward the bench. He stopped inches from the sideline and bent over to tie his shoelaces. Spartan defenders failed to notice that Johnsos was still on the field of play and, therefore, an eligible receiver. On the snap Johnsos ran straight down the sideline and Brumbaugh heaved a deep spiral that Johnsos ran under at the thirty-yard line. He sped into the end zone with no one within fifty yards of him. Halas had introduced the "sleeper play." It would be exploited by deceit-ful coaches for decades to come.

It had been that kind of season. Every team but Staten Island and the Cardinals were counted among title contenders. The Cardinals limped into Wrigley Field for the Thanksgiving game with only one viable weapon, Joe Lillard, the only black player in the NFL. Cardinals owner Robert Jones said, "Look at Lillard, our colored boy. He is one of the best backs in the league, yet his entire college experience consists of a fresh-man year at Oregon State."

After defeating Brooklyn the previous week, the Bears desperately needed a victory over the Cardinals. The Bears offense awakened again for a 34–0 victory on a day when the sporting press focused more on the fighting than the 143-yard rushing day by Nagurski. Lillard gained only three yards on twelve carries.

Three days later the Bears recorded their sixth tie of the season at Portsmouth. Nagurski and Glenn Presnell, the Portsmouth running back, traded touchdowns. The Bears were 4–1–6 with two games remaining against the Giants and Packers—teams you didn't want to face late in the season. Amazingly, the Bears were still clinging to hopes of a championship.

The Bronk almost single-handedly delivered the victory over the Giants, scoring the lone touchdown and making tackles all over the field. In typical fashion, the Bears won 6–0.

The snow arrived on Monday. It fell night and day for seventy-two hours, and Chi Town spent the next two days digging out. Snowplows worked Wrigley Field, and when the machines were finished, the white stuff was piled five feet high along the sidelines. Another blizzard hit town Sunday morning, and Halas would have considered canceling the game if the NFL title were not on the line.

In spite of their early-season scoring woes, a Bears victory over Green Bay would tie Chicago with Portsmouth for the '32 league championship. All Green Bay needed for its fourth straight outright title was a win at Wrigley Field. It seemed appropriate that the Bears and Packers were meeting for the twenty-fifth time in the rivalry.

About five thousand fans trekked to the corner of Clark and Addison that Sunday afternoon and cloaked themselves in blankets and long woolen coats. You could barely see them through the blinding snow. Most of the fans huddled beneath the steel awning along the third-base line. It was the only game to be played that December 11, 1932, as the other teams had completed their seasons. All radios were tuned to WGN in Chicago.

The players enjoyed reasonably good footing early in the game. But as the fierce winds blasted off Lake Michigan, snow clouds hung closer and closer to the playing surface. Snow was being lifted from the five-foot embankments and blown onto the field. By the second quarter the field was like a skating rink.

Chicago's only offense was Nagurski. Green Bay rode the broad shoulders of Hinkle. Inch-long cleats were screwed into the bottoms of their shoes. Both Nagurski and Hinkle heaved and grunted and managed to move their teams into scoring position in the third quarter. But the swirling gusts pushed field goal attempts hopelessly wide of the posts.

The Bronk took command of the game in the fourth period. He plowed for eight yards, six yards, three yards, four yards, and ten yards. He once landed on his stomach and slid another eleven yards. The public address announcer said, "And Nagurski slides into second base." The Bronk's face was plastered with ice. Late in the afternoon, the temperature plummeted to minus two degrees.

Hewitt wished for a leather helmet. "Now I know why you bastards wear those things," he said. "My ears are freezing."

Nagurski drove seven yards through the Packer line to the fourteen, where, on fourth down, Halas instructed Jones to call for the field goal. Tiny Engebretsen was kicking toward the south end zone with the wind at his back. The fat ball barely fluttered over the crossbar.

Green Bay marched to midfield and Nagurski recovered a Hinkle fumble. On the next play, the Bronk tunneled through the Green Bay line, collided forehead to forehead with Hinkle, regained his balance, and snowplowed fifty-six yards to the end zone. With less than a minute to play, the 9–0 victory was safe. Engebretsen had saved his best effort for the three-pointer; his extra-point attempt sailed wide right and almost hit the baseball press box.

Thanks to the peculiar standards of the time, the 6–1–6 Bears tied Portsmouth, 6–1–4, for the championship. This is how the standings appeared in the Monday newspapers:

|  | W | L | T | Pct. |
|---|---|---|---|---|
| CHICAGO | 6 | 1 | 6 | .857 |
| PORTSMOUTH | 6 | 1 | 4 | .857 |
| GREEN BAY | 10 | 3 | 2 | .769 |

The vagaries of league rules cost Green Bay a fourth straight championship. In those days, ties did not count in the percentage column. Today a tie is considered half a win, half a loss. Here's how the teams would have finished according to the percentage formula of modern football: (1) Green Bay, .733, (2) Portsmouth, .727, and (3) Chicago, .692.

But what the hell. The deadlock between Portsmouth and Chicago set the stage for the first championship game in the history of pro football. Commissioner Joe Carr loved the idea. A championship showdown would create the kind of buzz the NFL desperately needed. The dailies would finally make some room for pro football on the front page. Why shouldn't the NFL finally have its day in the sun?

How ironic that another blizzard was headed toward Chicago.

# 9

# The Circus

The aroma of roasting peanuts and cigar smoke pervaded the air as fans hustled through the stadium doors to escape the bluster of a snow-covered city, men wearing long overcoats and fedoras, women tightly bundled in woolen coats and sweaters. They all had braved the fierce cold to catch a glimpse of the game that had everyone talking.

Chicago Stadium, the giant gray palace on West Madison, was the place to be this Sunday evening, exactly one week before Christmas in 1932. The city was buried in snow—the drifts waist high in some areas—thanks to the third blizzard in ten days. It was the kind of snow that swallows automobiles and jams trolley cars. George Halas had pulled off a coup, moving the game at almost a moment's notice from snowbound Wrigley Field to an indoor complex that was heated. Completed just three years earlier, the Stadium was the permanent home of the Chicago Black Hawks and a place frequented by Ringling Brothers and Barnum & Bailey. The National Football League was breaking ground with its first official indoor game.

It might have seemed appropriate to the NFL detractors that the first title game would follow on the heels of a circus. Days earlier, clowns had cavorted, elephants had defecated, and midgets had been shot from cannons. More than a hundred rail cars were required to move the circus to the next town.

P. T. Barnum and J. A. Bailey made piles of Ben Franklins entertaining millions of Americans. Would they have ever dreamed up a circus attraction like Portsmouth versus Chicago? Likely not. But to the men who had gathered in a Hupmobile dealership in Canton, Ohio, back in 1920 to invent the NFL, theirs was the Greatest Show on Earth.

Chicago Stadium was a fabulous venue for the time, a concrete monstrosity that consumed an entire city block and stood four stories tall. Nothing outside New York City was comparable. An electric sign sixty feet high and ten feet wide radiated in the darkness and provided a magnet for street traffic. The marquee simply read THE STADIUM. It would have been impossible to stand within five city blocks of those powerful bulbs and not be drawn to it like a bug to a light. Near the roof were limestone bas-relief sculptures that depicted athletes in classical poses. The long vertical windows were recessed and illuminated by colored lights.

Most of the fans arrived by the trolley that rumbled up and down West Madison Street. City crews had labored for days, plowing and shoveling the heavy snow until the electric cars could navigate the streets once more. Given the conditions, another town might have declined this invitation; pro football still occupied a cold spot in the public heart. But not Chi Town. Not the city of big shoulders and thick skin and a warm flask in the hip pocket. Mathias "Paddy" Bauler, the tavern owner turned city alderman, was right: "Chicago ain't no sissy town."

Those who had experienced Chicago Stadium knew to brace themselves as they entered the arena. The building literally shook when the Barton pipe organ was at full tilt. It contained 3,675 pipes, six keyboards, and 828 keystops. It could generate a sound equivalent to a twenty-five-hundred-piece brass band.

Al Megard was the master of the pipe organ. As his fingers sprinted across the keys, he was barely visible inside the three-sided organ walls, which were five feet tall. He looked more like an engineer inside a locomotive. Megard had learned an important lesson about the Barton organ one evening during a heavyweight title fight at the Stadium when a riot broke out. Fans were incensed that a local fighter had been robbed by a controversial split decision. Chairs flew and heads were split open. Al decided to open all of the keystops and play a rousing rendition of the

National Anthem. Cranked to full blast, the pipes produced a sound so powerful that it broke lightbulbs and shattered windows. But it quelled the riot. The rowdies seemed to forget what they were doing.

Now, as fans took their seats along the lower level, they noticed a pungent odor. It was a smell unbecoming to the NFL's new sense of respectability—animal droppings left over from the circus. Players who were warming up, catching passes and shagging punts, felt it sticking to their cleats. Glenn Presnell, the Spartans' fleet halfback, tripped and fell in the soft stuff. He rose with a black stain on his white pants. Portsmouth coach Potsy Clark caught a whiff of Presnell and yelled across the field to the godfather of pro football, "Hey, George, this place smells like horseshit. I mean elephant shit. Didn't you guys think about raking this field?"

Halas was just happy to have six inches of dirt covering the concrete floor—dirt he didn't have to pay for. The Bears owner was practically broke. Though he was thrilled to have defeated Green Bay in the regular-season finale, this finish to the season would bring relief to his bank account. He hadn't been able to meet the $2,500 commitment owed to the Packers for the game at Wrigley Field a few days earlier. He gave Green Bay's treasurer a thousand in cash and a promissory note for fifteen hundred. It would not be the last time he would be late fulfilling a contract. In 1932 a championship season did not equate to big bucks. He had given away more tickets to some regular season games than he had sold. He had yet to break the news to Nagurski and Grange that he was short on their salaries. For the second straight year the Bears stars would be going home for the off-season with IOUs in their pockets.

Without Chicago Stadium Halas would be swimming in a Chicago River of red ink. Oh, the Portsmouth game could have been played at Wrigley Field after snowplows had worked night and day for most of the week. But snow piled high in the stands was another matter. No more than a few hundred fans could have found a place to sit. Bears fans were hardy souls, but paying good money to sit on wet snow for three hours might have been asking too much.

If Halas considered his own situation to be a financial nightmare, he just needed to look across the field. The Portsmouth Spartans more than lived up to their nickname. The team was so strapped that the players were required to supply their own pants, socks, and shoes. Father Lumpkin, one of the best ends in the NFL, could not afford socks, so he wrapped his feet in adhesive tape provided by the team. When the tape got dirty, he peeled it off and rewrapped.

Speed was the name of the game in Portsmouth. When the paychecks were handed out Monday morning, players raced each other to the bank. Gate receipts rarely covered the team's payroll, and about half of those checks were certain to bounce. The Spartan players lived in boarding-houses for two bucks a week and most of the players doubled up. When the players did have the money, they barely had the energy to spend it. Potsy Clark put his team through their paces night and day. He instructed the players to keep their shoes handy when the team was traveling by bus. If he spotted open land alongside the road that had yet to be planted, he would order the bus driver to stop for a quick practice.

Near the end of the '32 season star tailback Dutch Clark had realized that he was eight hundred dollars short of salary, thanks to the bad paper handed out by Sidney Plutowksy, the club treasurer. Portsmouth was about to play Green Bay in a game that would determine their place in the final standings.

"Either give me my eight hundred or I'm going to Colorado," Clark told the keeper of the books.

"I'll write you a check," Plutowsky said.

"I got enough of those in my drawer. Fork over the cash or I'm gone."

The team still had some cash left over from a game played against the Bears the previous week. Plutowsky counted out six hundred dollars in one-dollar bills that Dutch stuffed into his pants, overcoat, and suit coat. Some of those bills were sticking out of his pockets when he boarded the bus.

Dutch Clark never counted on the Spartans playing an additional game against the Bears—much less one for all of the marbles. He had already taken a job as the basketball coach at the Colorado School of Mines, and the season was about to tip off. So the man who took the snaps from center, did all of the passing and punting and most of the running, was absent when his team took the field for the biggest game in the history of the NFL.

"Where's Dutch?" Halas yelled across the field.

"Ain't here, and it's none of your goddamned business," Potsy Clark snapped.

"Just wondering," Halas said. "You know, it's a good idea to have your best player around for big games."

Clark was steaming. Like the other coaches, he hated Halas and all of his arrogance. "Don't worry, George," Clark said. "We got enough fellas to kick your dead ass."

Shoehorning a football game onto the floor of Chicago Stadium would require some imagination. Fortunately, the Bears and the crosstown Cardinals had taken a test run back in 1930 during an exhibition game, with the proceeds going to charity. The biggest charity, as it turned out, was the Bears and the Cardinals, who divvied up most of the receipts.

The field was only eighty yards long and forty yards wide. In comparison, a regulation NFL field was a hundred and twenty yards long (including end zones) and fifty-eight yards wide. Because the end zones required ten yards on both ends, the playing field at the Stadium was only sixty yards long.

New ground rules were drawn up: No field goals were allowed, and kickoffs were initiated from the kicking team's ten-yard line. Punts that bounced around in the rafters would be considered touchbacks. Each time a team crossed midfield, it was penalized twenty yards, in effect making the field a hundred yards long. The most significant rules change—one that would have lasting ramifications—involved the sidelines, which were only a few feet from the hockey boards. According to the archaic rules of the time, the ball was placed only a few feet from the sideline after a ball carrier or receiver was knocked out of bounds. But it was determined for this game that the ball could be moved fifteen yards toward the middle of the field if the offense was willing to suffer a loss of down.

The greatest worry this night was the playing field itself. Only six inches of dirt with some wood shavings and turf covered the concrete floor, and the loose chunks were certain to fly away as cleats dug into the soft surface.

Halas had other worries—like footballs sailing into the stands. The cheapskate would not allow kicker Tiny Engebretsen to practice his extra-point kicks during pregame warmups. During the '30 exhibition game at the Stadium, the Cardinals' Ernie Nevers had drop-kicked a field goal that sailed into the Barton pipe organ and bopped organist Ralph Waldo Emerson on the head. This was not Emerson the nineteenth-century poet, essayist, and transcendentalist. This was just a guy named Ralph Waldo Emerson who doubled as the staff organist at radio station WLS.

Thirty minutes before kickoff, bookmakers worked the crowd, walking up and down the aisles shouting the ever-shifting odds. The Bears had opened as 3–1 favorites, but Chicago money had moved it to 5–1. Bookmakers searched the stands for members of the Capone gang but could find none. Both Jack McGurn and Frank Nitti were conspicuously absent.

A fat man in the lower section flagged down one of the bookmakers. "Give me a grand on the Bears," he said.

"I ain't got a grand."

"Go find it," said Fat Tony Cirillo, the brim of his fedora pulled down to obscure his identity. "This money's comin' from McGurn himself. He couldn't be here. But this money had better be down. See."

With trembling hands the bookie accepted the thousand-dollar bill. He quickly moved the odds to 7–1, hoping to discourage more heavy action on the Bears.

It was little wonder that the Bears were attracting big plays from the wise guys. The defense led by Nagurski, Hewitt, and Grange was tough to penetrate. The Bears had allowed only forty-four points in thirteen games, an average of 3.4 points per contest. Opposing offenses averaged barely thirty yards a game.

The untimely departure of Portsmouth's Dutch Clark made the Bears seem like a lock. But the Spartans had a lineup of unsung players like Lumpkin, former Nebraska All-America Presnell, and a 237-pounder named George Christensen, the best tackle in the league in the eyes of his peers. Ox Emerson, the other tackle, was not far behind. The players that Halas had warned his Bears about was Ace Gutowsky, the 195-pound fullback from Kingfisher, Oklahoma, a man who could block, run, and pass. Gutowsky also had led the league in interceptions for the '32 season.

Every seat in the house was occupied on this night, and the crowd was estimated at twelve thousand. Fans were so close to the action that they could reach out and touch the players. It was like occupying a slightly elevated seat smack-dab on the sideline. They could smell the sweat mingling with the animal dung, hear the grunts and the pounding feet, feel the G-force of the collisions.

Brute Trafton placed the ball on the tee for the opening kickoff.

Trafton was indeed the Chicago kickoff specialist and planned no monkey business. He booted the ball over the end line and it hopped into the stands and into the arms of a fan, causing Halas to slam his hat to the ground for the first but not the last time that night.

Chicago bettors held their collective breath as the Spartans moved meticulously down the short field—Presnell right, Gutowsky left, Presnell up the middle. In the absence of Dutch Clark, Presnell shifted to tailback and took the deep snap from center. The Bears had underestimated his speed, and, in spite of the compressed field, Presnell was flying around the ends, almost scraping the hockey boards as he picked up large chunks of yardage. Facing fourth-and-goal from the two-yard line, Presnell faked to Gutowsky off tackle and was sailing around right end, with no defender around him, when his cleats broke through the circus mush and scraped the concrete floor. This sudden loss of torque caused him to fall on his face six inches from the goal. The Bears piled on. Chicago's offense took over on downs.

Across the field, Potsy Clark bellowed, "Goddamn your field, George. Goddamn you!"

"Shut up, Potsy!" Halas yelled back. Then he laughed. "Hey, Potsy! That sounds like a *girl's* name."

Little did Clark realize that Halas was taking mental snapshots of his every move. The Portsmouth coach was breaking one of the longstanding rules of the NFL by signaling in plays to Presnell from the sidelines. Coaches were prohibited from calling plays, much less relaying them by hand signal. But Halas was not worried about the blatant disregard of league rules. His eyes were riveted on Clark because he was memorizing the signals.

Late in the second quarter Presnell peered at Potsy between plays and waited for the signal. One of the Spartans walked past and obscured his view. Presnell shrugged both shoulders and turned up his palms to signify that he had missed the call. Trafton yelled, "Hey, Glenn, he wants you to run Ace off tackle again." Presnell's heart sank. The Spartans might never score if the Bears already knew their plays.

When Chicago had the ball, Brumbaugh fed it to Nagurski play after play, and the Bears offense moved at four and five yards a clip. But Jones was often content to pooch kick on third down. Twice in the third period, punts bounded off the rafters for automatic touchbacks, the receiving team taking possession at the ten-yard line. The Bears drove deep into Portsmouth territory late in the third quarter, but Brummy fumbled a snap and Christensen recovered. Portsmouth had two scoring opportunities die with interceptions.

The game seemed destined for an appropriate conclusion—yet another scoreless tie—when safety Dick Nesbitt leaped and intercepted a Presnell pass at midfield and rambled down to the seven-yard line, where he was knocked out of bounds. The Bears chose to move the ball fifteen yards away from the sideline, thereby forfeiting a down. On second down, the Bronk hammered off left guard to the one. On third down, he lost one, and the ball was on the two-yard line. Brumbaugh sent the Ghost in motion around left end on fourth down, hoping a linebacker or two would tag along. But Nagurski instantly read the intentions of the Portsmouth defense. Ten men were stacked at the line of scrimmage. None moved when Grange began to circle around left end.

The first person to notice Nagurski's great field awareness had been Doc Spears back at Minnesota. This is how he described it: "Nagurski's as smart as a mule in the field. Ever watch a mule in the field? Well, he misses nothing. A bird flies from a tree . . . a rabbit scurries through a hedge . . . a man comes through a gate at the far end . . . the mule sees them all, even though he doesn't appear to be looking at them. That's the way it is with Bronko on a football field. No player on the opposite team can make even the slightest move without him seeing it. He never has played quarterback because we haven't needed him in that position. But what a quarterback he would make!"

The Bronk was supposed to slam into the line between the right guard and tackle. Instead, he ducked his head, lowered a shoulder, and threw on the brakes. To the surprise of everyone, including Halas and the coaches, the Bronk retreated two steps, jumped, and delivered a soft pass to the back of the end zone. It went straight into the hands of Grange, who almost dropped it. The Redhead, standing at the end line, was as surprised as everyone else. But he managed to stick out both hands at the last instant and snare the pass for a touchdown.

Potsy Clark shot onto the field like a rocket. He screamed, pulled his hair, chased the referee, and cursed Halas, all at the same time. The Spartans coach was enraged by what he interpreted as a violation of the rules. Passes in that era were to be thrown no closer than five yards from the line of scrimmage. The Bronk was about two yards back when he hopped and delivered the ball to Grange.

As Clark tried to lodge his complaint, Halas sprinted onto the field and stuck his nose in the opposing coach's face. "You don't know a goddamn thing about rules, Potsy," Halas said.

"You sonofabitch," Clark screamed. "You've been stealing my signals."

"Damn right. Better dream up some new ones."

The officials caucused, but referee Bobie Cahn of New York determined it best not to reverse a touchdown on the home turf, where gangsters roamed. Escaping Chi in this snowy mess was going to be tough enough.

Portsmouth was sinking fast. Neither Presnell nor Gutowksy had gained a single yard in two quarters. Presnell had been intercepted five times. His next two attempts fell incomplete. Punter Mule Wilson set up to punt in his own end zone. Wilson, quite aware of Trafton's punt-blocking ability, received the snap from center Clare Randolph with jittery hands. He promptly dropped the ball, and it rolled out of bounds for a safety. The Bears led 9–0 with four minutes to play.

Halas had waited the entire game to pull one of his shenanigans. On the ensuing kickoff, he eased closer to the sideline, stuck out his foot, and tripped Gutowsky as he ran past with the ball. Neither Cahn nor the other officials noticed. But Clark went off like a roman candle.

"This game is being played under protest, George," he hollered from the Portsmouth sideline.

"Protest this," Halas yelled back, saluting Clark with a single finger.

No wonder the headline across the top of the *Portsmouth Times* on Monday read, SHAM BATTLE ON TOM THUMB GRIDIRON.

After the game, Bear players trekked through the snow to the Cottage Lounge for the postgame celebration. Nagurski, Grange, and Trafton were mobbed by fans at the bar. Around midnight, George Halas walked through the door. The Bears owner normally celebrated with a small group of friends and rarely socialized with the players. But this night was different. Trafton led a chorus of "For He's a Jolly Good Fellow," and it clearly pleased Papa Bear. That night, Halas knew in his heart that he should return to full-time coaching.

Chicago fans and the sporting press loved the NFL championship almost as much as the Cubs' back-to-back World Series titles in 1907 and '08. One sportswriter wrote, "Watching this game from the Stadium was the difference between sitting ringside at a heavyweight fight or in the last row of the upper deck. All the sounds of human beings smashing human beings were right out there and very real." Wilfrid Smith wrote in the *Chicago Tribune,* "The professional football championship of the United States is the property of the Chicago Bears." The NFL's dirt-cheap currency had been minted overnight into bigger bills.

The Chicago dailies validated the Bears and their NFL championship with tall headlines the next morning. It was Frank "the Enforcer" Nitti who crashed the party. Nitti, now in charge of the remnants of the Capone gang, was shot three times Sunday night as the game was being played. Cops had raided the gangster's office on the fifth floor of the LaSalle-Wacker building. The cops burst through the office door and ordered the six hoodlums to raise their hands. All but Nitti obeyed. He quickly stuffed a piece of paper in his mouth and attempted to swallow it. Sergeant Harry Lang leaped over the desk and tried to stop him. Nitti pulled a gun and fired three times, striking Lang twice. Lang and Sergeant Harry Miller returned fire, striking Nitti three times, once in the neck.

Nitti, known as "Screwy" and "Chi-Chi," was still conscious when he was rolled into Bridewell Hospital about an hour later. He asked for a priest and his father-in-law, a noted surgeon. When placed on the operating table, Nitti cried, "Oh, God, please save me this time!" He recovered and lived until 1943 when he put a bullet in his brain to avoid a jail sentence.

The other five Nitti men were placed in custody. Absent among the jailbirds was Jack McGurn. He had been attending the Bears-Spartans game, wearing a disguise, sitting next to Fat Tony Cirillo.

In Capone's absence, the gangster world was forever changing. Now the National Football League was due for an overhaul.

# 10

# Brave New League

Bronko Nagurski's controversial touchdown pass to Red Grange in the most famous pro football game ever played had the league fathers thinking. What if the rules could be adjusted to enhance passing? What if the NFL placed a greater premium on the value of scoring, on the value of entertainment?

The right man to drive these changes was none other than the new owner of the Boston Redskins, George Preston Marshall, a quirky man who wore a full-length raccoon coat, demanded that his players line up for publicity photos in war paint, and also produced a few theatrical shows in Washington, including a musical titled *Getting Gertie's Garter*. His first marriage was to a Ziegfeld Follies girl and his second was to a silent screen goddess, Corinne Griffith. Marshall knew little about football. He knew a lot about showbiz. This became evident with his halftime extravaganzas, which were worthy of Hollywood.

As the owners were about to adjourn from their annual meetings in the spring of 1933, Marshall stood and asked for permission to speak. What he had to say would raise the blood pressure of every man in the room.

"Gentlemen, you know far more about the game of football than me," he said. "But, gentlemen, the game you are playing is not entertaining. It is dull, uninteresting, and boring. This is how I look at it. We are in show business. And when the show gets dull, you throw it out. You put another one in its place. I want to give the public what it wants. I want to *change* the show."

Marshall proceeded to propose rules changes that would add hash marks to the field, liberate the passing game, and move goalposts from the end line to the goal line. The fat ball would be slimmed down so it could be thrown for both distance and accuracy. He also demanded that the NFL be split into two conferences for the purpose of staging a championship game each season.

As he spoke, a somnolent crowd became unsettled and loud. Fists pounded the table and cigar ashes were spilled. Then George Halas stood and addressed the fractured assembly. What he had to say would never be forgotten: "Men, we all know that Mr. Marshall is a little different than us. But these are some issues we need to address. It wouldn't hurt to change our game. I find all of these proposals pretty damn satisfactory. I am behind each and every one of them."

No one in the room was more surprised than Marshall. Halas had fought the brash Boston owner from the day he strutted into the league. Every idea he had previously proposed had been shot down by Halas. Now, though, Halas was ready to seize this opportunity to restructure the game. With record unemployment and America's economy out of control, the entertainment dollar had never been more precious. Never had it been more incumbent on a sports league to entertain. Halas could have jumped up and kissed the bombastic Marshall when he launched his campaign.

Normally, a man like Marshall would not have appealed to a salt-of-the-earth type like Halas. But the Bears co-owner was crippled financially, and the odds of his losing control of the team loomed larger with each passing day. When Marshall pushed for more liberal offensive rules, Halas seconded each motion. Why not? College football was outdrawing the pros five to one at the time. This alliance between Marshall and Halas came straight out of the blue. The men were as different as champagne and Old Style beer. Halas could barely stand the sight of Marshall swaggering up and down the Boston Redskins sideline in that stupid coat. But it was time for a change.

The first order of business was the writing of the "Bronko Rule."

Nagurski's touchdown pass against Portsmouth had created the NFL's biggest buzz since the Red Grange tour back in 1925. Suddenly a stodgy set of owners could see the value of encouraging the forward pass. Henceforth, it would be permissible to throw the ball from any spot behind the line of scrimmage. The second item on the agenda was adding hash marks; the pros would be following the colleges by spotting the ball ten yards from the boundary lines. Then the owners did away with the five-yard penalty for an incomplete pass and killed the change-of-possession rule for an incomplete pass in the end zone. The goalposts were returned from the end line to the goal line, and the fat ball was reduced from fifteen inches in circumference to eleven inches, making it far easier to grip and fling.

One of Marshall's brightest ideas was to split the league into two conferences, eastern and western, thus setting up a championship game every year. More teams would be involved in the conference races, and the fans would have a reason to follow each game more closely.

On that day the NFL managed to rise from the Dark Ages and become a viable league. The years ahead would be vibrant and filled with imagination. The Fat Ball era had finally died. Pro football, a sport built on verve and masculinity, would take the next step: It would become a thinking man's game.

In spite of Marshall's forward thinking, a dark side of the man emerged during these meetings. After the rules changes were passed, Marshall stood and, with a somber expression, said, "Gentlemen, I want all of the Negroes out of the game. Now. They are bad for business. They are bad for our image. What are out-of-work white people supposed to think when they look out on the field and see a bunch of damned nigrahs?"

Black players had been part of the league since its inception in 1920. Fritz Pollard, a 165-pound tailback for the Akron Pros, was the league's first black star, and he led his team to the very first league championship. Duke Slater, an All-America at Iowa, had the longest tenure of any black player—1922 through 1931. Integration had caused few problems in the NFL. There were a few fights and some foul words. But overall, everyone got along.

Some of the league owners resisted the change. But the measure banning black players passed with ease.

Halas shook his head but kept his mouth shut. He had enough problems of his own. Dutch Sternaman, the Bears' co-owner, finally proved that he was not bluffing. He ordered Halas to buy his fifty percent of the club or lose the Bears altogether. Sternaman was broke and needed the cash. He no longer cared about the Bears.

Sternaman wanted $38,000 for his share. Halas had nothing close to that in the bank.

Halas looked everywhere for money. Ralph Brizzolara, his childhood friend and a Bear executive, sold some Swedish stock and came up with $5,000. Wrestler Jim McMillen, a close Halas friend, kicked in another five grand. Halas's mother was able to provide another $5,000. The biggest investor was none other than George Trafton's mother, who supplied $20,000. But Halas, who had been forced to pay off some debts, was still short by five grand. The clock was ticking. Sternaman's lawyer had demanded the money by noon on August 9. At eleven that morning, Halas still did not have the money. Finally, he received a call from C. K. Anderson, the president of the First National Bank in Antioch. The bank was willing to loan $5,000. The Bears had been saved.

# 11

# Revenge

Just the mention of the name Nagurski inspired a numbing fear. This was never more evident than on a cloudy afternoon at the Baker Bowl in 1933, when the Philadelphia Eagles dreaded the thought of tangling with the toughest man in football.

Born that season into the NFL, the Eagles were the property of Bert de Benneville, the scion of Pennsylvania wealth; de Benneville was shortened to Bell, a name that would hold rank in pro football for several decades. Bell would climb the ladder to the office of the commissioner in 1946.

Little was expected from the Eagles in '33. The roster was filled with castoffs, misfits, drunks, and rejects from the local colleges. The Eagles took their name from the Blue Eagle symbol of the National Recovery Administration, an integral part of the New Deal. It could be said that the public held as much faith in President Roosevelt's fledgling recovery program as it did in the new Philly franchise.

The crowd of five thousand had come not to see the Eagles or Red Grange, for that matter. They had come to see the Bronk. Late in the first quarter, a rookie linebacker by the name of John "Bull" Lipski made the mistake of placing himself in the path of Nagurski, who dipped the left shoulder and rammed it into Lipski's jaw in the same vicious manner that Jack Dempsey had hammered the giant Jess Willard in 1919. Lipski crumpled like a bag of dry cement. His arms went one way, his legs the other, and his head struck the ground with a thud.

The NFL had yet to introduce the injury time-out. There would be no patience for an unconscious player. The trainers dashed onto the field with the clock still ticking and snapped ammonia capsules under Lipski's nostrils, and when his eyes popped open, his rag-doll body was lifted into a standing position. His legs were like jelly as the trainers wrapped their arms around him and hurriedly dragged him toward the sideline.

Carl Brumbaugh called the Bronk's number on the next play, a sweep around left end. He rumbled behind a bone-crushing block by Bill Hewitt. Nagurski swung to the outside, burst into the open field, cut toward the sideline, and spotted what appeared to be three defenders in his path. He didn't realize it was the two trainers hauling Lipski away. They had yet to cross the boundary line. The Bronk lowered his right shoulder and plowed into all three men, scattering them like bowling pins; Lipski was hurled three feet over the sideline and his head slammed into the ground, knocking him out once more.

Nagurski, unfazed by the collision, thundered down the sideline until he was knocked out of bounds some twenty yards later. As he rose, he looked up the field to see the two trainers sprawled motionless on the grass and Lipski down again. Then it hit him: He had plowed under three innocent bystanders. He walked slowly to the Eagle sideline, removed his helmet, and said in a high-pitched voice, "I am sorry. You fellas really should get out of my way while I'm running."

It was common for the Bronk to express pity for the men he sent to la-la land. He might be distressed for days about sending an opponent to the hospital. After his rookie season, when he sledgehammered more than a dozen players into unconsciousness, he made an honest effort to alter his tackling style; for a while, at least, he stopped whacking them in the head.

Despite his occasional remorse, the Bronk still scared the bejesus out of his opponents. To further his frightful image, Nagurski had taken up wrestling in the off-season. A promoter named Tony Stecher from Minneapolis had approached him with the prospect of making some extra money. First, Stecher would have to teach him some techniques. They worked in the ring for several days as Stecher, a former world champion, got the best of Nagurski. Finally, Stecher said, "What makes you such a great football player?"

"Blocking and tackling," Nagurski said.

"Then tackle me," Stecher replied.

It was the wrong thing to say.

Nagurski rumbled across the ring and plowed into the wrestler. Stecher suffered a badly broken right leg along with a concussion and had to be hospitalized for several weeks.

The Bronk had intimidated a lot of NFL players, but not Clarke Hinkle of the Green Bay Packers. He was a hard-hitting package of slab muscle. The Bronk felt no empathy whatsoever for Hinkle, whom he considered a dirty player. He was also ticked off that Hinkle was gaining a reputation as the second coming of Nagurski himself.

The previous season, during a game at Green Bay's City Stadium, Nagurski was streaming mad at Hinkle, who had sent a couple of Bears players to the bench with cheap shots. So the Bronk instructed Brute Trafton not to block Hinkle on a dive play.

"Just get out of the way, Traf, and let me at that sonofabitch," he said. Nagurski piled into the Packer linebacker with the force of a freight train. Hinkle's lights went out. He suffered a broken nose and a gashed chin.

Now it was Hinkle's turn to settle the score with Nagurski when the Bears and Packers met for the first time in '33. The Big Nag would not have Trafton at his side. Halas had finally convinced the rowdy center that his legs would no longer handle the rigors of a thirteen-game NFL season and it was time to hand the job on a full-time basis to Ookie Miller. Trafton was tired of arguing with Halas and hung up his cleats. He made the trip with the Bears anyway, to his favorite spot of all—Green Bay. For years Trafton and Packer fans had sparred both physically and verbally, and now he planned to stand behind the Bears bench and give them hell all afternoon.

In the first quarter, Hinkle dropped into punt formation on third down with the option of kicking or running. He spotted a crease in the Bears defense and took off. As he veered toward the right sideline he spotted Nagurski in typical balls-out pursuit. He could hear the Bronk's heavy breathing and he asked his legs for more speed. But Nagurski was faster and had the angle on his prey. It appeared certain that Hinkle would be knocked out of bounds short of the first down, but at the last second he pulled a Nagurski, pivoting and delivering the blow instead of taking it. To the astonishment of all who witnessed it, Hinkle drove his left shoulder into the Big Nag's jaw. Nagurski fell in a heap near the sideline and lay unconscious until the trainers sprinted onto the field and broke ammonia capsules beneath his nostrils. The Bronk jerked awake and shouted, "Where is that sonofabitchin' Hinkle?" The Packers fullback was on the ground just beyond the first-down marker and feeling woozy. But he managed to rise to his feet and return to the Green Bay huddle. Nagurski was not so lucky. His nose was pushed sickeningly to the left side of his face, and his jersey was coated with blood. There was a sharp pain in his right hip. He had to be helped to his feet, and he wobbled to the Bears bench, where he would spend the rest of the afternoon.

The sight of Nagurski stumbling off the field ignited a long roar from the crowd of twenty-three thousand fans.

"Get that bum off the field," they yelled. Bronko did not hear a word of it.

Green Bay fans sensed the pendulum finally swinging back in their favor. Chicago had gained the upper hand in the rivalry the last two years. But the Bears were not the same team without Nagurski. Neither team could score in the first half. Halas gathered the Bears in the north end zone at halftime for his pep talk. The coach was interrupted several times by whiskey bottles hurled from the stands. It was Trafton's job to return fire.

Green Bay shifted to a rookie lineup in the third quarter. Quarterback Arnie Herber tossed a fifty-yard rainbow to Ben Smith, who caught the pass and stepped out of bounds at the one-yard line. Buckets Goldenberg plunged into the end zone off left guard and the Pack led 7–0.

Neither offense was going anywhere for the rest of the third quarter, or for the first ten minutes of the fourth. With five minutes to play, Packer kicker Bobby Monnett attempted a field goal that would have sealed the victory. Hewitt blew between the guard and tackle like a gust of wind and blocked it. The Bears were still alive.

At the end of practice each day, the Bears tried a trick play called the "Stinky Special." Hewitt would take the handoff on a play that was disguised as an end-around. He would stop at the last second and heave a long pass to Luke Johnsos, the other Chicago end. Hewitt was known as a rugged blocker and tackler with a granite jaw. No one would have ever expected him to uncork a long one.

The play was called the "Stinky Special" because Hewitt, as a rookie, had only one set of clothes, and they could become smelly. He had one pair of white corduroy pants that turned gray, one pair of saddle oxfords, and one blue Michigan sweater with a big yellow M. Some of his teammates took to calling him "Stinky" behind his back. Most did not call him "Stinky" to his face because they were scared stiff of him.

Stinky swept left end with the Packers in full pursuit. Then he stopped, planted his foot, and whipped the forty-six-yard pass to Johnsos, who was standing alone at the goal line. Manders kicked the PAT and the score was tied at seven.

As the clock ticked away, the Green Bay offense sputtered and backfired and Lambeau seemed resigned to a tie. Less than a minute was left when Herber retreated into punt formation. Hewitt, who lined up at left end, couldn't care less whether he was ruled offsides this time. The Bears' only hope was for him to smother the punt. He gambled and won, literally swiping the ball off the foot of the kicker. The helmetless Hewitt seemed to cover the twenty yards to the end zone with the speed of a Red Ruffing fastball. Jack Manders delivered the extra point, and Chicago had the 14–7 victory.

As he ran to the bus, Halas grinned at the sight of Lambeau slumped on the Green Bay bench, staring at the ground.

●  ●  ●

When Red Grange saw the picture of George Musso sporting a mustache and wearing a Millikin College basketball uniform, he said, "This guy will never make it. He looks like a walrus." But Halas was fascinated with the data printed alongside Musso's name: six-two and 257 pounds. If he made the Bears roster, Musso would become one of the largest players in the history of the NFL.

Halas prided himself on discovering obscure talent at distant outposts. Most pro coaches were happy to sign studs from the eastern powers and midwestern colleges like Notre Dame, Michigan, Minnesota, and Illinois.

Few set their sights on the southern or western states. But Halas loved the little schools, regardless of their location. Millikin was located down in Decatur, Illinois, where the Bears were hatched as the Staleys in 1920.

Halas splurged. He sent five bucks to Musso to cover traveling expenses from Decatur to the Bears preseason camp being held outside Chicago for the first time. Musso would need three dollars for a rail ticket from Decatur to South Bend, Indiana. Halas took one look at the walrus as he stepped off the Wabash Line and offered him $90 a game, about average in that day for a lineman. But after watching him stumble about the practice field, no one believed he would ever earn a game check.

"That kid is fat, slow, and ugly," Halas told Grange. "You were right."

One of the greatest mismatches at camp was Musso versus Hewitt. Musso possessed the slowest feet in camp, Hewitt the quickest. The "Off-sides Kid" made Musso look like an overgrown seal.

Musso, with a face like the meringue on a lemon pie and an oddly proportioned body, was a sight to behold. He was wider than a beer barrel, and he jiggled when he walked. There was little muscle tone. But thanks to his athletic background, he had reasonably good physical coordination. He had won twelve letters in three different sports—football, baseball, and basketball—and must have been doing something right.

Football and George Musso almost never made a connection. The son of a Collinsville, Illinois, coal miner, he had worked long hours in the mines. Friends had to intercede to persuade his dad to send Big George to high school. The teenager never told his father that he had gone out for the football team. The elder Musso almost had a conniption when he learned his son had earned a football scholarship to Millikin, and in spite of the protests, Musso boarded the train to Decatur and never looked back.

During a 1929 Millikin game, he faced a scrappy 175-pound guard who would find fame as a sportscaster, actor, and politician. The much larger Musso had little trouble handling Ronald Reagan that day as Millikin defeated Eureka 45–6.

Surprisingly, almost none of the Musso potential revealed itself at the Bears' camp. The only factor working in his favor was his girth. Hewitt was able to outquick the walrus, but he couldn't penetrate the massive wall composed of thick gut and larded chest. Halas thought long and hard about what to do with his new tub of goo. Musso was lucky to have a uniform when the Bears broke camp and boarded the train back to Chicago, where Halas summoned him to his office and offered to send him to a minor league team in Cincinnati. So distraught was the big man that tears formed in his eyes. He went home and pondered his plight. Oddly, Musso had befriended Nagurski, a quiet man who was drawn to extroverted people—witness his close friendship with Trafton. So amused was Nagurski that he invited Musso to share an apartment with him and defensive back George Corbett for the '33 season.

"Bronk," Musso said over dinner, "coach wants to send me to the minors. He says I can't play ball up here."

"Ah, George can be a hard guy," Nagurski said. "But he's pretty fair. Give it some time."

The Bronk went to see Papa Bear the next day.

"George," he said, "what's this about giving Musso the axe already?"

"Kid can't play, Bronk," Halas replied. "He's just out there killing grass."

"Boy's still got his baby fat," Nagurski replied. "Give him some time, George. By golly, he's a load. Just think. We might have another monster on our hands."

They agreed that Musso would stay with the team for a few games and that Grange and Nagurski would work with him, helping to develop his footwork. In spite of his initial thumbs-down, the Ghost had grown attached to the fat, jolly kid.

"You won't regret it," the Bronk told Halas.

Halas would have shrugged off another player, but not Nagurski.

Neither the fans nor the press was aware that Halas had actually started a youth movement during the Bears' summer training camp in '33. But the players were certainly aware of it. It seemed that Halas was cutting a veteran player with each passing day.

Ten of the twenty-eight players who suited up for the Bears in 1932 were axed. This baffled the survivors. It was the code among the veteran players that they would take care of each other during training camp. If one of the older guys was struggling, the others would hold him up rather than knock him flat. The players could not figure how Halas was locating the deadwood on the team. He stood on the sideline during practice, the worst possible place to judge talent.

One afternoon Halas called his players into the training camp auditorium and turned out the lights. Then before their very eyes flickered a film that had been shot during the morning practice. No football coach at any level had used film as a means to critique his players. Now they knew that every action on the practice field, along with the games on Sunday, would be strictly critiqued. It also worked to motivate the players.

No team in the NFL during that '33 season could match the Bears' first unit—Hewitt and Bill Karr at the ends, Link Lyman and Dick Stahlman at the tackles, Zuck Carlson and Joe Kopcha at the guards, and Ookie Miller at center. The halfbacks were Gene Ronzani and Keith Molesworth. Brumbaugh was beginning his fourth season as the starting quarterback, as was Nagurski at fullback. Defensive substitutions were Grange and George Corbett at halfback for Ronzani and Molesworth. Johnsos spelled Karr at end. Nagurski and the helmetless Hewitt never left the field. They were sixty-minute men.

Chicago reeled off six straight wins to start the season. The second time the Bears and Packers met, Hewitt had another Herculean day, shutting down the left side of the line as he had back on September 24 when the *Green Bay Press-Gazette* reported, "Hewitt was a team by himself. . . . Green Bay would send two or three men after him, but Hewitt would smash through all of them to break up the play." Green Bay led 7–0 with four minutes to play when Brumbaugh tossed a twelve-yard touchdown pass to Johnsos, and Jack Manders added the extra point. Then the Bears marched sixty-seven yards to the Packers eight-yard line, where Manders booted a thirteen-yard field goal with less than a minute to play. The Bears had come from behind again to beat the Packers, this time 10–7. Again Lambeau sat on the bench at the end of the game with his head between his knees. It was Chicago's fourth win in six games against the hated Pack.

On November 5 the Bears traveled to Boston to meet the Redskins at Fenway Park. Boston's flamboyant owner, George Preston Marshall, roamed the sideline alongside the coaches. The Redskins had spent the better part of the week cooking up schemes to send Nagurski to the hospital. As it turned out, Marshall was not the only one. Lone Star Dietz, the head coach, was the most outrageous personality in football. Dietz, of Sioux and German descent, learned his football under the fabled Pop Warner at the Carlisle (Pennsylvania) Training School for Indians. He was a tackle and teammate of Jim Thorpe and had invented the "Indian block," which would become better known as the cross-body block. Lone

Star chose the right time to unveil the block against heavily favored Harvard in 1911, when Thorpe ran wild and the Indians pulled off one of the biggest upsets in the history of college football by the score of 18–15.

Lone Star climbed rapidly through the coaching ranks and led Washington State to a 14–0 victory over Brown in the 1916 Rose Bowl. Almost every newspaper in the country carried the photo of Dietz strolling the sideline in tuxedo, stovepipe hat, and cane. With Dietz on the sideline, you never really knew what to expect, for his bag of tricks included triple reverses and fake fumbles. But his favorite was the "squirrel cage" on kickoffs. After the deep man caught the ball, the other ten players would surround him and the ball would be slipped to lineman Turk Edwards. Then all of the Boston players would take off running up the field, pretending to hide the ball behind their backs. The kick coverage team didn't know which one to tackle and certainly didn't expect a 235-pounder like Edwards to have it. He was normally left free long enough to rumble fifty yards or so up the field before somebody figured it out.

Now, as the Bears hit Beantown, Dietz decided to put a contract out on Nagurski. He instructed Redskins tackle Jack Riley to allow himself to be blocked whenever the Bronk ran the ball to his side of the field. Riley hated the idea, but decided not to buck his volatile coach.

Early in the game Nagurski took the handoff and prepared to plow into the left side of the line when Riley was shoved aside by Link Lyman. To his surprise, roaring up from about ten yards deep was Ernie Pinckert, one of the hardest hitters in pro ball. The collision had the Big Nag wobbling on rubbery legs to the sideline and taking a seat on the bench.

When his head cleared at halftime, though, the Big Nag wanted back in the game. On his first carry he charged off left tackle, and Riley literally took a seat on the ground. Pinckert blasted the Bronk. This time Nagurski needed help from the trainers to reach the sideline. He did not return for the rest of the game. The Redskins pulled off the monumental upset by the score of 10–0 before 22,820 fans, the biggest crowd to witness a pro game in Boston. As the final seconds ticked down, Marshall had the gall to dance on the sideline.

"I will get even with that bastard," Halas shouted, shaking his fist.

Portsmouth would be a crossroads game. Talk about grudge matches—this would be the first meeting of the teams since the controversial NFL title game of the previous season. Coach Potsy Clark still accused Halas and Nagurski of cheating to win. Now seeking revenge, the Spartans would be mad as hell as they marched into Wrigley Field on a fiercely cold day amid blowing snow.

Tailback Dutch Clark, who had missed the '32 title game, still had not returned to the team, choosing to concentrate on his coaching job back in Colorado. Once again Glenn Presnell, the 190-pound dynamo, would run the offense from the tailback position of the double-wing offense. At that moment, Presnell was the NFL leader in passing, scoring, and field goals and was third behind Johnny Blood and Nagurski in rushing yards.

Presnell took the game straight to the Bears, scoring both of Portsmouth's touchdowns in the first two quarters and the Spartans led at halftime 14–0. The Bears were sinking fast. Presnell was the master of deception when handling the ball, and his sleight of hand kept the overly aggressive Nagurski off balance.

With sleet mixing with the snow, the field turned to ice in the second half. Nagurski, his inch-long cleats chewing up the ice, carried the ball on nineteen of the Bears' twenty-one plays in the third quarter. He exploded into the end zone on a five-yard touchdown run midway in the quarter. Manders then added a field goal of thirty-three yards minutes later to cut the lead to 14–10.

Then came the Bronk once more. The Spartans could hear his cleats puncturing the ice crust and could hear his heavy breathing and loud grunts. He tore into defenders, driving them several yards up the field. As the fourth quarter was winding down, Nagurski broke loose at the forty-yard line with only one player between him and the end zone. Presnell, knowing his only hope was to jump on the Bronk's back, rode the big man for ten yards down the field. Nagurski rose and patted Presnell on the back. "Nice tackle," he said. "But it won't happen again."

His legs churning and chunks of ice flying, Nagurski turned the corner around right end on the next play and set his sights on Presnell, the final obstacle in his path. He tucked the ball under his right arm and reared back with his left forearm, clubbing Presnell under the chin and sending him into a back flip. Nagurski scored easily, and the Bears had come from behind again to win 17–14. The Chicago dailies were starting to call them "the storybook Bears."

The 10–2–1 regular season was polished off with wins over the Cardinals and Packers and a 17–7 victory over Portsmouth. Now they were the inaugural Western Division champions, headed for a title showdown with the New York Giants.

• • •

"The only way to stop Nagurski is to shoot the sonofabitch before he leaves the dressing room." That line was uttered by Giants coach Steve Owen as New York and Chicago prepared to play for the NFL championship game on December 17 at Wrigley Field.

The Giants coach lived by a simple philosophy, which spoke to his admiration of Nagurski. "Football is a game played down in the dirt by two people," he said. "The one who scraps the hardest is going to win." He also said, "Pro football was invented by a mean sonofabitch, and it's meant to be played that way." The S.O.B. he was thinking about was Halas.

It was Nagurski's opinion that Mel Hein, who stood six-two and weighed 200 pounds, was the best defensive player in football. Though he played center and linebacker, he possessed the speed of a halfback.

It was Hein's opinion that Nagurski was the best player in football. "Every time I think about tackling Bronko, I can almost feel the pain," he said. "I always drop my shoulder to try to stop him. But he runs me flat. I never have found the right way to tackle that big ox. If you try to hit him high, he'll run over you. If you try to hit him low, he'll trample you to death. He's the best."

For the final game of the year, Nagurski was running behind a vastly improved offensive line. The tutoring of Musso by Grange and Nagurski had paid off. "Moose," as he was now called, had become a powerhouse almost overnight at right tackle, winning a starting job the eighth week of the season.

It was a beautiful afternoon as the game began, and it quickly became evident that neither team was ready to gamble. Manders, now called "Automatic Jack," kicked field goals of sixteen and forty yards, but the Giants had the halftime lead of 7–6 thanks to a twenty-nine-yard touchdown pass from Harry Newman to end Red Badgro. Ken Strong made the extra point.

Manders kicked yet another field goal in the third quarter to give the Bears a 9–7 lead.

Pro football at the time was a sport desperately in need of a little razzle-dazzle. The Bears never expected Owen to be transformed into a riverboat gambler. But he had a card up his sleeve when the Giants began their next possession near midfield. All of the New York linemen set up to the right of Hein, making him an eligible man. Instead of setting up for the deep snap, Newman made one of his rare appearances under center, like a T-formation quarterback. Newman took the ball from Hein and placed it back between Hein's hands. Then the Giants quarterback backpedaled madly, as if retreating to pass. Seven Bears, including Nagurski, took up the chase.

Now standing alone in the middle of the field, Hein casually tucked the football in his shirt and started walking. No one in the stadium noticed that he developed a sudden beer gut. Before the play, Newman had said to Hein, "Take it slow and don't rush it. Nobody'll know that you got the ball." But Hein could not help himself. After ten yards he broke into a slow trot, and then into a gallop. Suddenly the fans at Wrigley Field spotted Hein and started pointing at the big Giants center. Keith Molesworth was the only defensive back in the vicinity, and there was no guarantee that he could catch one of the best all-round athletes in football, a man who could outrun most backs. But he saved the day by dragging Hein down. The Giants later scored on Max Krause's one-yard plunge over the goal line, and they grabbed a 14–9 lead on Strong's point-after kick.

Chicago decided to counter with Nagurski. The Bronk carried the ball nine straight times and moved the ball all the way to the New York six-yard line. The Giants braced for another Nagurski smash. But the Big Nag threw on the brakes at the last instant, just as he had done against Portsmouth a year earlier. He leaped and tossed an end-over-end basketball pass to Bill Karr in the right corner of the end zone, and Chicago led 16–14 on Manders's extra-point kick.

Like Nagurski, Newman was virtually unstoppable through the air. He completed passes of thirty and twenty-one yards to end Ray Flaherty. On the next play, Strong sprinted around right end for fifteen more. Then Newman slipped into the huddle, dropped to one knee, and drew the next play in the dirt. He would hand off to Strong around left end and the halfback would run through a hole in the line. But Strong was stopped at the line so he lateraled back across the field to Newman. As Newman took off around left end running for his life, Strong hauled ass to the end zone. Before crossing the line of scrimmage, Newman stopped and lofted a pass into the left corner, where Strong waited by himself. New York 21, Chicago 16. Ten minutes remained on the clock. The lead had changed hands five times.

It was time for the Bears to play Bronko Ball once more. They moved the ball down the field in short, powerful bursts. Brumbaugh mixed in a few short passes. A quick toss to Hewitt moved the ball to the New York thirty-three. Again Nagurski faked a plunge into the line, then jumped and flipped a ten-yarder to Hewitt over the middle. The helmetless wonder ran five yards, pivoted, and lateraled the ball to Karr, crossing behind him. This little piece of trickery completely fooled the Giants. Karr sprinted into the end zone untouched. Manders's kick made it 23–21, with seconds to go.

Nobody left the park. They had seen enough of Newman's passing to know the Giants could come back. The Bears were keeping one eye on Newman and the other on Hein. They were ready for anything, including the center sneak.

On the first play of the drive, the Giants shifted all of their linemen to the right side of Hein, making him eligible for a run or pass. Nagurski smelled the center sneak once again. But Newman took the snap from Hein and pitched to Dale Burnett. The Bears forgot about Hein. Burnett bobbed and weaved in the backfield while Hein, who was open at the fifteen, waved his arms madly. All Burnett had to do was throw the ball in the vicinity of Hein for a certain touchdown. But the ball slipped out of the back of his hand. The Giants could not believe their eyes.

There was time for one more play, and the Giants had one last sleight of hand. Newman completed a desperation pass over the middle to Badgro. Grange moved in for the tackle. Then he saw what was developing. Hein was only two yards behind Badgro, ready to take a lateral. So the Ghost used his head. He wrapped his arms around Badgro's chest, pinning down his arms. Badgro couldn't shovel the ball to Hein. As the Ghost and Badgro fell, the gun sounded. The game was over.

It was one of the greatest heads-up plays anyone had ever witnessed. No one was questioning why Halas had kept an over-the-hill Ghost around. Grange was worth every dime he'd ever earned. Nagurski might have replaced him as the league's marquee player, but the Bears would not be back-to-back champions without Grange.

Chicago had yet another reason to celebrate. Prohibition had finally perished twelve days earlier. The repeal of the Eighteenth Amendment ended a drought that had lasted thirteen years, ten months, and nineteen days. It officially expired at midnight on December 5. The election of President Franklin D. Roosevelt in November 1932 had doomed the Volstead Act. Full repeal of Prohibition was a welcome relief in the Windy City, where gang warfare had raged out of control and where blood had run in the streets since 1920. It was estimated that more than a thousand men had died in Chicago as a result of the bootlegging wars.

Al Capone had gone to prison in 1931, as had several other crooks, but Chicago had been forever changed by Prohibition. For decades mobsters would control the city. But Chicago still had the Bears. And the future never seemed brighter.

For years the players had been celebrating at the Cottage Lounge on the North Side. This night would be different, though. There would be no Capone or Frank McGurn in the crowd, and everyone would be drinking the legal stuff. The first to arrive at the bar was Trafton. Naturally, he offered the first toast of the evening.

"Once again, a toast to the Ghost," he said. "But, Nagurski, you're still the man with the most."

The Bronk actually smiled.

# 12

# Bunyan

B ronko Nagurski strode powerfully across the frozen range, his rifle
slung over his right shoulder, his backpack strapped to his upper
frame, his breath rising like steam. The snow at dawn was piled high for
hundreds of miles across the Big North Woods as the sun rose over the
vast timberline. The blue sky was without blemish. The distant whistle of
a lumber train shrilled as it rumbled through the forests, hauling wood to
the paper mill.

The stillness of the morning was out of keeping with the Arctic blasts
that had roared down from Canada the last nine days, burying the Borderland in a deep blanket of snow and crippling hamlets from the North
Dakota border to Ironwood, Wisconsin. Icy winds had shooed most of the
citizens of International Falls toward their own warm hearths or into cozy
saloons. Whiskey and the boilermakers blunted the rough edges of a winter depression.

The Bronk could never remember suffering from the winter blahs.
Nor could he ever recollect standing still long enough to worry about such
things. To surrender to the subzero temperatures, to hover over a wood-
burning stove, was to be held captive for a third of the calendar year. It
was not the Nagurski style. Besides, this winter wonderland, with all of

its harsh conditions, was his favorite playground. Almost twenty years had passed since the six-year-old had killed his first deer, had strung up and gutted and dressed the carcass all by himself, the venison providing the family with some fine winter meat. It was nothing for young Bronislau to take off alone through the woods with his trusty .30–30 Winchester and to return home with some tasty kill. The kid could shoot.

When he was young, they'd said that the young Nagurski could have run all the way to Winnipeg and back without stopping. The legs slabbed with muscle were a testament to that notion. One of his many jobs was to run from lumber camp to lumber camp delivering messages from the paper-mill bosses to the lumberjacks. There were more than a hundred camps at the time. No wonder his body was sinew and bone and little else.

The stories told about the Bronk, even as a child, were remindful of the mythical character that had once roamed the Big North Woods—a giant named Paul Bunyan. He was treetop tall with the strength of an entire army. It was said that one bright morning Bunyan discovered that the million or so logs he and his men had cut were now landlocked in a northern Minnesota lake. Bunyan ordered his great Swedish blacksmith, Ole, to make an enormous shovel. He started to dig a canal all the way to the Gulf of Mexico. He shoveled so hard that the sun was darkened by a total eclipse. The dirt that flew over his right shoulder became the Rocky Mountains; the dirt that piled up to the left became the Appalachians.

Nagurski, like Bunyan, was the epitome of hair-on-the-chest maleness. Now, at age twenty-five, the thrill of the hunt was thick in his veins. He had been planning this trip since returning home the previous week. The sun had yet to rise over Chicago on the morning after the dramatic victory over the New York Giants when Bronk boarded a train and roared northward. That two close hunting buddies had backed out at the last minute, citing the frightful weather, would not deter the hard-willed Nagurski from tracking the big stag that had eluded him the previous hunting season. He knew that Big Boy was still out there, strutting through the dense forests.

The Bronk had left the farmhouse thirty minutes before dawn. He had poked a log into the potbellied stove, tied the laces of his Pak rubber-bottom boots with leather tops, pulled on his woolen leggings, cinched his backpack, buttoned his duck-down vest, zipped his red mackinaw, slid the hunting knife into his belt, tied the laces of his Stagg pants, flung the harness of the .300 Savage with lever action over his right shoulder, and headed out the door without waking a soul. It was thirty-seven degrees below zero when he bounded down the front steps. It was three days until Christmas.

This excursion by foot to the log cabin on the peninsula on the northeast side of Kabetogama Lake would require most of the day. He would encounter deer, wolves, moose, grouse, partridge, and hungry black bears weighing up to six hundred pounds. Few humans would dare tackle the elements of northern Minnesota in these conditions. It was enough to make Nagurski smile.

The dried beef in his backpack would tame his growling stomach until he could bag a couple of rabbits and boil them on the woodstove at the hunting cabin. The big meal would come later when he strung up Big Boy on a line behind the cabin, gutted him, dressed him, and carved up the hindquarters.

This would have been an easy trip in the late spring or summer. The Bronk and his buddies would have piled into the green Ford, driven the five miles to Black Bay, launched the johnboat, puttered along the ten-mile channel before emerging into the broad expanse of blue water known as Kabetogama Lake. Then they would have set their sights on Sugarbush Island. A half mile beyond the island on the shoreline at Nashata Point stood the cabin.

This journey in the dead of winter was akin to marching into Siberia. No wonder the big man was the lone human on the road this morning, his knees driving, his arms pumping, his head down, his breath smoking, and his body tilting forward in the manner of a hard-knocking fullback. The thick, soft powder had not been disturbed. The first five miles through fresh snow would challenge every muscle in his steely frame. But Black Bay would provide a more solid footing for the next ten miles. After reaching the mouth of Kabetogama Lake, he would cross the final two miles to the northern shore. The thick layer of ice over the lake would allow him to make good time. If only the clouds did not return, along with the harsh winds, the snow, and the sleet. The temperature would slowly rise on a clear day, possibly all the way to minus twenty. But if the dark clouds blew down from Canada, bearing yet another storm, it could fall to minus sixty degrees in nothing flat.

A man traversing five miles of powder, and twelve miles of frozen lake, faced the real prospect of frostbite and death. But this was the kind of challenge the Bronk had embraced since his rugged upbringing. This day he would trace the steps of the French *voyageurs*, who dared to pioneer this land and all of its obstacles during the late 1600s. The *voyageurs* did most of their traveling during the warmer months by boat but were never discouraged by the hard winters. They forged ahead on foot across a chain of frozen lakes for hundreds of miles. The same could be said of the Ojibwa Indians, a hardy tribe that traded in pelts, skins, and furs. They were bold and fearless.

Not until the late 1800s would people of other nationalities attempt to garner the resources of this region, a strange patchwork of dense forests, swamps, lakes, and northward-flowing rivers. It was some of the most inaccessible land in the forty-eight states. The *voyageurs* battled the frozen trails of upper Minnesota en route to the plains and finally to the Rocky Mountains.

The only sound Bronko could hear was the snow crunching beneath his boots. Occasionally, the lonesome whistle of the forest trains penetrated the silence. Alas, this was a good time to be alone. There were many thoughts on his mind. Just yesterday, Mike Nagurski had invited the Bronk to join him in the living room of the farmhouse and share some potato whiskey. That is when the bad news came down. "The bank is about to foreclose on the farm," the elder Nagurski had said. "We are going to lose everything."

The Bronk knew that his father had been in dire financial straits since the downturn of the local economy four years earlier. Trouble at the paper mill had virtually crippled the Falls, leaving more than half of the town unemployed. Even the lucky ones who kept their jobs at the mill had seen wages slashed from $50 a week to $28.

Edward Wellington Backus, once described as a man of "towering persona and stature," had constructed the paper mill in 1910. Backus once called International Falls the "City of Destiny." It took less than a decade for him to establish himself as the world's second-largest paper producer, and his worth was estimated at $100 million. But by the late twenties his empire was in ruins, thanks to unpaid back taxes that forced him into bankruptcy. The onset of the Great Depression further damaged his earning power at the paper mill. In truth, the stubborn Backus had failed to develop a well-trained organization and was without credit reserves. He had listened to no one's advice but his own. In the end his own ego destroyed his grand scheme.

Mike Nagurski had been a staunch citizen of the community for almost two decades. He was a half inch taller than his son but not nearly as broad-shouldered or as heavily muscled. The dominant feature of his face was the thin, beakish nose. Bronko's nose was wide with thick bone and cartilage. Both men possessed enormous hands and heads. Bronko wore a size-eight leather helmet. (It was once said that Paul Bunyan's head was so large that his wife combed his hair with a crosscut saw.)

Citizens of the Falls often remarked on how the oldest Nagurski child resembled his father, both in stature and energy. Bronislau admired his father, and it saddened him to know that this man with so much pride and honor had fallen so hard.

With the failure of the paper mill, and the arrival of the Depression, Mike was forced to close the store, the sawmill, and the construction business in 1930. He faced the dilemma of a lifetime. Bootlegging was virtually the last game in town. The field was fertile, but risks were high. Stills had sprung up across the farms and forests with the arrival of Prohibition in 1920, and bootleggers had quick access to some fine Canadian whiskey just across the border. Canadian brewers and distributors responded to the Volstead Act by sending a virtual tidal wave of beer and whiskey into the United States. The booze was smuggled in by train, automobile, boat, and even plane. The rough-and-tumble frontier types were not about to stop drinking just because an amendment had been added to the U.S. Constitution. The editor of the local newspaper wrote, "Gasoline is nineteen cents a gallon, hair tonic a buck-fifty and liquor five dollars a quart. It doesn't matter what you drink. They all taste alike." You could buy booze from the same dairy that delivered milk. When a local drugstore burned, the cops discovered 150 kegs of moonshine in the basement. One raid on Crystal Beach, about five miles from the Falls, netted twenty barrels of booze at fifty gallons each. Authorities estimated that was enough liquor to provide every man, woman, and child in the Falls with twenty-five drinks apiece.

The patriarch of the Nagurski family resembled many desperate men of the time. Soon the Feds would get the goods on him and threaten to send him to Leavenworth. He would agree to cease and desist and accept a low-paying job at the paper mill. Weeks later, Backus was forced to shut down operations completely. The plant closed for more than a year.

Father and son would sip the white-hot moonshine whiskey and talk for hours about this financial quandary and how to save the family. Money had to come from somewhere, and it had to come fast.

"I will buy the farm from you and take up the payments," the Bronk said. "You will not lose it."

They agreed that the deed would be transferred to Bronko's name.

The Bronk's greatest frustration was that he didn't have more money in the bank. Most of the contractual promises made by George Halas back in 1930 had been broken. Bronko had signed the largest financial contract in the history of pro football as a rookie at $5,000 per season. Not only had Halas reduced his salary each year, in spite of his great seasons, the Bronk had returned home each December with an IOU from the owner in his pocket. The Bears might have been the most successful and popular team in the NFL, but Halas could not make ends meet. Nagurski was due to make only $3,500 in the 1934 season.

That afternoon the Bronk sent a telegram to Halas. It read simply, GEORGE SEND MONEY STOP BRONKO.

Bronko had managed to sock away enough cash the past four seasons to cover the purchase of the farm. But writing a check for the property was just a down payment on the future. Other family expenses were certain to arise. His sisters, Stephanie and Jennie, were soon to graduate from high school and had been promised a college education. Mike Nagurski had made that pledge when he had money in the bank, along with borrowing power.

Other financial burdens would soon befall the Bronk. There was the auburn-haired woman with the Myrna Loy looks, the one he planned to marry. Bronko and Eileen Kane had started dating not long after meeting in 1929 before his final college game. He had been burning up the rails and the highways to St. Paul, where Eileen was a student at St. John's College. Now Bronko worried whether his bank account could support a wedding, much less a large family. Eileen was a devout Catholic. Where in God's name could he come up with more money?

Professional football had finally gained some public respect, but the Bronk worried about the future of the game. He was at first ashamed to participate in a scandalized sport that had been vilified by virtually every college president, coach, and sportswriter in America. One afternoon during that first season with the Bears, he was walking back to his hotel at the

Wellington Arms when he happened upon a group of kids playing tackle football on the playground. One of them yelled, "Hey, let's play pro ball! Let's play pro ball!" The Bronk was naturally curious to learn their interpretation of "pro ball." That is when they stopped blocking and tackling and reverted to a game of two-hand touch. Neither team put much of an effort into the game. The Bronk felt sickened at the sight of it all.

He was so ashamed of the reputation of the professional game after his first season that he wouldn't even talk about his experiences during a visit to the Minnesota campus.

"People don't believe this is an honest sport," Nagurski once said to Red Grange. "People make fun of us, Ghost."

Grange shook his head. "The same people who make fun of us are the ones who would trade places with us in a heartbeat," he said. "They're just jealous."

There were times when Bronko felt guilty about playing a game for money. Oh, he loved practicing during the week and playing on Sunday, and the camaraderie of his teammates was the most gratifying part of the job. He was lucky to have such friends as George Trafton, Carl Brumbaugh, and Grange around to teach him the ropes. And to win two league championships in his first four seasons, well, that was something he could have never dreamed up.

But the Bronk also worried about what common folks really thought of him. What did they say about him around the Falls? Did they think he acted high and mighty, like the big cigars from Chicago? Surely they didn't think he was getting rich playing football.

Just a few days earlier, he was relaxing at one of the local watering holes called the Red Mule when a familiar scene played out. A drunken lumberjack approached him. "So you're the great Bronko Nagurski," he said. "You don't look so tough."

Lumberjacks were known to drink, gamble, and chase whores for several days without sleep. Most were determined to squander every penny of their paycheck before returning to camp, and the Falls was the kind of wide-open town that could accommodate every one of their desires. Craps, poker, and blackjack could be found in brothels and saloons around the clock. You could also head up to Rainy Lake, where the horse races were staged during the winter months on the rock-solid ice. Several of the hotel owners and saloonkeepers owned racehorses, and when the Canadians or the big-city tourists came to the Falls the stakes could get high.

Girls were always available at the hotels and brothels for the pleasure of the lumberjacks. In the summer, when prostitutes flocked to the Falls during the fishing season, tents with hundreds of cots were set up around the town.

Most lumberjacks lived miserable lives and had little or no self-esteem. Beating up the legendary Bronko Nagurski would have meant free drinks for weeks and a huge dose of self-respect.

Nagurski tried to ignore the drunken man who had just challenged him. He reeked of booze and sweat and was actually bigger than Bronko. He possessed a muscular frame himself after years of swinging an axe. When the man persisted, the Bronk said, "You sure you want to do this?"

"Yeah, you bastard," the lumberjack growled.

The jack never saw the right uppercut coming. It caught him flush under the jaw and sent him flying across the room and into a wall that splintered into several pieces. As he flew headfirst into the dark of night and straight into a snowbank, the bartender shouted, "Timberrrr!"

It was the fifth or sixth time—no one was sure—in the last four years that Nagurski was forced to prove himself to the lumberjack colony. It was done reluctantly each time. As usual, his tormentor did not even bother to return. Bleeding from a gash over his eye, he stumbled down the street to the next bar, probably looking for a smaller man to unleash his frustration upon.

"Make sure he pays for the wall," Nagurski said to the bartender.

"Don't worry. I'll have the sheriff pick him up if he doesn't come back."

It didn't take an Einstein to realize that Nagurski was the toughest S.O.B. in the valley. He was also the greatest thing ever to hit pro football. For years, players were regarded as lazy thugs. But stars like Nagurski and Grange served to change that image. The Bears had provided a new model for NFL teams—a hardworking, blue-collar bunch that actually practiced and had team meetings each day.

Still, Bronko knew that the NFL and Halas would discard him like worn-out cleats when he was injured or grew too old to play the game. He could not help but worry that he would someday meet the same fate as Grange. He admired the Ghost more than all others. Grange had had it all—money, fame, beautiful women, and incomparable talent—but it was all as fleeting as the last snowflake of winter. The Ghost needed but three years to blow a quarter million dollars, an obscene amount at the time. He had stood on a pedestal alongside four other luminaries of the twenties—Jack Dempsey, Babe Ruth, Bill Tilden, and Bobby Jones. Now he stood at the door to obscurity. The public, of course, remembered his fabulous final season in college in 1924, along with that first barnstorming tour with the Bears. But the rest of his pro career was mostly forgettable. The 1934 season would be the Ghost's last dance, and he was certain to spend most of it on the bench.

The Ghost and the Bronk had sat together during the celebration at the Cottage Lounge after Chicago defeated the Giants 23–21 for the 1933 championship.

"Bronk, you are the greatest football player I've ever seen," the Redhead had said.

"No, Ghost, you're the best. And they'll always remember you that way."

The Ghost was not lying. Nagurski was the name synonymous with football, the Babe Ruth of the sport. But it confounded Nagurski no end that the sporting press, after slamming pro football all those years, was now calling him the savior of the game. He was roundly compared in terms of popularity with movie stars like Tom Mix. He would have never expected, much less imagined, this kind of adulation. Wilfrid Smith had written in the *Chicago Daily Tribune,* "Bronko Nagurski is undoubtedly the unanimous choice as the greatest player in professional football." That was the consensus.

"I don't know if I like all of the fame that comes with this game," Nagurski said to Grange one day.

"Bronk, you'd better get used to it," Grange had said. "There's plenty more fame to come."

"Yah," the Bronk said. "But maybe I don't like the fame."

"Look at it this way," Grange said. "Fame is a woman who'll walk on you when you're down. But when you're winning, she's the kind you'd like to take around."

"Maybe I don't like those kinds of dames."

The Ghost could only shake his head and laugh.

Not only was Nagurski the greatest runner and blocker of the age, a third tool had been added to his game—passing. It was not unusual for him to take the handoff, fake into the line, and stop at the last second before flipping a quick strike to a back or an end. His passes had provided the winning points in both the 1932 and '33 league title games.

Those who studied the game knew that Nagurski's fourth tool—defense—might have been his greatest strength. The big man ran down ball carriers from sideline to sideline, driving their leather helmets into the ground. The scariest sight in pro football was Nagurski at linebacker, digging in his cleats with teeth clenched and the steely eyes staring ahead. No player was more revered or respected by opposing players.

So why, at this very moment, was the Bronk's life so upside down? Why was he bearing a heavy heart across this frozen land of northern Minnesota?

After five miles on the powdery road, his calves and thighs were burning. But now he was taking his first few steps on Black Bay, where the ice provided better footing and was easier on the legs. So many thoughts had poured through his head the last two hours that he had failed to take stock of where he was. And now he could hear the barking of dogs. *Dogs?*

Headed straight for him were a half dozen malamutes barking their lungs out. And standing behind the tail-wagging canines astride the runners of the sled was the ever-smiling George Esslinger, who was driving the dogsled westward along the bay and straight toward the big man. Esslinger pulled the team up a few feet short of where the Bronk stood.

"Well, if it's not the great Bronko Nagurski!" he yelled. "The greatest player in the history of football. And the man who can*not* swim. And the man now standing smack-dab in the middle of a goddamned frozen lake."

Bronko could only shake his head. George Esslinger was one of the most colorful characters of the Big North Woods, a friendly sort who used to race his dogs from Manitoba to Minneapolis and owned a case full of trophies for his efforts. He had recently bought a lake resort not far from the Nagurski cabin.

"Where the hell did you come from, heh?" Nagurski said.

"Straight out of the clouds," Esslinger said, laughing. "Yah. And you didn't even see me coming. If I'd been a bear, I'd a bit you."

"I'd a bit you back."

"Bronk, you'd better turn back. You'll freeze your buns off before you get to the cabin."

"Well, I guess that makes two of us crazy sonsabitches."

"Yah, and you still got a dozen miles of frozen lake. And you can't even swim."

"Have you ever seen ice melt at forty below, George?"

The Bronk had discovered at an early age that he couldn't float. He may have been unstoppable on the football field, but he was not unsinkable. Family and friends surmised that since his body lacked measurable fat cells, and that muscle and bone are heavy, the boy was born to sink. But he never developed a fear of water and spent the better part of the warm months fishing from a boat or on the shore. The damnedest sight was a young Bronko in the middle of Rainy Lake as a boy straddling logs as they were sluiced to the paper mill. He would jump from log to log, rarely losing his balance. If he did happen to fall off into the water, he simply grabbed a log and pulled himself back up. In the middle of summer, he was regularly spotted in the middle of the lake—a half mile from either shore—jumping from log to log, oblivious to fear and his own sinkability.

The greatest fear of a hunter or hiker on a frozen lake is having the ice break apart beneath him. The shattering of the ice of a frozen lake resounds like rolling thunder. If ever you hear it and you manage to survive it, you will never test your luck again—unless your name is Bronko Nagurski.

It happened the first time when he was eight years old. The Bronk was daydreaming and walking across the ice into the mouth of Kabetogama Lake when the rumble started. It sounded like a freight train blasting straight down the middle of the immense lake. The ice fractured in every direction, huge blocks of ice breaking off and rolling. The Bronk stood more than two hundred yards from the bank, so there was no need to make a mad dash to safety. He waited for the ice to break apart around him, then balanced himself on one of the largest blocks. The sinker had found a fine float. He bestrode it for more than two hours until it delivered him safely to the rocky bank, where he pulled himself up and began the long trek home. He was so unfazed by what others would have considered a harrowing experience that he didn't tell a soul for two weeks.

Standing on the edge of Black Bay now, talking to George Esslinger, Bronko felt the black cloud above his life begin to dissipate. George loved the wilds of northern Minnesota almost as much as Nagurski. Kabetogama Lake was five hundred miles of rocky shoreline and twenty-five thousand acres of crystal-blue water. It was born of an ancient glacier that had scoured the Canadian Shield.

As they talked, a bull moose about a hundred yards away raised his head and surveyed the scene. They could hear the howls of a hungry wolf.

Bronk could not remember the last time he smiled. But he was smiling now. "George, how many deer have you seen this winter?" he asked.

"More than you'll ever kill. Too bad the damned football season had to last so long."

"Yah, so true. So true, George."

Esslinger had come to the Borderland two years earlier from Canada. He was a dockhand and guide at Rock Point Resort on Gapa's Landing until the place burned. So he bought it, rebuilt it, and was now making a living off the resort during the spring and summer months. During the winter months, when sensible folks stayed home by the fireplace, he drove the huskies around and around the frozen lake, having the time of his life. In the summer he put wheels on the sled and transported tourists to Gapa's Landing from International Falls.

"You must be the craziest man alive," Esslinger said.

"Yah, but not as crazy as you, George," the Bronk said.

"Grab on," Esslinger yelled. "You'll either freeze or fall in a hole and drown."

The Bronk didn't want a ride. He wanted to walk the final dozen miles across the white ice beneath a speckless cerulean sky. So many issues needed to be processed through his brain. He could always think more clearly at this magnificent lake surrounded by the great forests. He was drawn to this place like an eagle to the mountains. He didn't need to explain to anyone why he fled the big city at the end of the football season and caught the fastest train going north. He would always come back to this unspoiled land. It was in his blood. And he would die here.

Nagurski preferred to be alone, like the wolf that howled somewhere in the distance. But he could never turn down a ride from happy-go-lucky George, whose very presence had already helped to lighten his load a bit.

"I'll take a ride," the Bronk said, climbing aboard. "But you think six huskies is enough to carry our wide asses?"

"Yah. Straight to hell and back."

"Okay, let's go for a few miles."

George yelled, "Mush!" and they were gone lickety-split across the giant rink.

•　•　•

Big Boy appeared from the brush like an old ghost from nothingness. The dawn's early light streaked through the aspen, white pine, and spruce, casting long shadows across the floor of the forest. Big Boy was showing off his superiority with his rack held high and glittering in the sunlight. He stood on a tall ridge. The Bronk was forty yards away in a low crouch, sitting in a swale as still as a muscled-up 230-pound man could. One flinch and Big Boy would be halfway to Canada before he could get off a shot.

It was somewhere between thirty and forty below zero at six that morning, and the Bronk fought to control his chattering teeth. He knew the buck with the razor-sharp senses felt the presence of danger. His head flinched. His ears soaked up the slightest sounds; his eyes devoured every inch of the woods. *The sonofabitch has six eyeballs, yah.*

Bronko lifted the .300 Savage without making a sound. This was the tough part. His hands had to remain steady. He was going to get one good shot.

The rifle with five shots in the cylinder and one in the chamber was light and agile. It was the Bronk's favorite. He had purchased it from a friend after his second season with the Bears. The barrel was stainless steel, and the lever action was quick and smooth.

The Bronk locked Big Boy's upper rib cage into his sight, allowed some air to leak from his lungs, and squeezed. At that instant, the big stag leaped over the brush. The bullet, aimed for the heart, sailed inches below his girth and ricocheted off a stump. His life had been saved; standing still for another half second would have meant sudden death. The beautiful beast would now be lying in a large heap. Instead, the Bronk saw the white tail flare widely, a signal to the other deer in the vicinity to run like hell. He wondered if he would ever see Big Boy again.

"You were mine," he said angrily to himself. "I worked for you. And you got away. *Again.*"

• • •

Built in the spring of 1931, the cabin was the realization of a lifelong dream. The Bronk could have lived here year-round and never missed the world passing him by. He would have never read another newspaper, never watched another game, never again fretted over the glory.

It was situated about fifty feet from a rocky cliff and faced southwest across the lake. Behind it for a dozen miles was nothing but dense forests where the biggest deer in Minnesota frolicked.

The cabin sat on a peninsula that separated Kabetogama Lake to the south and Rainy Lake to the north. Both lakes boasted clear, blue water and tremendous fishing in the summer and winter. Ice fishing from December through February attracted hardy souls from across the Midwest in pursuit of the large northern pike. Summer fishing opened in early May with the lure of the five-pound walleye, drawing thousands to the border lakes. Naturally, the best fishermen were the black bears that hunted the redhorse suckers along Sucker Creek and Clyde Creek, just north of the Nagurski cabin. In the fall, the redhorse suckers swam upstream and laid their eggs below a four-foot waterfall. They became easy targets of the bears when they tried to traverse the waterfall. That is why so many of the black bears were approaching six hundred pounds.

The cabin, constructed of logs and regular lumber, was the work of Harold Kerry, Ray Manley, and Bronko. They had been friends for several years. Kerry, a forester for the paper mill, was Nagurski's best friend. The fourth member of the regular hunting trips was a man known only as Quigley, or "Quig." He rarely left the cabin, because he had little interest in hunting or fishing. His passion was cooking, and the biggest eater he'd ever seen was Bronko Nagurski.

Quig would say, "You kill it, you clean it, and I cook it."

Not only was the Nagurski cabin the first on the northern reaches of the lake, it was by far the sturdiest. Unlike the others, it was finished with painted Sheetrock. It was twenty by twenty feet, with three sets of bunk beds along the walls. There was a woodstove for cooking and an oil stove for heat. There was an outhouse in the back.

As he boiled the rabbits on the woodstove at noon that day, the Bronk heard a buzzing in the sky but ignored it. He was convinced that nothing or no one was out there in this kind of weather. The mercury had risen to the daytime high of twenty-five below, and not even a hardy ghost from the *voyageur* past would be knocking about in this weather.

Then he heard the buzzing again and could tell it was moving closer. The big man pulled on the thick coat and stepped onto the front porch. He lifted his meaty right hand to block the glare of the sun and his mouth flew open.

"You are crazier than all shit," he said, his eyes riveted to the sky. "I have never seen anything or anyone like you. You damned fool."

What he saw was a yellow Piper Cub J-3 rocking across the sky piloted by Francis Einarson. The wheels had been replaced with airplane skis. It became apparent that Einarson was trying to find a place to land on the frozen lake. From four hundred feet, the pilot cracked a window and dropped a four-pound piece of cast iron known as the "iron bomb." Einarson would need to find another place to land if the iron ball broke through the ice. But the weight fell rapidly and struck the ice without penetrating it.

Einarson circled the lake and banked just north of the island, heading due west. The plane was a yellow speck on the blue sky. The Bronk forgot about the rabbits on the stove and took off running across the ice, waving his arms, trying to show his friend the smoothest track on the ice. Setting down on the frozen lake would not be that difficult this day, thanks to a clear sky. But on gray days, it was easy for the pilot to misjudge the distance to the ice and to either overfly the lake or slam the skis into the rock-hard surface.

Einarson pulled back on the throttle and began his descent. He worked the rudder stick between his legs that controlled the elevation. He was down to seventy miles per hour. The Bronk waved his arms wildly, pointing to a smooth area that the pilot had already spotted. The plane sailed over the glowing whiteness and the skis set down perfectly on the frozen surface between Sugarbush Island and Nashata Point. Einsarson shut off the engine and cracked the door.

"What in God's name are you doing here?" Bronko shouted. "Do you have any common sense at all?"

"Yah," Einsarson said. "I came to get your ass. Bad storm blowing in from Canada. You could be stuck here for weeks."

"Worse things have happened."

"Bronk," Einarson said in a serious tone, "tomorrow is Christmas Eve."

"Oh, my God," Nagurski said. "I—I . . ."

"I heard about your troubles. I mean your dad's troubles. You got a load on your mind. And I bet you let Big Boy get away. Again."

Bronko suddenly remembered the rabbits. He turned and ran across the white ice toward the cabin, yelling, "Gotta go. Lunch is burning."

Nagurski managed to save the rabbits by pouring more water into the boiling pot. He turned toward Einarson as he walked through the front door.

"You didn't think to bring some water," he said.

"No, but I did bring this," he said, pulling a pint jar of potato whiskey from his coat pocket.

"Good," Bronko said. "I need a bracer."

Rarely did either man drink to the point of intoxication. But circumstances now called for stronger measures. They drank and their gullets burned with the firewater. The Bronk's head began to buzz, and a warm, relaxing feeling washed over his body. No longer did his troubles seem so complex.

"By the way, I picked this up at Western Union for you," Einarson said.

It was a telegram from Halas with a Chicago dateline. MONEY COMING, it read. BE THERE BY NEW YEAR'S.

"Thank you, George," the Bronk said, directing his words at the yellow slip of paper. "And you will be giving me a raise next season."

Nagurski took another draw on the moonshine, and a fire ignited in his stomach lining. He peered across the table at his good friend and saw him twice.

"Francis, it looks like I might need a second job," he said. "Got any ideas?"

"How about professional wrestling?" Einarson said.

Nagurski laughed. "Now that's not a bad idea for a man who's been drinking. Only one thing, friend. I tried that shit last year."

Francis smiled. "You know, Bronk, I think you should take wrestling seriously. Those promoters are after you. They can't all be wrong. They've been chasing you since you got out of college. Maybe there's some money in it after all."

Darkness fell over the peninsula, and they lit the kerosene lanterns and talked well into the night. The moonshine burned all the way down. Francis was making some good points about the prospects of professional wrestling. It drew good crowds in spite of the Depression. The more they talked, the better Nagurski liked the idea of seeking a second paycheck from wrestling. After draining the final drops of the potato whiskey, the men fell into their bunks. The Bronk dreamed about flying off the ropes and body-slamming big, burly wrestlers.

They awoke the next morning to yet another blue sky and light winds. The sun was peeping over the timberline when Francis rose from the bunk bed with a dull ache in his head and a ringing in his ears. Both men greeted the day through a hangover fog.

"That storm will be here by noon," Francis said.

"Let's get out of here," the Bronk said. "Crank her up, heh?"

The Bronk took one last look behind the cabin to see if Big Boy might be lurking in the woods. He wondered if another accomplished hunter might be stalking the mighty beast and if he would ever see his prize quarry again. He knew that Big Boy rarely strayed more than two miles from the cabin. But it was too late in the game, especially when a new blizzard was coming, to pursue him this morning. It frustrated the Bronk that he couldn't get one more crack.

The Bronk would sit in the passenger seat behind the pilot. To make room, Einarson had to remove the second rudder stick. Squeezing a six-foot-two and 230-pound frame into the passenger seat required some work. The plane itself weighed less than a thousand pounds. But they were into the sky less than fifteen minutes later. Far to the north they could see the clouds gathering over Canada. The Bronk made a mental list of a dozen tasks he would need to accomplish that day. First, he would need to drop by the Kane residence to apologize to his fiancée, Eileen, for almost missing Christmas. He would also deliver some gifts.

Then he would have to begin the task of saving the Nagurski family.

# 13

# Sneakers

George Halas stood on the sideline at the Polo Grounds on a miserably cold and wet December day and growled like a bear.

"Stomp their goddamned toes, Nagurski!" he hollered. "Break those sonsabitches' toes!"

Halas could barely stomach this charade. The New York Giants were on the ropes in the 1934 NFL championship game, and now they were cheating. The sight of these rogues trotting back onto the field for the third quarter wearing white gym shoes sent Papa Bear into a rage.

"Basketball!" Halas shouted. "This isn't goddamned basketball!"

He waved referee Bobie Cahn over to the Chicago sideline.

"Make 'em take off those damned shoes, Bobie," Halas said. "They're trying to trick us."

"Now, George," Cahn said. "Why don't you have your boys change into some sneakers and everything'll be fair and square?"

The Bears had not packed gym shoes for the trip to New York. Halas knew that it was a mistake. Rubber-soled shoes would grip the ice-covered Polo Grounds better than the long, pointed cleats. Chicago's special cleats, made of Bakelite, were being ground down by the ice. The

Bears would be skating across the field by the fourth quarter. Sneakers could make all the difference in a close game.

The quick thinking of Giants end Ray Flaherty had inspired the change in footwear. His college team at Gonzaga had once won a game on an ice-covered field in Seattle wearing sneakers. He'd suggested the switch to Giants coach Steve Owen, who pondered the possibilities. An hour before the game, Owen got on the phone, calling every sporting goods store he could find in the phone book. All were closed. Then he called his good friend Abe Cohen, a tailor who made all of the sports uniforms at Manhattan College.

Owen, from the oil patch of Cleo Springs, Oklahoma, had a round belly and a thick drawl. He thrived on snuff and steaks and worked in the coalyards during the off-season.

"Dang it, Abe, we need us some sneakers," he said. "I don't care if you got to steal those suckers. Just go find us some danged sneakers."

Cohen knew where gym shoes could be located. He hailed a taxicab.

"Manhattan College," he told the cabbie.

Cohen just prayed that somebody had left the back door of the gymnasium unlocked. They had. A group of students were playing a half-court game when Cohen sprinted into the locker room. He quickly discovered that the gym shoes were stored in the players' individual lockers. Naturally, those lockers were locked. So he dialed Owen's number at the Giants' coaching office.

"Break the danged locks," Owen demanded. "I don't give a damn. I'll take responsibility for everything."

Cohen arrived at the Polo Ground in the second quarter with a box filled to the brim. Owen decided to wait until halftime to make the switch.

"I don't have time to explain this to you," Owen told the players. "Just put the doggone things on."

Halas went ballistic as he watched the Giants trotting out for the second half. His anger was inspired mostly by jealousy. Early that morning, just past dawn, it had registered with the Bears coach that the playing surface at the Polo Grounds would be like an ice rink. He was walking down Broadway to early Mass when he felt the Arctic blast. Newspapers were flying and hats were spinning along the sidewalks. On returning to the hotel an hour later, Halas called around to the sporting goods stores and, just like Owen, had no luck.

The field in the first half had been a combination of ice and mud and the Bears' cleats managed to supply some traction. They led the Giants 10–3 at halftime, having tripled New York's offensive yards in spite of two Nagurski touchdowns being wiped out by penalties and two missed field goals by Automatic Jack Manders. Halas had felt certain his Bears were on the brink of a third straight championship game. The Bronk had been unstoppable. He scored on a one-yard run that counted in the second quarter following a thirty-five-yard catch and run by halfback Gene Ronzani. Even the flag-happy officials couldn't screw this one up.

A miracle would be in order if the Giants were to come from behind to beat the Bears, a team the national sporting press considered the greatest in the history of the NFL. The Bears had outscored opponents in the regular season 286–86. The offense powered by Nagurski and rookie Beattie Feathers was almost unstoppable. Outside of the Detroit Lions, the Bears were miles ahead of the competition on defense.

New York's only advantage in the championship game was the home field, and it did not seem to matter at the moment. The crowd of thirty-six thousand at the Polo Grounds roundly booed the Giants on their way back onto the field for the third quarter. That is when Halas spotted the sneakers. He cupped his hands and yelled, "Stomp their goddamned toes, Nagurski."

Rain had pounded New York for three days, and the Polo Grounds, the world's largest sponge, sucked it up. Though the sky had cleared, the wind was blasting, and the mercury read nine degrees at kickoff. The winter sun hung just above the bleachers of the south end zone and still shone on the north end of the field. But at the south end of the field, in the deep shadows, the watery soil was freezing faster than a raindrop at the North Pole.

The original Polo Grounds had been constructed in 1883 on the northern edge of Central Park. This newest version, informally known as the Polo Grounds IV, went up in 1911 between Coogan's Bluff and the Harlem River. It boasted a massive double-deck grandstand that seemed to rise to the sky. The Yankees along with the baseball Giants and football Giants had shared it for several years. Babe Ruth used to lace pop flies into the right-field seats. The distance down the right-field line from home

Bronko's last game with the Bears, the 1943 championship game against
the Washington Redskins. *Courtesy of the Bronko Nagurski Museum*

Mike and Michelina Nagurski (left) with friends and a string of
northern pike in International Falls in 1929. *Courtesy of the Janice
Nagurski collection*

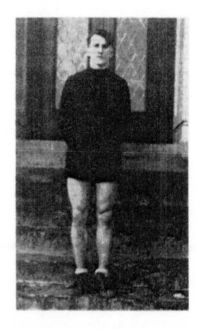

Bronko as a young man. *Courtesy of
the Bronko Nagurski Museum*

Bronko as a junior football player
at International Falls High School
in 1924. *Courtesy of the Janice
Nagurski collection*

Bronko Nagurski as a college senior in 1929
(note the Minnesota good-football drop that
was the equivalent to a letter jacket).
*Courtesy of the Janice Nagurski collection*

East-West Shrine Game, 1929. *Courtesy of the
Bronko Nagurski Museum*

Wrigley Field before a game in the 1940s. *Courtesy of the Chicago Bears*

The Bronk. *Courtesy of the Chicago Bears*

Chicago Bears stars huddle around broadcaster Red Grange (77) in 1934. (L-R) Bronko Nagurski (3), Jack Manders (10), Beattie Feathers (18), and Link Lyman (13). *Courtesy of the Koochiching Museums*

George Trafton. *Courtesy of the Chicago Bears*

Bulldog Turner. *Courtesy of the Chicago Bears*

Red Grange. *Courtesy of the Chicago Bears*

**The champs of 1932.** *Courtesy of the Chicago Bears*

**Bronko with baseball, football, and Olympic great Jim Thorpe.**
*Courtesy of the Bronko Nagurski Museum*

Bronko Nagurski in front of the outfield wall at Wrigley Field before his first game in 1930. *Courtesy of the Chicago Bears*

A poster from 1937 featuring Bronko Nagurski. *Courtesy of the Chicago Bears*

The champs of 1940. *Courtesy of the Chicago Bears*

A game program from 1943. *Courtesy of the Koochiching Museums*

The champs of 1943. *Courtesy of the Chicago Bears*

Bronko at Timber Terminal. *Courtesy of the Bronko Nagurski Museum*

Bronko returns to International Falls. *Courtesy of the Bronko Nagurski Museum*

Bronko and bust at the Pro Football Hall of Fame. *Courtesy of the Bronko Nagurski Museum*

plate was only 283 feet. The Yankees beat the Giants in the 1921 and '22 World Series at the Polo Grounds: Giants manager John McGraw became so angry with the crosstown rivals and their celebrated lineup that he kicked the Yankees out of the stadium, terminating their lease, and forcing Jacob Ruppert to get busy finishing his own venue in the Bronx—Yankee Stadium.

The Giants' Ken Strong, one of the best kickers in football, was wearing a pair of sneakers when he put foot to football for the second-half kickoff. The ball glanced off the side of his shoe and spun like a top all the way to the sideline. Strong laughed. Halas even chuckled. Strong teed it up again and knocked a line drive about twenty yards downfield where the Bears opened the third quarter on offense at their forty-yard line.

The Bears were ankle deep in muck. Thanks to the long cleats, their powerful run offense could handle the mud—but not the iceberg just past the fifty-yard line. Each time they moved into Giants territory and crossed into the shadows, they started slipping and sliding like middle-aged men on snow skis for the first time. The line of demarcation between mud and ice was the fifty-yard line. The Giants, however, enjoyed good traction on both ends of the field.

Now, on the opening drive of the third quarter, the Bears crossed midfield and could move no farther. They punted. The Giants made two first downs and punted. The Bears ran three plays on the ice and punted again. Then New York made two more first downs and was forced to punt once more.

Late in the third quarter, when the Bears crossed the fifty and embarked upon the miniglacier, a frustrated Nagurski pulled off his shoes and slung them one by one to the sideline. His cleats had been worn to a nub. At Halas's urging, he had tried and failed to crack some toes. Now he would attack the slick surface in his stocking feet. The plan worked. The Giants had been rolling into Nagurski's legs and knocking him off balance. Now, with better footing, he was powering forward and was starting to gain three and four yards a pop. He singlehandedly moved the Bears offense inside the Giants' ten-yard line, where, in the final seconds of the third quarter, Automatic Jack kicked a twenty-four-yard field goal.

The Bears led 13–3 as the teams switched ends of the field for the fourth quarter. The Bronk ran to the sideline for a dry pair of socks. That's when his teammates and coaches could see the soles of his feet were bleeding.

Several Bears players started peeling off their shoes. Like the Bronk, they were willing to sacrifice anything to save the championship.

• • •

Six months earlier, during the hot Chicago summer, the season had not seemed so promising as the Bears found themselves baby-sitting a bunch of college boys.

The inaugural NFL-College All-Stars game was the brainchild of *Chicago Tribune* sports editor Arch Ward, who was more promoter than journalist. Ward had also finagled the first baseball All-Star game, played in Chicago the previous July. Arranging a game between the defending NFL champions and the College All-Stars was far less complex than bringing together the National and American Leagues. The baseball All-Star game required that Ward beg the approval of autocratic baseball commissioner Kenesaw Mountain Landis and then campaign for every single vote from the owners. He was successful in both efforts. And what an afternoon they enjoyed at Comiskey Park on July 6, 1933. Forty-seven thousand fans showed up to see Babe Ruth drive a two-run homer into the right-field seats to give the American League a 4–2 victory over the Nationals.

NFL owners initially rejected Ward's proposal to match the defending NFL champions against College All-Stars selected by the press and the fans. They worried about the potential humiliation of losing to the amateur bunch. That was before Halas and Pittsburgh owner Art Rooney stepped forward and exhorted the others to embrace this marketing opportunity. Every newspaper in the country would run an account of the game, and the NFL could count on eighty thousand showing up at Soldier Field.

Supporting this midsummer football fest was not necessarily in Halas's best interest. He had everything to lose and little to gain. If the All-Stars happened to win, the Bears would be the laughingstock of pro sports. Proponents of the college game from Columbia to Stanford would say, "I told you so." Sports editors who had relegated NFL game stories to the bottom of page six would be vindicated. Halas knew that if his Bears lost this game, the newspaper boys would be lighting cigars, shaking hands, and slapping each other on the back, and the NFL would have been dealt a blow from which it might never recover.

The *Tribune* trumpeted the game for several weeks, ensuring a huge crowd. But most of the stories were slanted toward the college angle. Only Nagurski drew any mention from the writers, and most of that copy focused on his years at the University of Minnesota.

Throwing his hat into this ring was solid proof that Halas was placing the league above the team. And that was saying a lot. Halas loved the Bears more than life. Furthermore, Halas was not about to get rich from this game. The Bears were sacrificing a lot for the sake of the game.

Now he had yet another tough chore ahead of him. He had to convince his players that playing the College All-Stars was a once-in-a-lifetime challenge. He knew his grizzled Bears, after winning two straight NFL titles, couldn't care less about an overhyped exhibition game staged on a hot and sticky night when they should be drinking beer and chasing dames.

Bill Hewitt showed his true feelings for the All-Stars: "They got more triple-threat All-Americans than the movies. They're a bunch of sissified frat boys. That's all."

It was true that the College All-Stars had five players from the same frat—Phi Delta Theta. But they were loaded with talented players like Tennessee All-America running back Beattie Feathers, Northwestern end Edgar "Eggs" Manske, and Iowa halfback Joe Laws, winner of the *Chicago Tribune* silver football, the forerunner to the Heisman Trophy.

The All-Stars had gathered in Chicago two weeks before the game and worked as if preparing for the biggest game of their lives. The Bears, in spite of a packed house of 79,432 at Soldier Field, approached the game as if it were one big circus. The team's mascot, a half-grown black bear, walked around the field fifteen minutes before kickoff, eyeing the crowd. Then he headed straight for the Chicago bench, where he stood on his back legs and promptly guzzled three Cokes from the team's ice cooler without burping.

As the game began, the contrasts in style and attitude were evident. The college boys were wild-eyed and demonstrative, the Bears machine-like and low-key. Both teams produced lengthy drives in the first half without scoring. Halas had predicted to the press that Nagurski would be

the only Bears player going full tilt, and he was right. It also became emi-
nently clear that the College All-Stars were scared to death of him. Eggs
Manske tried to block the Bronk and was launched high into the air and
three yards backward. Nagurski seemed unfazed, as if he had swatted a
fly. The same play was called and Manske stammered, "N-now you hold
on. G-get somebody else to block that big bastard."

With the College All-Stars on defense, Chicago tackle Moose Musso
found little resistance from the man he was trying to block.

"What's wrong with you college boys," the Moose yelled. "Don't
none of you want to tangle with my man the Bronk."

Late in the second quarter, Nagurski hammered the ball virtually the
length of the field on twelve straight carries, only to have Keith
Molesworth fumble at the collegiate nine-yard line.

The Bears moved the ball to the All-Star nineteen-yard line in the
fourth quarter, when Carl Brumbaugh spotted an open Hewitt in the end
zone. But the pass was overthrown and Laws intercepted.

The All-Stars tore off large chunks of yardage against the Bears
defense—running away from Nagurski—but lost three fumbles and
missed two field goals. The game ended in a scoreless tie. But given the
magnitude of their celebration, you would have thought the college boys
had won thirty-zip. Players danced and banged each other on the shoulder
pads. Coach Noble Kizer, his chest thrust forward, addressed the press:
"Our bunch was good enough to win, and it was due to bad breaks that
they didn't win!"

The Bears responded to the tie with a collective shrug.

"We play those guys ten times, we win nine and there's one tie,"
Hewitt said. "We'd kill them in a real game."

The Bears were just glad it was over.

•  •  •

The year 1934 was one of pain, upheaval, and conflict. The Great Depression rolled along like a mighty river. President Franklin D. Roosevelt's
New Deal had put little change into the empty pocketbook of America.
But nowhere was the economy slumping harder than in Germany. Chaos
and poverty in Germany led to the single greatest political move of the
century: After the death of President Paul von Hindenberg on August 2,

Adolf Hitler seized control of the country. No sooner had the dictator been anointed than the German forces took a new oath of allegiance: "I swear by God this holy oath that I will render to Adolf Hitler, Führer of the German Reich and People and Supreme Commander of the Armed Forces, unconditional obedience, and that I am ready, as a brave soldier, to risk my life at any time for this oath." The Nazi storm was brewing.

On the North Side of Chicago, John Dillinger lived fast, loose, and free. Dillinger had robbed banks, killed cops, and broken out of jail twice, but he remained the man about Chi Town. He was a regular at Cubs games and dined at the Seminary Restaurant. Dillinger was leaving the Biograph Theatre on Lincoln Avenue after seeing *Manhattan Melodrama*, starring William Powell and Clark Gable, when he walked straight into a trap. Ten cops were waiting around the corner. He took off running. Shots rang out. A bullet tore through his right eye. Public Enemy Number One was dead. An hour later, Dillinger's decomposing body was placed in a window display at the Cook County Morgue, and thousands of curious Chicagoans stood in line to view the body of the daring criminal.

While the rest of the country contended with record unemployment, and the Dust Bowl destroyed Midwest farming, Chicago never stopped buzzing. The Great Depression was unparalleled in magnitude and scope. But Chicago, a town built and rebuilt on speculation, at least acted undeterred. Movie theaters across the city advertised "refrigerated air." The Museum of Science and Industry, constructed in 1893 for the World's Columbian Exhibition, was refurbished at a cost of eight million dollars, an unthinkable amount for the time. Now the Century of Progress Exhibition roared into its second year, with more than a hundred thousand people streaming into the fairgrounds each day. Thirty-eight million people would attend the World's Fair: The biggest draw was the Midway, a name that would inspire a moniker for the Chicago Bears—Monsters of the Midway. George Halas loved it.

"Bronko Nagurski is like a monster," he said. "He has monstrous hands, a monstrous head, and a monstrous neck. Yeah, we are the Monsters of the Midway."

No one was ever certain who coined "Monsters of the Midway." But for decades Halas would stand by his theory of the Nagurski influence.

Chicago at least had warmed to the Bears. Halas's team would likely never replace the Cubs as the city's top sports attraction. But turnstiles were turning, and people were talking. An entire city had developed an infatuation with the broad-shouldered fullback who wore the number three.

The Bears, as it turned out, were much like the gritty and resilient city that had embraced them. Chicagoans had a long history of fighting back. This was never more evident than during the Great Fire of 1871, when the big story was not the fire itself, but how the city rebounded from the fire. The rebuilding began while the ground was still hot.

The Great Fire had begun on the west side in Mrs. O'Leary's barn, and it tore through the city for two days with whirling pockets of gas and air that knocked down buildings and sent survivors running for safety. The fire burned north across the business district, jumping the Chicago River twice. It took down Potter Palmer's grand hotel, Marshall Fields's Marble Palace, many of the city's brothels, and the brand-new *Tribune* building. Three hundred people were killed in the fire, and seventeen thousand buildings destroyed. A lengthy drought and an overabundance of structures constructed from pine and cedar combined to create the conflagration. For two days flames seemed to lick the sky. Almost one-fifth of the city was left in ashes and ruins.

The Great Fire would change Chicago forever, as Chicagoans were infused with the can-do spirit. The day after the fire, the *Tribune* declared, "CHEER UP . . . looking upon the ashes of thirty years' accumulations, the people of this once beautiful city have resolved that CHICAGO SHALL RISE AGAIN."

A city constructed of wood was replaced with one of steel and stone. Halas, in effect, would copy that post-fire blueprint in forging the rock-hardened Bears into a dynasty. Nowhere was the metaphor of steel and stone more evident than in the presence of Bronko Nagurski. In the year 1934 he was everything that Chicago stood for. He was the new Jack Dempsey and Babe Ruth and Red Grange rolled into one. And in the midst of America's turmoil, he was a symbol of hope.

These two-fisted Bears, led by Nagurski, captured the city's imagination. They were a tough, blue-collar bunch that never backed down. It was the other team's players that went to the hospital. The Bears were so tough that even their quarterback refused to wear a helmet. Portsmouth coach Potsy Clark once called Carl Brumbaugh "the smartest quarterback in the league." That was an apt description—considering that Brummy was the best ever to operate the complex T-formation. But Brummy was not a predictable sort. He could be reckless, zany, and strong-willed. No quarterback was more aggressive on defense or hit as hard as Brummy. This is how the *Chicago Sun-Times* once described him: "Here was Carl Brumbaugh, the dark-skinned daring quarterback whose insane recklessness won more than one game with the Bears."

The superstitious Brummy practiced a few odd rituals. He was the holder for Automatic Jack Manders, the best kicker in the league, who once made seventy-two straight extra points. Each time Automatic Jack lined up and Brummy knelt to take the snap from center, he would turn and spit on the toe of the kicker's shoe. So long as Jack was automatic, that little custom was not about to change.

Brummy loved being the center of attention. He once admitted, "I love the football so much that I hug it like a child. I love to run with it. But now I believe that I am getting smarter. I give it to Nagurski."

He could be as vociferous as his own coach. Halas was madly cursing the officials one afternoon in Brooklyn after the Bears had been assessed three straight penalties. The last flag had backed them up all the way to their one-yard line when Brumbaugh hollered to the bench: "Hey, George, keep it up! Go ahead and cuss some more. Get it out of your system. Hell, they can't penalize us but a few more inches anyway."

Halas admired Brumbaugh's grit. It was obvious through the years that Halas chose players for the Bears who reminded him of himself. Halas was determined and plucky and obsessed with winning. He was known to totally block out the real world when the football season rolled around. The night before a Bears game, a friend approached Halas at a cocktail party and said with a wink, "George, we were just talking and somebody said something about your grandfather being a horse thief."

The coach did not blink. "Yeah, sure, sure," he replied. "But if we can score first tomorrow, we're going to win. The thing is, we've got to score first."

He was not above cheating. Once, when a fumble skittered out of bounds during a game against the Giants, the official dropped his hat at the spot on the sideline and hustled to retrieve the ball. Halas trotted over and kicked the hat two yards up the sideline—in the Bears' favor. The official never noticed. But Giants owner Tim Mara, who had witnessed Halas's dropkick, was screaming from the grandstand like a madman.

Like Nagurski, Halas was a drawing card. Fans in the east grandstand were so close to the field that they could hear the coach's foulmouthed banter with the officials. Referee Jim Durfee lived for the chance to verbally spar with Halas and, whenever possible, he jumped at the opportunity to penalize the Bears right in front of their bench. One afternoon, as he began marching off a five-yard penalty against Chicago, Halas hollered, "What is that for?"

"Coaching from the sideline." Calling plays from the sideline was illegal in those days. Halas was in clear violation.

"Check the rule book," Halas shot back. "That's a fifteen-yard penalty, not five."

"Not the way you've been coaching, George," Durfee said with a smirk.

One afternoon Durfee was stepping off a fifteen-yard penalty against the Bears when Halas cupped his hands and yelled, "You stink!"

Durfee kept on walking, marking off another fifteen-yarder. He then turned and shouted to Halas, "How do I smell from here, George?"

The Bears would play their first four games of the 1934 season on the road. The Cubs would occupy Wrigley Field through September and possibly into October if they happened to reach the World Series. Halas once had adored the Cubs so much that he named the Bears in their honor and signed a long-term lease for the use of their ballpark. But things had changed. Now he found himself rooting against the Cubs. He hated being shut out of Wrigley. Playing the first four games of the season on the road was a huge disadvantage. The Bears were not even allowed to practice at Wrigley Field with the baseball season in progress. They worked out on a rough patch of ground next to a factory a few miles from downtown. Two-time defending champions deserved better, Halas thought.

As it turned out, the Cubs' season ended in late September, thanks to a third-place finish behind the Cardinals.

The Bears would catch the Chicago and Northwestern to Green Bay to open the '34 season. Trips to the small town in northeastern Wisconsin made Halas think: *I love Chicago. But wouldn't it be nice if every fan in Chicago, just like every fan in Green Bay, cared about nothing but football, football, football?*

The scene at Green Bay's City Stadium on a cool, crisp September afternoon was next to heaven. The bleachers were so close to the field that the fans could hear the grunts and feel the bone-crushing collisions. They hated the Bears more than any other team, and this pleased Halas no end. Green Bay, after dominating the series in the late twenties, had lost five and tied one of its last seven games with Chicago; and this was a Packer team boasting of All-Pros like Johnny Blood, Mike Michalske, Cal Hubbard, and Clarke Hinkle. Halas knew he was giving Curly Lambeau an ulcer. His only disappointment was that the Bears now played the Packers only twice a season instead of the three times each season since 1926.

Halas had another ace up his sleeve in one Beattie Feathers, the speedster from Tennessee, a rookie who defined the term *triple-threat*. In a 1932 game against Kentucky, he had punted twenty times for a forty-eight-yard average, passed for forty yards, and rushed for a touchdown in a 7–3 victory. The dark-skinned and handsome Feathers was half Cherokee.

Feathers carried ten times for fifty yards in the first three quarters against Green Bay. But with the score reading 10–10, Halas decided to ride the Big Nag to the wire. Nagurski carried the ball six straight times to open the fourth quarter. The crowd yelled for Hinkle to knock him out of the game again as he had done in '33. But Nagurski, who had a score to settle with Hinkle, was now a man possessed. He hammered the line behind a Musso block and flattened Hinkle, who was seeing stars as he stumbled off the field. Nagurski, with a full head of steam, was virtually impossible to stop. From the thirty-four he rumbled straight up the middle, blasting through a wall of defenders and into the open field. Three Packers jumped onto his back at the fifteen-yard line, and he carried all three into the end zone. Then he shook off the trio like a bull ridding his backside of horseflies.

With the Bears leading 17–10, the Green Bay offense was going nowhere without Hinkle; three plays netted two yards. The Pack punted, and Chicago had the ball again at its own forty-yard line. The Packers' defense cringed at the thought of more Nagurski. They were battered and bloodied. They were ready for postgame boilermakers.

Nagurski carried eight straight times until the ball rested at the one. He finished the Packers off with a dive play behind Musso into the end zone. It was the perfect way to start the season—a 24–10 thumping of the hated Packers. The Bronk, in the fourth quarter alone, had gained eighty yards. Dating to the previous season the Bears had won six in a row.

Halas was chuckling again as walked toward the gate at the north end of City Stadium. He stopped to drink in the sight of Lambeau slumped on the Packers' bench, hat in hand, crying again.

• • •

Nagurski was the engine that drove the Bears, but Halas had developed a keen eye for judging talent, and the entire Bears lineup was flexing some serious muscle. The best ends in the league were Bill Hewitt and Bill Karr. It could be argued George Musso and Link Lyman were the best tackles. Charles "Ookie" Miller was an All-Pro center. Guard Joe Kopcha, who would soon graduate from Rush Medical School, was working on his third straight All-Pro season. No team had a better half-back rotation than Red Grange, Keith Molesworth, and Gene Ronzani. Brummy stood above all the rest at quarterback. Automatic Jack was, at least, semiautomatic.

The latest Halas prize was Feathers. Papa Bear knew this kid possessed a dangerous brand of speed. No one in the NFL could match it. But what initially caught Halas's eye was that Feathers faithfully followed the blocks of Nagurski as if his life depended on it. He looked like a rabbit in lockstep with a bear. In tandem, the Bronk and Feathers rolled down the field, Nagurski scattering defenders like bowling pins with Feathers running where the pins once stood. In the open field Feathers took off like a rocket. You could almost see the vapor trail, a reminder of the great days of Red Grange in the twenties.

Back in August, during the All-Star game, Feathers could not believe his eyes as he watched Nagurski operate. He noted that defenders folded their tents when the Bronk set his hard eyes on them. They could care less about making the tackle. They just wanted to brace themselves and survive the blow. Now, come hell or high water, Feathers was going to follow the big man into the open field, where he would then gallop like the Ghost of yesteryear.

Kopcha, the master of the pun, was joking around with the Chicago sportswriters one day when he said, "I bet you've never seen Feathers on a Bear."

After opening the season with an impressive win over the Packers, the Bears defeated the Cincinnati Reds, the Brooklyn Dodgers, the Pittsburgh Pirates, the Chicago Cardinals, and the Reds for a second time by the combined score of 131–17. One play in the Cincinnati game that resulted in no yards and no points was one the Reds would never forget. The Bears' Bull Doehring, the lefthander with the strongest arm in football, was sweeping left end when he fired a twenty-yard bullet into the end zone for end Luke Johnsos. It was unforgettable because of the way Doehring threw it. As two Reds reached for Doehring, he did a reverse corkscrew and fired a behind-the-back rocket. But Johnsos, who was both nearsighted and unready for this circus throw, dropped the ball.

It was not the first time Doehring had been so daring. During a West Coast exhibition tour the previous winter, he had fired a fifty-yard touchdown pass behind his back straight into the hands of Bill Karr in the end zone. No one could believe their eyes.

The Bears were like a high-wire act that required no safety net. They could do no wrong. Feathers and Nagurski were now a magnet that was stealing headlines from the other pro sports. Bowling, a major sport at the time, attracted barrels of ink in the Chicago dailies, but the Bears were knocking the pin-busters off page one.

Feathers and the Bronk were like a horse and carriage, wieners and sauerkraut, Astaire and Rogers. This togetherness had been carried to a new level. Each day before practice at Wrigley Field, they waited until the other Bears had dressed and were on the field before they walked side by side down the tunnel. On game days they were the last two on the field and ran shoulder to shoulder to the Bears sideline as the crowd roared its approval.

The Bears had a 6–0 record and an eleven-game winning streak when Green Bay came back to the Windy City. Wrigley Field was a sold-out madhouse. Chicago felt like a town on the brink of a championship fight. It was late October, and the snows had yet to arrive. But a storm was in the air.

Behind the thunderous blocks of Nagurski, along with the great Chicago line, Feathers tore through the Packers for 155 yards on fifteen carries. He rushed seven yards for one touchdown and caught a fifteen-yard pass from Brumbaugh for another. The Bears defeated Green Bay 27–14, and Feathers's rushing total for seven games was now more than seven hundred yards. All the talk was about a thousand-yard season, something that had never happened in football.

Game eight was a rematch of the NFL title game of the preceding

December. That went straight to the wire and was saved by the heady tackle of one Red Grange. But even the Giants could not handle the one-two punch of Nagurski and Feathers, who broke yet another NFL record by exceeding a hundred yards on the ground a fourth time. Feathers finished with 116 yards on sixteen carries, and the Bronk contributed another 76. The Bears won easily, 27–7.

Earlier in the season, Nagurski had extracted revenge from Green Bay's Clarke Hinkle. Now it was Ernie Pinckert's turn to suffer.

The Bears railed to Boston to play the Redskins at Fenway Park in the season's ninth game. The Redskins had stunned the defending NFL champions the previous year at the old baseball park, and Halas had not forgotten the humiliation of watching owner George Preston Marshall dancing on the sideline, nor could he forgive Ernie Pinckert for his cheap shot that knocked Nagurski out of the game.

Pinckert was the brother of fabled psychic Jeane Dixon, who would one day claim to have predicted the assassinations of Mahatma Gandhi, Martin Luther King Jr., and John F. Kennedy. Pinckert, however, possessed no crystal ball. On this day in 1934 he never saw it coming. Nagurski eighteen-wheeled the big Boston fullback, who landed on his head and lay on the ground like a limp rag. Pinckert was carried unconscious from the field on a stretcher.

The Bears throttled Boston 21–0, and Halas decided to keep the team in Beantown a few days before hopping the train down to New York for the second meeting of the season with the Giants.

Nagurski had been laying the lumber to opposing players. But now his body was starting to feel the wear and tear of a long, hard-fought season. The meanest S.O.B. in the valley had an aching back. He was also suffering from a nagging soreness in his right hip, which had been slightly dislocated during the collision with Hinkle back in '33. He also had two knots on his upper back that doctors could not explain. The Bronk was having trouble getting in and out of bed. Halas was worried.

On the train trip to New York, Halas arranged for the trainer of ex-heavyweight champion Jack Dempsey to work on both Nagurski and Ookie Miller, who suffered from various ailments. Massage tables were set up in one of the cars, where the trainer would rub down both men. Halas supplied a bottle of Absorbine Jr. to rejuvenate their aching muscles.

Miller was a cutup in much the same mold as George Trafton, who was now two years retired from football but still busting up bars. Nagurski would have nothing to do with Miller, the man he accused of stealing Trafton's job. The Bronk and Ookie had not exchanged a pleasant word in three years.

"I wonder if Nagurski will ever talk to me?" Ookie had asked Brummy one day.

"Not in this life," Brummy said flatly.

Ookie and the Bronk were lying on adjacent tables. The room was quiet, and it quickly became evident that Nagurski was not in the mood for conversation. But the outgoing center was ready to try anyway.

"Bronk, you know we haven't talked much," Miller said.

"I don't talk much to anybody," Nagurski said.

"Well, I see you talkin' to the Ghost and Brummy and Moose, and I know you and Trafton talked a lot."

"They are my friends."

"The Ghost is my friend. Hell, he's my roommate."

Grange had once told Nagurski, "You know, Ookie's not a bad guy. You're just pissed he knocked the Brute off the roster."

It was true. Nagurski hadn't given Ookie much of a chance. But Bronk knew in his heart that Miller was a good ballplayer who blocked his ass off. The Bears running game was second to none, and Bronko could hardly complain about the effort of the Chicago line. It was said in pro football that a lineman was just a back without brains. But the Bears had guys who could talk with the best of them. Moose and Hewitt were two of the funniest and most opinionated people outside of Trafton he had ever met.

The Bronk gave some thought to what the Ghost had said about Ookie. It wouldn't hurt to have a few words with the guy. But as the trainer with the strong hands dug his fingers deeper into his aching back, he felt himself fading into darkness. When he woke up an hour later, Ookie was sound asleep on the other table.

Ookie got his nickname as a kid because because he couldn't say "cookie." To Halas, he was slightly kooky. This became evident when the Bears traveled to New York in 1932 for a game against the Giants, and Miller missed the Saturday night curfew—by five hours.

At four o'clock that morning, when he finally returned to the team hotel, Ookie found a note from Halas taped to his door. It read, "Ookie, when you get in, come see me.—George."

Ookie picked up the phone and dialed the room of guard Tiny Engebretsen, his partner in crime that night. When Tiny answered the phone, Ookie said, "We're in trouble," and then told him about the note on his door.

"I'm not in trouble," Tiny said. "I didn't get any note."

"Oh my God!" Ookie said.

Ookie and Engebretsen had been out sampling some of New York's nightlife. They picked up two flappers in short skirts along the way, and that wiped out any chance of making curfew. They stumbled into the hotel lobby two hours before dawn with big smiles. Then Halas's note brought Ookie crashing back to earth. He thought about knocking on the coach's door, but opted to postpone his punishment until breakfast.

The sight of a nervous Miller picking over his food that morning pleased Halas. The coach was beaming as he approached the table.

"Hey, Ookie, did you have a good time last night?" Halas boomed.

"Well, coach, you see, I've never been to New York City—"

"Don't worry about it, kid. It'll only cost you a hundred dollars."

Ookie crumbled inside. He barely had enough money to pay rent and the bills, and now he was losing an entire game check.

"I don't think I'm going to play today," he told Brumbaugh.

"Ah, go ahead, kid," the quarterback said. "George fined me once for the same thing. I played a good game. He gave the money back."

That day Miller had the best game of his rookie season as the Bears routed the Giants. Halas came by his locker after the game and patted him on the shoulder.

"Ookie, I think I'll fine you every game," he said. "You play better."

Perhaps. But Ookie never got his money back.

Now, two years later, the Bears were back in New York, having arrived at Grand Central Station the morning before playing the Giants in the biggest game of the '34 season. Ookie was still missing curfews and gambling on the train, but no one could question his performance on the field. He had been selected All-Pro in '33. But the Big Nag still wasn't talking to him.

It was typical New York weather for mid-November—blustery with snow in the forecast. Typical of the times, the coaches had mapped out conservative strategies. When the game kicked off at one o'clock that Sunday afternoon, neither Halas nor Owen had a single passing play in mind. The massages from Dempsey's former trainer had made Nagurski feel young again.

The Giants, in spite of losing five of the last six to Chicago, were not intimidated in the least by the Bears. They featured a lineup that was as big and rugged as the Monsters. They scored on the first play of the second quarter to culminate a rough-and-tumble fifty-nine-yard drive that included not a single pass. With passing whiz Harry Newman out with an injury, the Giants had turned on the power. Ken Strong, who had gained twenty pounds, was now one of the most powerful runners in football. He scored the opening touchdown on a three-yard run.

A freakish play to open the second half made Bears halfback George Corbett want to dig a hole and crawl into it. Strong's kickoff landed in the end zone, but thanks to some reverse English, the ball bounced back onto the field and settled at the two-yard line. Corbett, thinking it was an automatic touchback, picked up the ball, strolled back across the goal line and touched the ball down. The officials saw it differently. They ruled it a safety. New York now led 9–0.

Later in the third quarter Feathers returned a weak punt thirteen yards to the Giants forty-six. Ronzani carried for twelve yards, and the Bronk plowed over the Giants all the way to the twelve-yard line. Chicago was on the move but still could not block Flaherty, the big, roughhewn left end. Brummy was ticked off in the huddle. "We've got three hundred plays and nothing to take care of Flaherty," he said harshly. Brummy turned to Ookie and said, "You snap the ball directly to Feathers. Bronk, you knock the shit out of Flaherty. And you, Feathers—you big Indian— if you've ever run in your life, run now."

He did, too. For a touchdown. Manders kicked the extra point and the Giants' lead stood at 9–7.

A Chicago prayer was answered late in the game when Giants running back Max Krause hit a wall of Bears and fumbled into the arms of Link Lyman at the New York thirty-three. A minute was left on the clock. After short bursts by Nagurski and Manders, the Bears faced a fourth-and-two at the twenty-five. Brumbaugh decided to forgo the long field goal and Nagurski gained ten yards straight ahead, keeping the ball squarely in the middle of the field. As the Bronk returned to the huddle, he patted Ookie on the hip and said, "Nice block, kid."

The clock was still ticking. Ten seconds . . . nine . . . eight . . . seven . . . when Manders lined up for the twenty-three-yard field goal attempt. Brummy turned and spat on his kicker's toe. Manders's kick split the uprights for the 10–9 victory as time expired.

In the jubilant Chicago locker room, a wide-eyed Ookie walked up to Brumbaugh and said, "I can't believe he finally talked to me!"

Brummy chuckled. "I told you he would."

No one was more excited than Halas, who danced about the locker room and yelled at the top of his lungs. Somebody brought in a case of beer—legal stuff now—and the Bears poured it over each other's heads. They were celebrating their fifteenth straight victory.

Halas stood on a chair in the middle of the room and yelled, "Rules are off tonight! By God, this is something to celebrate. There'll be a party tonight at the Hollywood—on me!"

The Hollywood restaurant, one of the most popular nightspots on Broadway, was filled with dancing Bears that night. They drank and hollered, and Link Lyman jumped on the stage with the band, grabbed the microphone, and stole the show with his rich baritone voice. Even the bandleader was impressed and encouraged him to keep going. When he grew tired, and his voice became gravelly, Lyman playfully tackled the microphone stand and then jumped off the stage.

Halas dropped into the restaurant late in the evening to make sure his back-to-back NFL champions were behaving. He arrived about the time things were getting out of control. This worried Papa Bear so he asked for the tab.

"About eight hundred," the manager said.

"Cut 'em off," Halas said. "These boys have got to play some more football this season."

The next morning, the Bears packed for the long train ride back to Chicago and the final three games of the regular season. If they could shake off second-place Detroit, they would play for the championship again—most likely against the Giants.

Halas's custom was to pay the players on the train in cash. He had collected gate receipts before the game from Giants owner Tim Mara, who kept a thousand that Halas still owed him.

As the train rumbled and clacked, Halas walked from car to car, taking care of payroll. He made a point of saying to each player, "If I catch you gambling on this trip, I will fine *your* ass." The Bears owner had seen how the card games could devour a man's entire earnings.

He found Ookie Miller in the club car sitting with Brumbaugh and Moose Musso. He counted out the money to his star center and stuffed the rest back in his pocket.

"Wait a minute, George," Ookie said. "I'm a dollar short."

Halas glared at the center as if he were insane. "That's for the Absorbine Jr.," he snapped.

When Papa Bear walked away, Miller turned to Brummy and said, "Bet he didn't charge Nagurski."

"Damn right," Brumbaugh said. "You're learning the game, kid."

Fifteen minutes later, Halas burst through the door of the club car, where a game of five-card stud was in full swing. One by one, he pointed to each player around the table and shouted, "I'm fining you ten dollars! I'm fining you ten dollars! I'm fining you ten dollars!" Then he got to Nagurski. "Oh, I see you're winning, Bronk," he said.

Halas let the boys gamble for the rest of the trip as long as the Big Nag was winning.

The Chicago Cardinals were now owned by Charlie Bidwill, the man who came to Halas's rescue when he needed cash to buy out co-owner Dutch Sternaman two years earlier. Bidwill also appeared in the Bears' team pictures in 1931 and '32 before he bought the Cardinals, now the laughingstock of the NFL.

The Bears' sixteenth straight victory was indeed a 17–6 walk through Wrigley Field. But they also suffered the biggest loss of the season when Feathers was bounced out of bounds by three Cardinals early in the game. He suffered a badly dislocated right shoulder, and the Bears held their breath, wondering if his magical season was over. Up in the press box, the writers and statisticians put pencils to paper. They checked and rechecked his rushing totals. On that final carry Feathers had surpassed the thousand-yard mark. His totals were 101 carries for 1,004 yards, for an average of 9.9 yards per carry. The milestone had been reached.

Now, though, the Bears faced the rugged task of back-to-back games with the Detroit Lions, with the Western Division title on the line. The Lions were the old Portsmouth Spartans, who had shut down operations after the 1933 season. They were purchased by radio magnate George A. Richards and moved to Detroit. Life could only get better for the old Spartans, who had ridden a roller coaster to hell and back the last few years. They were winners on the field but losers in the wallet. For years, players had been racing each other to the bank, hoping to cash their weekly paychecks before the account ran dry.

If not for a 3–0 loss to Green Bay the previous week, the Lions, like the Bears, would be undefeated. But a win on Thanksgiving Day against Chicago would produce a tie for first place in the Western Division with one game remaining.

This was the same team that had taken the Bears to the wire in the 1932 title game at Chicago Stadium. Now, two years later, the old Spartans were gunning for revenge. This was a familiar roster that still boasted stars like Ace Gutowsky, Glenn Presnell, Dutch Clark, Father Lumpkin, Frank Christensen, and Ox Emerson. It was a power-laden unit that started the season by shutting out its first seven opponents—a streak that would never be matched. In that seven-game span, they did not allow an opponent to cross their twenty-yard line.

The Lions had slammed the door on their first seven opponents with a basic, no-gimmick 6–2–2–1 defensive alignment. This defense remained so dominant because the stud players had stuck around through the lean years when they could have been making more money pumping gas. Now the mighty Chicago Bears were coming to town to pose the greatest challenge of their football lives. All twenty-six thousand tickets to the game at Detroit University Stadium had been sold for weeks.

A Thanksgiving game was nothing new for the NFL. But it was the first of its kind in Detroit, and therefore a landmark event. The Lions on Turkey Day would become one of the longest-running traditions in the history of the NFL. Perhaps the most memorable Thanksgiving game had been the Red Grange debut at Wrigley Field back in 1925, when a record crowd of thirty-six thousand came to see the crosstown Chicago rivals play to a scoreless tie.

This would be a historic day for yet another reason. Radio mogul George Richards had strung together a ninety-four-station radio network to carry the Lions-Bears game. The announcers, Graham McNamee and Don Wilson, were the most prominent names in the industry. For the first time, millions of Americans would add football to their feast of turkey, gravy, stuffing, and pumpkin pie. This marriage of football, Thanksgiving, and a strong media voice would help to change the way Americans looked at pro football.

The demand for tickets, and the desire to pad his bank account, had prompted Richards to open the gates for standing room only that Sunday morning. On this sunny, cool afternoon, fans ringed the field five deep. Lions players knocked out of bounds were given a boost back onto the field. Bears players were kicked and scratched. Moose Musso was cracked over the head with a beer bottle as a wild fight broke out in the south end zone. Nagurski waded into the melee and had it under control before the cops could arrive with nightsticks.

"One of those sonsabitches bit me," the Moose told Nagurski.

"Next time, bite him back," the Bronk said.

The Lions were full of piss and vinegar at kickoff. Feathers's absence allowed the Detroit defense to focus on Nagurski. Brumbaugh was under strict orders not to pass. Four and five defenders ganged up on Nagurski at the line of scrimmage on every play, and his longest gain in the first half was four yards. It appeared the Lions-Spartans would finally break the Chicago hex.

The Detroit backfield that included Presnell, Gutowsky, and Dutch Clark could match the Bears straight up. Dutch Clark, the All-Pro tailback, had missed the '32 title game because of a college coaching commitment. Now he was running and passing the ball better than ever. The tailback in the single wing was the triggerman, and normally the biggest producer on offense.

In the first half Gutowsky scored on touchdown runs of three and five yards. Presnell, who missed one extra point, booted a twenty-one-yard field goal. The Bears managed a late touchdown before halftime with Nagurski slamming the line behind Miller and driving five Lions backward into the end zone. Detroit led at the half 16–7.

Detroit became too predictable in the third quarter. Nagurski snuffed running plays at the line of scrimmage. The Lions hoped to eat the clock by running the ball, but the Bronk and the helmetless Hewitt were ransacking this offense. The Lions were forced to punt time and again.

On offense Nagurski was a wrecking ball, taking the Lions' defense apart brick by brick. Bronko's surges moved the ball into field goal range late in the third quarter, and once more in the fourth. Automatic Jack made both kicks, trimming the lead to 16–13. Now the Lions were forced to take the ball out of the deep freeze. Clark completed three straight passes, and the offense was on the move again. But Hewitt, the Offsides Kid, was getting a bead on the Lions passer. He was offsides by at least a yard on a third-down play. No flags flew as he tipped Clark's pass high into the air. The ball tumbled into the arms of Chicago guard Joe Zeller, who ran for the end zone like a man with his pants on fire. He almost made it. Presnell caught him at the four-yard line.

The Bronk slammed into the line for no gain. Ditto on the next effort as practically every silver helmet rattled his rib cage. The ball was still at the four. A blind man would have known what was coming next. Somehow, though, it didn't register with the Lions. The Bronk took the handoff from Brummy and aimed his shoulder into the line. Then he stopped, jumped, and floated a pass to the back of the end zone where a wide-open Hewitt was waiting. Touchdown, Chicago!

It was precisely the play that had beaten this team back in the 1932 championship game—only Hewitt had replaced Grange at receiver. The stadium was so quiet that you could hear Halas's laughter all the way to the top row of seats.

The Bears led 19–16 with two minutes to play. Detroit University Stadium was silent. Halas alertly inserted Grange into the game as a defensive back. Nagurski, who rarely spoke during the game, gathered the defensive unit around him.

"Look," he said, "these boys are capable of moving the damn ball. Don't let any of those fellas get behind you. Let's kick some butt, heh."

Clark completed two quick strikes, moving the Lions to the forty, turning the crowd's ignition key on once more. Down on the field, the players could barely hear themselves. Presnell ran a double reverse for twenty more yards. The clock was ticking, with under a minute to play. Gutowsky gained ten yards on a quick trap, and the Lions called their final time-out.

The Bears lined up safety Keith Molesworth at the goal line, hoping to prevent the deep completion. Grange rotated closer to the middle of the field. Hewitt was going to beat the snap, even if it meant a five-yard offsides penalty. Halas was yelling at the top of his lungs, but no one on the field could make out what he was saying.

Clark hit Presnell over the middle for a gain of six. A pass to Gutowsky moved the ball to the sixteen. The next attempt bounced off Gutowsky's chest, stopping the clock with five seconds left. Clark took the deep snap knowing this would be the final play of the game. Presnell broke toward the corner, and Clark released the pass that now spiraled nose down, straight toward Presnell's hands. Grange moved slowly, desperately, toward the Lions halfback, limping like an aged man. Twenty-six thousand throats were at full throttle. Grange leaped as Presnell's fingers extended for the ball. The Ghost managed to get two fingers on the ball, slightly altering its course, and it wobbled through Presnell's hands. The football hit the turf as the clock struck triple-zero.

Madness reigned. Presnell and Grange tumbled into the sea of fans standing on the sideline and disappeared. A riot was about to break out. Nagurski and Hewitt alertly sprinted to the spot where the Ghost had vanished into the disorderly crowd. They plowed through this wall of humanity until they found Grange at the bottom of a pile, missing his helmet and with blood streaming from his nose. The Bronk threw forearms in every direction until the crowd backed off. Then Nagurski and Hewitt lifted Grange by his arms and carried him to safety.

"Get me out of here," Grange yelled. "I'm too old for this."

The Bears ran for the bus amid a hail of beer bottles. The Ghost was lucky to still be walking this earth.

• • •

Thanks to the strange scheduling of the time, the Bears and Lions would play a second straight game—three days later in Chicago.

The teams caught back-to-back rides on the train out of Detroit the day after Thanksgiving, and the conductors on each one prayed the trains did not somehow meet somewhere along the tracks. A brawl would surely erupt.

This was not the best way to end the regular season. The Western Division had already been settled, and Chicago had won the right to meet New York in one week for the NFL title. They had to survive the Detroit buzz saw once more. The Lions really had revenge on ther minds now.

The playing surface at Wrigley Field in early December was the color of a corn tortilla. As he warmed up for the game, Nagurski noticed an unfamiliar face on the sideline. The eyes belonging to that face were staring a hole through him. Then the man was walking toward the Bronk with a wide smile. He stuck out his hand and said, "George Richards, Bronk. I own these Lions. Just wanted to tell you, by God, that you played the best damned ball game in the history of this league on Thursday."

"Well, thanks," the Bronk said.

"Listen," Richards said. "I got a proposition for you."

Bronk had heard it all before. He looked into the eyes of this stranger and felt a con coming on.

"What kind of proposition, mister?" Nagurski said.

"Well, my son, I will write you a check for ten thousand dollars right now. But you've got to do one thing for me."

"What's that?"

"You've got to take off that uniform, walk out of this stadium, and never come back to professional football again."

Bronko laughed. Then he checked the expression of the Lions' owner. He was not smiling.

"Come on," Nagurski said. For a moment, Nagurski's mind drifted north toward home. *Oh, if he only knew how badly I need that money. I know this is a joke. But, God, if I could only get my hands on ten grand.*

Richards said nothing.

"Come on," the Bronk repeated.

Then Richards laughed—cackled, actually. "Shit, son, they'd throw me out of football," he said. "George Halas'd eat me for lunch. But, honestly, your retirement is the only way I'll ever win a championship."

It was true. Nagurski was the only obstacle standing between the Lions and a future Western Division title—possibly an NFL crown. They were stacked with enough talent to handle the Giants or the Packers on any Sunday.

America was paying attention once more to the Lions and Bears on this frosty afternoon at Wrigley Field. The wind was slicing off Lake Michigan, every seat in the house was filled, and once again Richards had arranged for a network broadcast. A sleety drizzle commenced as Automatic Jack kicked off to the Lions.

The crowd at Wrigley Field couldn't have cared less about the sleet or the wind or that the temperature had dived into the teens. It would be their last chance to see the Monsters of the Midway this year. League rules stated that the home field would be rotated for title games. Because last year's Giants-Bears title game had been staged at Wrigley Field, this one would be shifted to New York, even though the Bears had a far better record.

This day, Halas planned to live and die by the Bronk. A low-scoring game would suit him fine.

The first half ended in a scoreless tie. With Nagurski pounding the Detroit line, the Bears moved into Manders's range in the third quarter and a thirty-three yarder split the uprights. It appeared the score of three-zip would hold as the game moved deeper and deeper into the fourth quarter. Players from both teams were slipping and sliding on the icy surface. The punt was the favored play.

With two minutes to play, the Lions faced fourth-and-seven at their own forty-yard line. They chose to punt. The Bronk's eyes scanned the field for somebody to block, and he spotted Harry Ebding, one of the best ends in the league, roaring down the right sideline. Nagurski slammed into Ebding, who lost his footing on the slick track and fell. As the Bronk turned, he spotted an official who was calling a penalty on him.

"Holding, on the Bears," the referee said, pointing at Nagurski. "Ball goes back to Detroit. Automatic first down."

The Bronk felt sick to his stomach. Detroit had the ball back at midfield.

Dutch Clark took the deep snap from center and pitched to Glenn Presnell, who swept right end. Presnell stopped just inches behind the scrimmage line and cocked his arm. The Bears defensive backs had been sold on the running play. They never expected a pass on this ice rink. Detroit wingback Ernie Caddel, crossing from the other side, was twenty yards down the field and ten yards behind the closest Bear when he hauled in Presnell's pass and trotted toward the end zone. A game once dominated by the Bears was now the property of the Lions by the score of 7–3.

Brummy could tell the Bronk, standing next to him, was filled with rage when they huddled following the kickoff. He could feel heat rising off of the man's body. The steam rising from Nagurski's nostrils was like smoke off a hot rivet. The ball was at the Chicago thirty.

The reticent Nagurski rarely spoke in the offensive huddle. But he said, "Brummy, that was my fault. If you've got one play that'll work for me, call it now."

Brummy had a dozen in mind, but he knew a shovel pass around right end would do the trick.

Two Lions dived for the Bronk's knees. Then two heads recoiled as if walloped by the iron fists of Jack Dempsey. Five yards up the field, two other Lions flung themselves at him and were plowed under. Now the Bronk held the ball in front of his chest in two massive hands and he pumped it up and down like a piston. The ice crunched beneath his pointed cleats. The last Lion standing between him and the goal was Presnell, who muttered, "Oh my God," an instant before Nagurski tore through him like a tornado through southern Illinois.

Nagurski was trucking down the sideline thirty yards from the goal. Fans in the east stands swore they could feel his locomotion as he rumbled past. He didn't slow down when he reached the end zone. He blew past the end line and piled into the baseball dugout. A collision at full tilt with a brick wall might have killed another man. But Nagurski was merely wringing out that final bead of frustration. Then he was up the dugout steps and back on the field, trotting across the field to the thunderous roar of the Wrigley crowd.

The winning streak stood at eighteen games.

• • •

A week later, as the NFL championship game moved into the fourth quarter, the Bears stood on the mini-iceberg in the deep shadows at the Polo Grounds as the fourth quarter began. The stinging wind was straight out of the Arctic. This would be the biggest fifteen minutes of their lives. The Bronk along with Brummy, Moose, Stinky, the Ghost, and Automatic Jack were playing in their socks, praying for better traction, hoping to stem the momentum of the New York Giants. Leading 13–3, the Bears were one quarter from a third straight NFL championship. But the Giants were on the move.

Ken Strong was not a man anyone wanted to tangle with in this situation. He had come from the school of hard knocks. In 1929 he signed with the Staten Island Stapletons, also known as the Stapes. For a clubhouse they had an old shed with a cold-water shower and a few hooks that served as lockers. The playing field was hard enough to double as a parking lot. Nothing was tougher than a Stapes fan. In a game against the rival Giants, Strong was carrying around right end when Ray Flaherty put him in a headlock and started dragging him toward a chain-link fence that ringed the field. Strong yelled, "Let go, Ray!" but Flaherty kept pulling. He seemed angry about something. Strong finally wriggled free. He looked up to see a little old lady leaning over the fence and banging an astonished Flaherty over the head with an umbrella. Flaherty had thought Strong was the one doing the punching.

The Bears were now forced to deal with both Strong and Flaherty, along with the hot hand of quarterback Ed Danowski, who had replaced an injured Harry Newman weeks earlier.

Mixing the run and pass, the Giants moved from their thirty to the Bears' four-yard line in the opening minutes of the fourth quarter. That is where Eddie Kawal, backup center and linebacker replacing Miller, intercepted a Danowski pass. But the Bears' offense was going nowhere on the icy end of the field. Keith Molesworth punted from the Chicago end zone, and Strong returned the short, fluttering kick to the twenty-three.

Danowski wasted no time sending end Ike Frankian on a post route. He was camped near the goal line when Danowski's pass, buffeted by the wind, wobbled straight into the arms of Brummy. Frankian wrenched the ball away from Brummy, turned, and lumbered into the end zone.

The officials had no clue to what to call. No one had had a clear view of Frankian's theft. The back judge did not signal touchdown until Big Ike started running along the back line, holding his prize aloft for the crowd to see. It was Frankian's second reception of the entire season and the biggest of his career. The Bears' lead was down to 13–10. Brummy lay on the ground and pounded the ice until his hands bled.

The Giants had the ball back minutes later at the Chicago forty-six following another short Molesworth punt into the gusting wind. Strong looked like Nagurski as he powered around left end, broke three tackles, slid through the arms of the Bronk himself, and took off. Every Bear defender was sprawled on the ground when Strong crossed the goal. Most had bloody socks. Most were approaching exhaustion. Strong's point-after kick made it 17–13.

The Bears still had a small supply of energy left. The Bronk was boiling mad, and Brummy could see it in his eyes. Once more, Chicago's salvation would be the greatest football player to ever suit up.

It was Nagurski, Nagurski, and more Nagurski—straight up the middle. Seven straight carries for thirty-seven yards, all the way to the Giants thirty-five-yard line. The Bears were on the muddy half of the field. It was fourth-and-one. The Giants knew it would be Nagurski again.

The Chicago line paved a wide lane for the big fullback. It was a clean handoff. The Bronk was moving powerfully when he reached the line of scrimmage. Then he slipped and fell for no gain. Giants tackle Bill Morgan jumped onto Nagurski's back. Credit for that tackle alone would be Morgan's ticket to the All-Pro team that year.

Hundreds of hats flew from the stands. Thousands of fans started running down the aisles of the grandstand toward the playing field. They ringed the sidelines. They pushed and shoved their way into the Giants' bench area, and Owen became separated from his team. The sideline was so thick with bodies that Owen found himself trapped and moving along with the mob. It almost seemed safer to be on the field with Nagurski than in the midst of these rowdies.

In the final five minutes the Giants dominated the Bears. They could not be stopped. It had been a brilliant idea to shoe the Giants in sneakers. Strong sprinted twenty-one yards on a reverse for a late touchdown, and Danowski added the exclamation point with a two-yard quarterback sneak. He was yanked to his feet by a horde of rowdies who had crashed the field. With the cops no longer controling the crowd, the game was called with fifty seconds to go. The bloodied Bears limped to the locker room as New York went wild. The final score was 30–13.

After the game, Strong said, "If they'd had new cleats in the second half, they would have walloped us."

Or maybe a box of sneakers.

Some of the Bears players openly wept in the locker room. The dream season had ended in a frozen hell.

"I'm old and worn out," Link Lyman said wearily. "This was probably my last game. God, I would have loved to swagger about and tell my grandchildren and all of the folks out in Nebraska, 'Boys, I played on an undefeated team—the greatest team that ever played football.'"

Meanwhile, the Giants and all of New York City partied as if New

Year's Eve had arrived early. A five-foot-two tailor would receive his share of the credit. Lewis Burton wrote in the *New York American,* "To the heroes of antiquity, to the Greek who raced across the Marathon plain, and to Paul Revere, add now the name of Abe Cohen."

• • •

The 1934 NFL season would never be forgotten. Pro football officially dropped out of the soup line that year. Nearly one million fans had witnessed the fifty-eight NFL games, and the Associated Press reported that in its annual poll sports editors had voted pro football the fastest-growing sport in America. Radio had become a powerful marketing tool. The Bears contributed greatly to the historical year with the first-ever unbeaten regular season. Beattie Feathers became the first man ever to reach a thousand yards rushing, and the Bronk had contributed 586 yards and seven touchdowns.

A week after the heartbreaker in New York, Nagurski tried valiantly for two days in sub-forty-degree temperatures to bag Big Boy. This time, his shot was wide right. After Christmas, the Bears headed west in what would be the farewell tour for Red Grange. The *New York Times* reported that nine seasons in the NFL had left Grange "battered and worn," noting that the "circuit has become a little too fast for the galloping redhead and he has seen little action this year."

In truth, Grange had not been an offensive threat in years. Perhaps no coach but Halas would have brought him back from his horrible knee injury. But no one ever questioned his value as a defensive player. He saved the '33 championship by halting a last-second lateral, and he lifted the Bears to the '34 title game when he tipped a pass through the hands of Glenn Presnell with no time remaining.

His final game was played on January 27, 1935, at Hollywood's Gilmore Stadium. It was a rematch of the championship game, though no one took it very seriously. These games in the California sunshine were played for what they were worth—exhibitions. The Bears cruised to a 21–0 lead with a lot of second stringers enjoying some playing time.

Late in the game, with the ball at the Chicago twenty-yard line, Brummy stepped into the huddle and said, "Well, guys, this is it. Red's final play. Let's make it a good one." Brumbaugh then called T-right, forty-five. It was Grange carrying over right tackle behind Moose Musso.

As they broke the huddle, Brummy said to Red, "When you get to the end zone just put the ball between the goalposts and run to the bench."

Even Grange knew something was up: *How could they possibly expect me to run eighty yards on these legs?*

The hole was wider than Route 66 through Los Angeles. Nagurski and Molesworth hustled upfield to block the defensive backs. No one touched the Ghost as he took off on his final historic run. But by midfield, his shoes were starting to feel like concrete blocks. Now he could hear heavy breathing behind him. He was almost walking by the New York forty. Then a 230-pound tackle named Tex Irvin, once described as "so slow you could have timed him with a calendar" dragged Grange down at the thirty-nine.

Yes, it had been arranged with the Giants that they would let the Redhead score. But with the old warrior moving at a snail's pace, Irvin had no choice but to tackle him. That is where the long run ended for the Galloping Ghost.

On that sunny day in Los Angeles, where Grange had once chased Hollywood starlets, and where his proud teammates now cheered him on, the storybook run of the Galloping Ghost finally ended.

# 14

# Crossroads

A mail courier arrived at the Bears training camp one day in late August of 1935 and dropped a heavy box at the feet of equipment manager Rennie Wykowski.

"Collect!" he demanded.

Wykowski examined the package but had no clue of what the contents might be. Papa Bear was forever experimenting with new ideas that spewed forth from his brain like water from a fountain. Any number of items might be lurking inside this mysterious parcel—a telescope for spying on practices, a magical liniment, a battery-operated bullhorn, or a newfangled kicking shoe. The box had no return address.

Wykowski summoned the team treasurer to pay the freight. An hour later, when practice ended, George Halas spotted the bulky container.

"What's this?" he asked Wykowski. "I didn't order anything." Halas tore into the bundle with both hands. Then his eyes widened as if he had found George Preston Marshall at the bottom of the box.

It contained more than a hundred worn-out sneakers of various shapes, colors, and sizes. Not a single one was fit to wear. Halas quickly closed it up and collapsed into a chair. His blood pressure was rising.

"I hope to God this is not an omen," he said with a sigh.

Halas suspected that Giants coach Steve Owen was the man behind this little scheme; no one loved a good laugh better than the country boy from Oklahoma. But Halas was not laughing. A dark mood pervaded the Bears camp, and it didn't help that a box filled with smelly sneakers with holes in the soles would reopen these old wounds. Halas could still see those fraudulent Giants moving surefootedly across the ice at the Polo Grounds in their dumb white gym shoes.

Six months after the Sneakers Game, the Bears were imploding. They were losing players left and right. As promised, Link Lyman had packed his bags and gone back to Nebraska. Beattie Feathers had yet to fully recover from off-season shoulder surgery, and doctors were not sure that he would ever be the same. The shocker of the summer came with the retirement of quarterback Carl Brumbaugh, who had been haggling over a new contract with Halas. He gave up the fight when Halas bumped his salary by only fifty bucks a game, to $150. He took a job as an assistant coach at the University of West Virginia.

Now Halas and trainer Andy Lotshaw were worried about the eroding physical condition of one Bronko Nagurski.

The Bronk had spent most of the off-season on the wrestling circuit as the main attraction at sold-out smoke-filled auditoriums from Minneapolis-St. Paul to Chicago Stadium. He defeated the likes of Ed "Strangler" Lewis and Henry Ordemann, a tough-as-nails old-timer. It was no secret inside the sport that promoters orchestrated the matches and appointed the winner of the match before the combatants entered the ring. Nagurski was selected to be the "good guy" against Cliff Gustafson, a disagreeable sort who often refused to take the fall. In fact, he was described by the press as the "pariah of the local wrestling organization."

Not only was it arranged for Nagurski to win the bout, he was supposed to lift Gustafson above his head and toss him from the ring. Crowds loved this kind of extracurricular violence. The Bronk's maverick opponent was not about to cooperate; he managed to wreck the script and win the bout by pinning wrestling's rising star. So what was the Bronk to do? He grabbed the referee by an arm and a leg and launched him over the ropes.

The long, grueling winter had left Nagurski bruised and tired. He limped into the Bears' summer camp two days late, looking like he needed a vacation. Months of being slammed onto the mat or into a turnbuckle was not what the doctor prescribed for a man with an aging and aching body.

Halas noticed Nagurski's slow, uneven gait as he lugged suitcases into the campus dormitory in South Bend. The coach got on the phone and found a masseur to work over his prized player, to get the kinks out of his back and hip. If the Bears were to reach the championship game a fourth straight year, the giant from the Big North Woods would have to tote a heavy load. Halas was willing to give him a few days off to heal before starting summer drills.

The Bears had only two weeks to prepare for a rematch with the College All-Stars. The NFL champion Giants had balked at the notion of traveling all the way to Chicago for the chance to be humiliated by a bunch of college boys. So Halas agreed to play the game. This year's All-Star team looked even better on paper than the team that had played the Bears to a scoreless tie the previous season. Among the big names were All-America end Don Hutson and a future politician by the name of Gerald Ford, a center from Michigan. The pros saved face this time by winning 5–0 before a crowd of eighty thousand at Soldier Field. That the Bears were granted an early glimpse of Hutson in the All-Star game was a windfall. Hutson was now the property of the Green Bay Packers, thanks to some creative contractual maneuvering by one Curly Lambeau. Anyone who had ever set eyes on the "Alabama Antelope" knew he was bound for greatness.

In the bidding for Hutson, Lambeau barely outlasted Shipwreck Kelly, the owner of the Brooklyn Dodgers. It had started at eighty bucks a game and had risen in five-dollar increments. Hutson actually signed contracts of $175 per game with both teams on the same day, but his Packers deal arrived on the desk of commissioner Joe Carr an hour before the one from Brooklyn.

The son of a railroad conductor in Arkansas, Hutson never dreamed of playing pro football while growing up in the Cotton Belt. His collegiate career ended with a four-catch, two-touchdown performance against Stanford in the January 1, 1935, Rose Bowl, a game the Crimson Tide won 29–13. He actually thought he was packing away football gear for the final time. He returned to Tuscaloosa, where he entered into a business partnership with a former teammate and roommate named Paul "Bear" Bryant; they were going to make a mint in the laundry business.

Bryant and Hutson had played opposite ends for the Crimson Tide, with Hutson the swift, acrobatic receiver and Bryant the street fighter.

The NFL had rarely crossed Hutson's mind because folks in the Deep South rarely talked about it. Alabama newspapers carried the NFL scores only once in a blue moon. Then one day after his senior season he received a telegram from Lambeau, and the next day Kelly's missive arrived. When Hutson told his pal "Bear" about the NFL's sudden interest, the big man said, "Just make damn sure they're paying you a good wage." Hutson's exposure to the world had been so limited that it was not until he arrived in Green Bay that he set eyes on his first saloon. Of course, every paved intersection in the northeastern Wisconsin hamlet had a tavern; some had four. Hutson surveyed the clapboard houses, the run-down practice facilities, and the crackerbox stadium with no locker rooms or public rest rooms and started planning for life after football. The business major at Alabama could see that pro football had a cash flow problem. He and his wife, Pam, were so confident of Hutson's NFL future that they rented a ten-dollar-a-month apartment and decided to bank every cent of his football paycheck and to live off the money earned from an off-season job—whatever that might be.

The Hutsons were surprised to learn they would be drawing paychecks from two banks after each game. Lambeau was so worried about word leaking about this "astronomical" contract that he had drafts written from two institutions—one for $75 and the other for $100. Not a single Packer player was making more than a hundred bucks a game, and most were pulling down seventy-five. Lambeau worried that the entire team might walk out if word spread of Hutson's deal.

In spite of his dim view of pro football, the Antelope could not have chosen a better time or place to make the leap. The fat ball era had passed, and teams were loosening up. You could grip and fling the new model that was tapered at the ends and easy to spiral. Green Bay had a tailback in Arnie Herber who was not afraid to uncork the ball and a coach in Lambeau who was willing to risk everything to slow down the freight train known as the Chicago Bears.

Lambeau had an abiding confidence in the skinny kid from the sticks. The Green Bay coach had sneaked into Alabama's pre–Rose Bowl practices in Pasadena to see Hutson make his one-handed catches. Even in college he could swing from a goalpost with one hand and catch the ball with the other.

In Green Bay Hutson would be teamed with one of the best passers in the history of the NFL. A tailback in the single wing, Herber had led the league twice in passing, once in '32 before the ball was slimmed down and again in '34.

Thanks to the College All-Stars Game, Hutson arrived at the Green Bay training camp just in time to miss all of the exhibition games and every preseason practice. His new teammates shook hands with him, but few hung around to talk. They took one look at this rail of a man and figured he would never make it.

Hutson did not start the regular season opener against the Chicago Cardinals and played less than a quarter. The only pass thrown in his direction was incomplete. He carried once on an end-around for no gain.

Two hundred miles to the south, George Halas read the account of the Cardinals-Packers game and knew that Hutson was nobody's decoy. The Bears would soon board the Illinois Central to Green Bay for the second game of the season at packed and rowdy City Stadium. Halas sensed an ambush.

The Bears had no choice but to cover Hutson with Feathers. Halas spent the better part of the week in practice preaching this sermon to the feisty kid with the bad shoulder: "I know you are fast. But Hutson is faster than you think. He lollygags around a lot. But, shit, son, the boy can fly. Do *not* let this man get behind you. Do *not* let him beat you."

"All right, George, all right."

As the Bears dressed for the game, Halas sat in a chair next to Feathers at the Northland Hotel and delivered the same message: "Keep an eye on this damned Hutson. Do you know why they call him the Alabama Antelope?"

"Yes, George."

The Packers always gathered around a radio to listen to the pregame remarks of one Emmet Platten, a Green Bay butcher who purchased fifteen minutes of airtime before every game and spent the better part of it critiquing the team. This day, he was taking out his frustration on the rookie from Alabama.

"I just want to know," Platten began, "how the Packers, a team in great need of talent, can spend all of that money on a skinny kid who doesn't even know if a football is blowed up or stuffed? We haven't beat the Bears since Christ left Chicago, and that was years ago, yah. Now we've got a cracker who's going to save us! I'll bet all the cheese in Wisconsin that the boy falls on his face."

All eyes were on Hutson as his teammates waited for a reaction. They were amazed to find him about half asleep, acting as cool as an Alabama cucumber. They didn't know that the Antelope had never been rattled. His wife had once observed that on their wedding day his manner was so composed and casual it appeared he had stepped into the church merely to get out of the rain.

This laconism was still on display when the Packers lined up for the first play of the game against Chicago. The ball rested on the Green Bay seventeen-yard line. When Hutson sauntered toward the line of scrimmage, the Bears noticed he was wearing no hip pads, and his shoulder pads were cardboard thin. He seemed as relaxed as a country boy with a toothpick clamped between his teeth strolling into a feedstore.

"Watch out!" Halas screamed from the sideline. "Get back, Feathers! Don't let that sonofabitch beat you deep."

Hutson lined up three yards outside of the left tackle. Johnny Blood, the NFL's all-time leading receiver, was flanked out ten yards on the other side of the field. Herber turned and set his focus on Blood. The Bears defense shifted to that side.

Hutson faked to the outside, planted his left foot, and shot toward the middle of the field. He ran past Feathers like he was standing still. As Hutson bolted into the open field, Halas ripped off his hat and fired it into the ground. The pass arrived over Hutson's right shoulder at midfield. Not a Bear was within thirty yards of the Antelope when he crossed the goal for his first NFL touchdown.

Halas watched Lambeau dance on the sideline and punch the air like a prizefighter warming up for round one. He turned and spit a stream of tobacco juice.

As Hutson trotted back up the field, and twenty-six thousand voices rolled across the prairie, Hutson said to himself, "I guess they know I can play now."

In this one-platoon era, most players lined up at corresponding positions on defense. So it was now time for Hutson to trot his bony six-foot-one, 185-pound frame over to the defensive end position, where the Bears planned to trample him.

Halas wanted to break this stickman in half. Chicago would line up in the straight T-formation and run the ball down his throat. The Bronk was like a snow plow as he led the blocking for Gene Ronzani around end and the Bears clicked off first down after first down. Quarterback Bernie Masterson, a halfback who had made the switch just that season, was under instructions to run the ball until the Packers puked. This plan would have worked even if Lambeau had not made his own adjustments. Iron Mike Michalske and Clarke Hinkle shifted their muscle to Hutson's side of the field and the Packers were able to shut down the Bears' steamroller. They even managed to limit Nagurski to two and three yards a carry.

Not since October 16, 1932, had Green Bay defeated Chicago, and that by the puny score of 2–0. The six-game winning streak was soon to become history. Green Bay's defense kept Automatic Jack out of field goal range and Lambeau's plan of eating up the clock with the running game worked: Green Bay 7, Chicago 0.

As Halas made the long walk to the team bus, and the crowd hissed and booed, all he could think about was that big box of sneakers.

• • •

The Bears could rest assured that they would rebound the following Sunday against the Pittsburgh (football) Pirates. The team was still being cobbled together by owner Art Rooney, the gambler extraordinaire who had won his franchise fee, along with a trunk filled with large bills, at the racetrack. This was the Pirates' third year of existence, and the roster was filled with out-of-work steelworkers who could barely walk and spit tobacco at the same time.

To make matters worse, Rooney wasn't much of a football man—at least not yet. When the Portsmouth Spartans failed to meet a gate guarantee with the Steelers in '33, the team owner said, "Sorry, Art. But go ahead and take Presnell." He was talking about Glenn Presnell, one of the most talented all-round players in the NFL. But Rooney failed to file the paperwork on the acquisition in time with commissioner Joe Carr and lost the rights to Presnell.

The Bears would be on the road for the first three weeks of the season.

This annoyed Halas to no end. Nothing, however, aggravated him more than the thought of having the Cubs back in the World Series in 1935. Naturally, the Bears were relegated to page six of the Chicago dailies, and advance ticket sales were lagging. It seemed like a black cloud was stalking them.

To make matters worse, the talk of the town was no longer Nagurski. It was Lewis Robert "Hack" Wilson, a feisty and stubby little man who led the league in home runs four years out of five. In 1930 he had shattered the major league record with 191 runs batted in, a record that still stands. And like Babe Ruth, he was a carouser and rabble-rouser, one who liked to drink all night.

Manager Joe McCarthy, hoping to rehabilitate Wilson, called the team together in the clubhouse one afternoon for what he called a scientific experiment.

He dropped a worm into a glass of water and it wiggled wildly. Then he dropped the worm into a glass of whiskey, and it died instantly.

McCarthy turned to Wilson and said, "Hack, what did you learn from that?"

"Well, Skip," Wilson said, "it means that if I keep drinkin' liquor, I ain't gonna get no worms."

In early September, at a time when Chicagoans should have been gearing up for the start of the football season, the Cubs were in third place behind the Cardinals. They came back to Wrigley Field for an eighteen-game home stand and won them all. Then the Cubs won three more in St. Louis to clinch the pennant before losing a meaningless game. The twenty-one-game winning streak still has no match.

Chicago was overcome with baseball fever. Bartenders served it, cabbies drove it, gangsters bet on it. Even the Marshall Fields–Potter Palmer set took the El north to Wrigley Field for a beer and hot dog and a glimpse of the hard-drinking leftfielder who blasted rockets into the bleachers.

Game six went to the bottom of the ninth inning, with the Detroit Tigers leading the Series three games to two. The score was 3–3 when Mickey Cochrane, who doubled as the Detroit manager, singled and advanced to second on a fielder's choice. Then Goose Goslin's bloop single fell between Cubs outfielders Billy Herman and Chuck Klein. Because Cochrane had guessed base hit, he had a big jump and scored easily. The Cubs had flamed out once more in the World Series.

It was Halas's hope that Chicago would now focus on the Bears. To his chagrin, they were now a thousand miles away at Forbes Field in Pittsburgh preparing to play the Pirates, a team that normally averaged three thousand fans for home games. But with Nagurski in town, the crowd swelled to ten thousand. Steel Town was not disappointed. On the third play of the game, Nagurski roared around right end and laid out two Pirates. Both men were still on the ground when the Bronk crossed the goal forty yards later. Both were unconscious and suffering from shattered clavicles. Like many of the Pirates, they had Nagurski's cleat marks all over their bodies. The Bears rolled to a 23–7 victory that afternoon without throwing a single pass.

The Pirates were scheduled to rail out of Pittsburgh the next morning for a three-game swing across the Midwest. In a Pullman section, several of the players were kibbitzing and enjoying a card game that had attracted a crowd. They were standing in the aisles and stretching on tiptoes to catch a glimpse of the action. Cards, poker chips, and beer bottles were spread across the table. As the train made a sudden turn, the Pullman car lurched, spilling bodies and beer bottles on the floor. Above the din rose the voice of halfback Warren Heller.

"Run for your lives, men! It's Nagurski!"

They could never get him out of their minds.

Philadelphians couldn't wait to see the human battering ram a few days later. Fifteen thousand fans—about five times the normal crowd—trekked to Franklin Field to see Nagurski rush for 121 yards and score three touchdowns in a 39–0 victory. Halas believed the Bears were back on track, and he couldn't wait for the train to roar back into the station at Chicago. It was going to be a championship season after all.

The amazing feat that occurred against the Brooklyn (football) Dodgers in the fourth week of the season cannot be found in any record book. It did not register on the scoreboard, and no statistical category will ever include it. But when it came down, Halas said to himself, "Thank God we're in Chicago so every one of these sonsabitches can see this!"

Twice in his career, Nagurski had run headfirst into the outfield wall at Wrigley Field. During the 1931 season, he had knocked a cop off his horse on the sideline at Wrigley Field. Twice he had thundered through the south end zone with such momentum that he flew down the dugout

MONSTER OF THE MIDWAY

steps and slammed into the abutment behind the bench. Once he piled into a cop car on the Wrigley sideline and peeled off the front fender.

This day, neither man nor beast was about to stop this Monster of the Midway. Nagurski was such a reckless force that even the sporting press struggled to find the words. Not in the history of football had such a powerful man laced up cleats. But Halas could never remember Nagurski hitting anyone harder than he did today. The Brooklyn trainers were almost exhausted from carrying player after player off the field.

As the Bears rolled toward their third straight victory, Halas was no longer depressed about the season-opening loss to Green Bay. He even stopped cursing the officials. This inner peace, though, would be shattered when he saw Nagurski limping back to the sideline after his third touchdown of the day.

"It's that goddamned hip, ain't it?" he said to the Bronk.

"Yah. Sonofabitch won't go away, George."

Halas had never seen the Bronk hurt. Oh, he had seen him bloodied, bruised, and punch-drunk from head-banging a brick wall. But he had never seen him hurt—until now.

• • •

Halas and trainer Andy Lotshaw sat in the waiting room at Chicago Memorial Hospital as the doctor walked down the hall with the large negative in his right hand.

He lifted it to the light and pointed to Nagurski's hip.

"It's more than a dislocation," Dr. Norman Krause said, looking at the X ray. "It's more than a hip pointer. It's a streptococcus infection that has settled into the hip and sciatic nerve. It's not good. It'll take awhile for even the great Bronko Nagurski to mend."

Halas held his hat in his hand.

"How long?" he asked.

"Maybe the whole season. This might end another man's career. But I know him. He'll come back."

"It's the goddamned wrestling," Halas said.

"It's a little bit of everything," the doctor replied. "Hell, George, he's got bumps all over his body. He looks like somebody took a pool cue to him."

"It's the goddamned wrestling," Halas repeated.

The doctor gave Halas a knowing smile. "George, he wasn't wrestling when he banged his head into that brick wall, now, was he?"

Halas shook his head and said nothing. Then his eyes moistened.

"He's all I got, doc. Grange's gone, Brummy's gone, Lyman's gone. Hell, even that goddamned Trafton's gone. Feathers ain't ever gonna be the same."

The doctor smiled again. "George, you've got a pretty doggone good team."

Krause was Halas's longtime friend. Their relationship dated to the twenties, when Halas was a tough little customer playing end for the Bears. Krause had repaired his ankle, knee, and shoulder.

"If there's anybody who can fix the Bronk, it's you," Halas said.

"George, the Bronk needs some rest."

The next game would be a rematch with Green Bay, no easy task without Nagurski. But a fired-up Bears team got the jump on the Packers as Bernie Masterson completed a forty-four-yard touchdown pass to Gene Ronzani. With Feathers and Nagurski on the sideline, Ronzani was no longer a heavy-footed blocking back. He was now the biggest producer in the backfield. The Bears led 7–3 midway through the first quarter.

Halfback Johnny Sisk had been on the Bears' roster since 1932 and hardly anyone knew his name. He averaged about thirty carries a season and had scored only twice. But like Ronzani, injuries had shoved him into the limelight. The Bears were facing a crucial third down when Sisk zipped through the line and darted fifty-four yards for a touchdown. With the Bears leading 14–3, the game at last seemed in the bag. That was until Arnie Herber fired a pass to Don Hutson in the fourth quarter and the Antelope zigged and zagged his way sixty-eight yards for a touchdown.

As fate would have it, Masterson fumbled on the next play. Green Bay's Ernie Smith recovered. Halas threw his hat to the ground and stomped it. Fifty seconds remained on the clock.

Arnie Herber completed a twelve-yard pass to George Sauer and an interference penalty moved the ball to the three. Herber faked into the line, jumped, and flipped a quick pass to a wide-open Hutson at the back line. Touchdown, Green Bay. The Bears had just swallowed a dose of their own medicine: Green Bay 17, Chicago 14. Halas watched Lambeau dancing on the sideline.

The season became a long and arduous struggle without Nagurski. The Bears beat the Giants and Redskins, but lost to New York in the rematch and then tied Detroit.

Chicago was 5–3–1 and all but eliminated from the Western Division race when the Bronk decided to make a comeback after five games on the sideline—against Detroit. It was risky business. The Lions hated him. After all, it was the Bronk and the Bronk alone who had kept Detroit from winning an NFL title the last four years. Detroit was now in a nip-and-tuck race with Green Bay for the Western Division title. They had no time for sympathy.

On the second play of the game, Nagurski limped into the line and was hammered by four Lions. Pain shot through his hip. He was slowly rising to his feet when he felt four hands lifting him. The hands belonged to Ox Emerson and Frank Christensen, two of the toughest hombres in football and members of the other team.

"I thought you guys hated me," Nagurski said.

"Nah," Ox said. "How could we hate the greatest player who ever lived?"

This was not sarcasm. Every time the Big Nag hit the ground that day, somebody in a blue jersey and silver helmet picked him up.

Chicago failed to score an offensive touchdown that day, and the Lions finally defeated the Bears, 14–2. It was the greatest day in the history of the Detroit franchise.

Meanwhile, the Bears were going nowhere fast. Nagurski continued to limp about the field with great pain, but rarely took a rest. The Bears would finish the season with back-to-back games against the crosstown Cardinals. The first game ended in a tie, and the Bears won the second. They finished the season with a 6–4–2 record.

Detroit completed the regular season with a 7–3–2 mark, at .700 (since ties did not count), and Green Bay at .666 finished thirty-three percentage points behind the Lions at 8–4.

The prediction of Lions owner George Richards had come to pass: The Lions would never win an NFL title until Nagurski went down. Behind the passing and running of Dutch Clark and Glenn Presnell, Detroit prevailed against New York 26–7 and walked away with its first league championship.

On the day after the season ended, the Bronk was walking down windy Michigan Avenue toward the train station with his hat pulled low. He happened upon a group of kids playing a roughhouse game of football. This was not a team game. It was one kid carrying the ball against about fifteen others. Needless to say, it was one-sided.

But one of the stocky kids, who had a big head and a solid jaw, tore through the line of tacklers with his knees pumping. He managed to stay on his feet and to break every tackle. He scored a touchdown.

The Bronk walked up to the proud ball carrier, who was bruised and scraped and whose nose was dripping blood.

"Hey, kid, what's the name of this game you're playing?" he asked.

"It's called Nagurski," the big boy said, thumbing his own chest. "And I'm Nagurski!"

The Bronk now swaggered to the station. His sore hip was feeling better already.

# 15

# Showtime

R edskins owner George Preston Marshall burst onto the professional
football scene at a time when America seemed as dark and gloomy
as a grainy eight-millimeter newsreel and football owners were about as
forward-thinking as Herbert Hoover. Strutting in his full-length raccoon
coat, his swagger evoked an image that hardly befitted the Depression
thirties. He was a tall and handsome man with a beaked nose, bushy eye-
brows, piercing eyes, and a thin mouth that rarely stopped motoring.

Given his lifestyle and his résumé, no one would have predicted that
Marshall was bound for a long and influential run in professional football.
He had a failed fling as an actor. He rode around in a chauffeured limou-
sine and invested big money in both Broadway and Hollywood produc-
tions. He also liked to meddle on the sideline.

One afternoon, he grabbed running back Cliff Battles by the jersey
when he returned to the bench.

"Look," he told Battles, "if you'd broken outside instead of inside,
you might have scored."

Battles just laughed and took a seat on the bench.

It was Marshall who had invented the NFL halftime show. Marching
bands had been a staple of college football for years. So why, Marshall

asked, should NFL crowds be left to twiddle their thumbs during intermission? He even invited Santa Claus to Fenway Park during the holiday season. It was clear from the day he walked into the league that Marshall had an eye for marketing and public relations and razzmatazz. He ordered his Redskins to dress up in feathers and headdresses and to wear war paint before the games. Only when the players complained that the facial paint was blocking their pores did Marshall call off the stunt.

There would be lessons learned. It was during the 1935 season that Marshall discovered that showmanship alone would not win football games. His zest to sell tickets led him to hire a local Boston sports hero, Eddie Casey from Harvard, to coach the team. The Redskins won only two of eleven games that season.

Months before the 1936 season got underway, he sought and won the services of former Giants end Ray Flaherty to coach the team. Flaherty had been known as a hardfisted, no-nonsense player with the great Giants teams under Steve Owen. He was determined to transform the Redskins into a workmanlike unit, emphasizing substance over flash. Before accepting the job, he demanded that his contract include a clause that forbade Marshall from coming down to the field during games.

But in November, with the Bears coming in for a game against the Redskins, Marshall could not control himself. From his box seats high above Fenway Park, he watched his team fall hopelessly behind. Halas was working his magic as he manipulated the officials. Everything was going Chicago's way. Finally, Marshall stood and marched down the aisle to the field, where he flew into a rage against the officials. This so incensed Halas that he sprinted across the field and started jabbing the Redskins owner with his right index finger.

"Get off the field, you sonofabitch," Halas hollered.

"George," Marshall said, "this is my field and my town. I can do as I please."

That is when Flaherty waded into the fray.

"Mr. Marshall, do I need to remind you that it's in my contract that you're supposed to sit in the stands?"

"Yeah, but Halas needs to shut his damn mouth."

"Go back to your seat," Flaherty said. "Or find another coach."

Marshall relented. As he walked back up the aisle, a fan threw a beer on the raccoon coat. Marshall responded with a left jab to the jaw and a right to the solar plexus. The fan crumpled to the cement floor.

Waiting for Marshall to return to the box was Corinne Griffith, the silent screen goddess and the owner's second wife. She was outraged by the entire scene. As he took his seat, she said, "I heard those mean things George Halas said. He should be kicked out of Fenway Park."

"Shut up, Corinne," Marshall said. "George Halas is my friend."

• • •

At age twenty-two, Joe Louis was living in a fashionable six-room apartment on the North Side of Chicago when promoters arranged for the heavyweight title fight of a lifetime with Max Schmeling, the big German slugger who had publicly embraced the Nazi regime but privately couldn't have cared less. Louis-Schmeling in July of '36 would be hyped as Der Führer vs. American Liberty. The whole world thought Louis would knock out Schmeling in the early rounds. In the last eighteen months, Louis had won twenty-seven fights, knocking out twenty-three of his opponents and defeating two former world champions. The fight was billed as "The Brown Bomber vs. the Terrific Teuton."

But Louis was having trouble handling prosperity. His training camp was set up at a resort in Lakewood, New Jersey, and he spent more time playing golf with the likes of Ed Sullivan, then a popular New York columnist, than embracing the drudgery of roadwork. And he had trouble keeping his hands off the attractive women hovering around his camp.

As fate would have it, Schmeling, the heavy underdog, bludgeoned the poorly conditioned Louis into oblivion. His face was swollen by the twelfth round, when Schmeling dropped him to the canvas. The forty-five thousand fight fans at Yankee Stadium could not believe their eyes as Louis was counted out.

It was reported in the *New York Times* that more than a half million gambling dollars were lost in Harlem on the fight. There was rioting and looting all over New York. That Schmeling was viewed as a model for Hitler's Nazi regime did not help American morale. Another war now loomed on the horizon. Italian dictator Benito Mussolini had just completed a meeting with Hitler to align the foreign policies of the two countries. An evil Axis was being forged. The world was a dangerous place once more.

Halas could not help but think about the prospects of World War II. He had promised himself that if another war broke out, he would somehow find the action. He had been relegated to playing baseball for a navy team during World War I, and missing the war was a source of great angst.

The 1936 season found Halas's Bears at a crossroads. Carl Brumbaugh had returned, but Halas made it clear that Bernie Masterson, now in his second season, was the starting quarterback. Brummy would spend the better part of his time tutoring Masterson in the intricacies of the T-formation. He gladly accepted the task, knowing it was better than coaching kids in the cold West Virginia mountains.

Halas wondered how long it would take to rebuild the dynasty. There were problems to be solved. It had become obvious that the oft-injured Beattie Feathers would never be the same; another thousand-yard season was out of the question. There were other holes in the Bears lineup. Halas had grudgingly approved the trade of guard Joe Kopcha to the Lions. Kopcha had asked for the trade, which would allow him to accept an internship at a Detroit hospital.

Moose Musso was the only dominating player left in the Chicago line. After his slow start during the '33 training camp, Musso had developed rapidly into an All-Pro. A Chicago sportswriter had asked about his secret to success: "I block for Nagurski," he said. "The Bronk waits for nobody. You block and get the hell out of the way. Or he'll break your back."

In the spring of '36, NFL owners had voted to institute a collegiate draft with hopes of spreading the talent and preventing the wealthier teams from corraling the best players each year. Cynics claimed that it was really a ploy to hold down salaries. In that first draft Halas surprised everyone by taking an unknown tackle from West Virginia by the name of Joe Stydahar. Brummy had given "Jumbo Joe" a strong recommendation and Halas listened. The Bears made several other key choices, including halfback Ray Nolting from Cincinnati. In the final round of the draft, Halas walked casually to the front of the room and said, "I saw a name I liked: Danny Fortmann. Now that name's got a good sound to it."

Whether he was kidding or not, Halas had found yet another monster in Fortmann. And he had rebuilt the Bears line with two brilliant strokes. Fortmann and Stydahar together would produce twelve All-Pro seasons. Both would be selected to the Pro Football Hall of Fame.

Eighty-one players were selected in the draft—nine by each team—but fewer than half signed contracts. The defectors knew they could make more money in menial jobs. The biggest failure of the draft was Philadelphia's not being able to sign the University of Chicago's Jay Berwanger, the finest all-around college player of the era. The rights to Berwanger, the first winner of the Heisman Trophy, were traded to the Bears. But Halas couldn't sign him, either.

While the owners were sorting out the college boys, Nagurski spent the off-season bouncing around the wrestling circuit of Minnesota, Wisconsin, and Illinois, playing both the good guy and the bad guy. It was hardly enjoyable. Wrestling fans could be intolerable. They liked to hold matches to coins before tossing them into the ring, hoping the wrestlers were desperate enough to pick them up and burn a finger or two. The Bronk could feel the wear and tear on his hip and shoulder and knees. The two knots on his back now felt like iron balls. But he was banking some extra money to keep the farm going back in Minnesota. He was engaged to Eileen Kane, and their wedding was less than a year away. Eileen was already talking about starting a family.

The Bronk's degenerative hip condition was a constant source of pain. But he had regained most of the power in his legs. Halas had reduced his salary again, to $3,250, and Nagurski was feeling even more frustrated when he had returned home during the off-season with another IOU in his pocket. He tried to purchase a new car in Minneapolis by using Halas's promissory note as collateral.

"A George Halas IOU doesn't carry much clout around here," the dealer said. "Show me some cash."

Nagurski had to wire the Bears owner, and Halas did come through. But haggling over money already owed him was starting to leave a sour taste.

The 1936 season looked like a crapshoot to Halas. That he had surrounded Nagurski with so many young players caused him sleepless nights. But at least he did not have to worry about the Cubs occupying Wrigley Field and dominating the sports pages in October. The Cubbies had finished second to one of the greatest New York Giants teams of all time, which included Bill Terry, Mel Ott, and the fabulous screwball pitcher Carl Hubbell.

Since the 1925 season, the Bears and Packers had always played either the first or second game at City Stadium. The Bears were filled with doubts as the Chicago and Northwestern carried them north to Green Bay for the start of the '36 season. The sporting press had almost unanimously predicted that Green Bay would win the Western Division title and beat the Giants in the NFL championship game. The passing combination of Herber to Hutson had become lethal. Chicago was a 3-1 underdog against a team that still boasted the likes of Clarke Hinkle, Buckets Goldenberg, and Johnny Blood.

But the game was upside down from the start. The Bears had a new star in Nolting, who tossed a touchdown pass to Hewitt, scored on a six-yard run, and boomed a couple of long punts; all of this occurred in ten minutes of playing time. The ruggedly handsome Nolting had chosen the Bears as a free agent because he didn't want to have to tackle Nagurski. Ironically, it was Nagurski whom he met head-on on the first play of an intrasquad scrimmage back in training camp. Nolting did not fare well, but neither did most of his teammates against the Bronk. At five foot eleven and 188 pounds, he possessed both speed and power along with plenty of guile. He was a perfect fit for the black-and-blue image of the Bears.

Ronzani, Karr, and Brumbaugh also scored touchdowns that day against Green Bay, and Nagurski rushed for 101 yards. Chicago won 30–3, and the sportswriters wondered if they had picked the wrong champ in preseason.

Nolting was showered with accolades from the Chicago newspapers. But that praise could not compare to what Nagurski had to say. Two days after the Green Bay game, while the Chicago players watched the game film, Nagurski made several mental notes. When the lights went up, he said, "Hey, George. Anybody who can block Hinkle like that would be starting for my team."

The Bronk was talking about Nolting. Naturally, he would start the next game at Pittsburgh.

That is when the jitters set in. On the third play of the game against the Pirates, Brumbaugh called Nolting's number. He would fake to Ronzani, spin, and hand off to Nolting on the counter play. But as Brumbaugh held out the ball, Nolting was not there to take it. The rookie had screwed up the play. Brumbaugh was fuming after being tackled for a six-yard loss.

"Where in the hell where you, freshman?" he said.

"I forgot the play."

"I'll teach you to forget."

Nolting carried the ball eight straight times on the same off-tackle play. Gaining four, five, and six yards a pop did not seem like punishment. *Man, I'm going to score another touchdown,* he said to himself. But with the ball at the Pirates' two-yard line, Brummy faked to Nolting and handed off to Nagurski, who easily trotted into the end zone untouched.

Brummy shouted at Nolting, "I guess that'll teach you to forget the plays, you stupid sonofabitch!"

Judging from the early results of the '36 season, Halas had already rebuilt the dynasty. The Bears defeated their first six opponents by a combined score of 119–32. Nagurski was a powerhouse once more. The Bears did not lose a step with Nolting replacing the oft-injured Feathers. Brummy and Masterson shared the quarterback position, and the T-formation offense operated without a hitch. Halas was impressed with the time and effort Brumbaugh had invested in teaching Masterson the complex offense.

As November rolled around, Green Bay had its sights set on revenge at cool and breezy Wrigley Field. The Packers' only loss had been to Chicago on the opening weekend. Packer fans swarmed the morning train for the two-hundred-mile trek south to Chicago and, after reaching the Michigan Avenue Station, grabbed the El to the North Side. They were like an army of green and gold winding down the wooden stairwell at the Addison station and pouring into the Cubs Grille, where the bookies were primed and ready.

Everyone knew that Hinkle would be a hard man to handle this time around. In the second quarter, with the ball resting at the Green Bay forty-one, Hinkle thundered into the line and smashed into the 258-pound mountain known as Moose Musso. Hinkle was thrown backward by five yards but landed on his feet. He shifted gears, dropped his shoulder, and slammed into the line once more. This time he was met head-on by Nagurski. Hinkle was thrust backward by three yards but remained upright. Then he spotted an opening between Nagurski and Musso and roared through it. No one could stop him. His fifty-nine-yard touchdown run turned the game in Green Bay's favor.

After Hinkle had crossed the goal, Musso chuckled and said to Nagurski, "That's the first time I've ever seen a sumbitch pass me three times on the same play."

Hinkle rushed twenty-one times for 109 yards that day, and the Packers defeated Chicago 21–10. The teams were now tied for the Western Division lead with 6–1 records.

After the game, Nagurski walked over to Hinkle and stuck out his hand. They had not shared a pleasant word in four years.

"Some of the best running I've ever seen," the Bronk said. "You're a hard fella to stop, yah."

"Shit, Bronk," Hinkle said. "You're the toughest sonofabitch I've ever seen. At least you didn't knock me out this time."

Chicago defeated the fading Giants the following week at the Polo Grounds 25–7. It was a sad season for the former NFL champs, who missed players like quarterback Harry Newman and end Ray Flaherty. It seemed that everyone was picking on the Giants. When Detroit fullback Ace Gutowsky was knocked out of bounds during a game at the Polo Grounds, he kicked a bucket of ice water on Owen. None of the Giants tried to retaliate. They were no longer in a fighting mood.

On November 15 at Fenway Park, when George Preston Marshall was cursed by Halas and thrown off the field by his own coach, the Bears won 26–0. The Redskins' hopes of finally winning a division title were fading fast.

The Bears remained on the East Coast the following week and dispatched the Philadelphia Eagles 28–7 as Nagurski rushed for three touchdowns and Nolting scored the other.

If they won the final two games, the Bears would be champions of the Western Division once more. Then they would have a shot at their third NFL title in five years. But there would be hell to pay on Thanksgiving Day in Detroit.

Back in late October the Bears had stung the defending league champions 12–10 at Wrigley Field, and Halas had rubbed Potsy Clark's face in it once more.

The Lions had shown Nagurski some tender care the previous season upon his return after the hip injury. But the gloves were off this time. The Lions were not completely out of the race for the division title, and with owner George Richards stringing together more than a hundred radio stations to broadcast the game, the Lions would have yet another reason to be motivated.

Again, Richards had sold standing room tickets on the day of the game.

More than four thousand fans ringed the field, raising the crowd to twenty-six thousand. Halas invited George Trafton along as a bodyguard. His job was to shoo drunken fans away from the Bears' bench. Detroit University Stadium was where Red Grange had almost lost his life when he tumbled into the angry mob on the final play of the game.

The Bears were ready for anything the Lions might dish out. Since falling upon some hard times, Halas had put the team back together one piece at a time. And it helped immensely that Nagurski was having one of his best seasons both at fullback and linebacker. The doctors were not sure he would completely recover from the severely damaged hip. But that Thanksgiving in Detroit, he sent three Lions to the sidelines with injuries and scored the first touchdown of the game on a thundering forty-four-yard run up the middle.

Detroit, however, had too much talent and resolve to lose at home to the Bears. Dutch Clark scored on a thirty-three-yard run and Glenn Presnell, one of the greatest all-around players of the thirties, scooted twenty-two yards around end for the other. Detroit won 13–7.

No one was ready for what happened three days later in the final game of the season. Not in seven years had the Bears lost to the crosstown Cardinals. But revenge is a powerful motivator.

The previous season, the Cardinals were trying to lock up the Western Division title when the Bears killed those dreams on a rock-hard field at Wrigley. So much ice had covered the field that Stinky Hewitt called it "a nice stretch of brick pavement." The Bears won 13–0.

This time the Bears seemed to have yet another victory wrapped up when rookie Joe Stydahar rambled ninety-six yards for a touchdown. But it was nullified by a penalty. The Cardinals managed to hold on for a rare 14–7 win over the Monsters of the Midway.

It was a season the Bears should have been able to celebrate. They outscored the opposition 222–94. Only three opponents scored more than ten points against them. Nagurski had one of his better seasons, finishing with 529 yards and three touchdowns. Stinky Hewitt led the league with 23.9 yards per catch and Manders in field goals with seven.

But Halas had to stand idly by and watch the Redskins and George Preston Marshall capture the Eastern Division title with a 14–0 victory over the Giants in mud and rain at the Polo Grounds.

Halas received a telegram the next day. It read:

GEORGE STOP GUESS WHAT STOP YOU GET TO WATCH US IN THE BIG GAME STOP GPM

Fortunately for Halas and his blood pressure, the Redskins lost to the Packers 21–6 in the NFL title game.

For years Marshall had criticized the fans and the paying customers for not supporting his football team. So, two days after the 1936 season, the Redskins packed their bags and moved to Washington, D.C.

The happiest day of Bronko's life arrived on December 23, 1936, when he married Eileen Kane, the love of his life, at St. Thomas Catholic Church in International Falls. It was supposed to be a small, private ceremony, but the local townsfolk flocked to the church anyway and the pews were packed.

When the groom was instructed to kiss the bride, Eileen virtually vanished inside the Bronk's enormous arms. The Bronk looked like a giant standing next to his petite wife. After the ceremony, the couple traveled all of about two hundred miles to Duluth for a quick honeymoon, then headed straight back to the Falls, where they began planning a family. Bronko Nagurski Jr. would be born one year and two days after the wedding—on Christmas morning of 1937.

# 16

# Farewell

On a warm afternoon in the spring of 1937, Sammy Baugh was relaxing at the family's ranch in Sweetwater, Texas, when a rider approached on horseback.

"Sam," the boy yelled, "come quick. You got a call from Washington down at the feedstore. Must be a senator or something."

Like many folks around Sweetwater, the Baughs did not have a telephone and took their long distance calls at the feedstore. A lot of people had been trying to get in touch with Baugh lately; at Texas Christian University he was recognized as the greatest passer in collegiate history. He could count a Sugar Bowl win over Louisiana State University and a Cotton Bowl victory over Marquette. But a senator calling all the way to the dusty West Texas town of Sweetwater seemed a bit far-fetched.

Baugh saddled up his horse and was at the feedstore in less than ten minutes. The store owner handed him the phone and said, "The fool on the other end must be a Rockefeller. This'n's costing him a fortune."

A group of men wearing boots and blue jeans and chewing toothpicks huddled a few feet from the phone. They heard Sammy say, "Now, Mr. Marshall, I've never even heard of the goddamn National Football

League. But if you want to pay me eight thousand a year to throw a danged football around the lot, I'm all ears."

George Preston Marshall had recently selected Samuel Adrian Baugh as the sixth player in the '36 NFL draft. The NFL's greatest showman was determined to make an immediate splash in his new town—the nation's capital. Both the rules of pro football and the climate were right for a quarterback known as "Slingin' Sam" Baugh, who had come within an eyelash of leading the Horned Frogs to a national championship in '35.

At TCU Baugh had played for a coach named Leo "Dutch" Meyer, a short, bespectacled man who wore dark suits, a fedora, and flashy ties. He was the first college coach in America to let the leather fly. Marshall and the Redskins were ready to improve upon Meyer's blueprint.

Marshall loved the nickname "Slingin' Sam." Little did he know that it had not come from football, but from the way Baugh threw a baseball from third to first. Surely, though, someone would have hung the name on Baugh even if he had never played baseball. Standing in the pocket, he held the football at his waist instead of the ear. His arms were like long whipcords, and his hands large enough to choke a steer. Baugh would raise the ball to his right shoulder and then sling it sidearm across his body, much like a third baseman fielding a bunt and trying to cut down the runner at first. A critic might call it slapdash. But this unconventional style allowed Baugh to throw from any position or any angle. It made him the master of passing on the run. He could throw off the back foot, the front foot, or with both feet off the ground. He often looked like a contortionist as he twisted his stringbean body and let the ball fly.

Grantland Rice once wrote that Baugh "fired the leather with as much speed as Dizzy Dean ever knew." It was true that Baugh's passes traveled with great velocity and almost always spiraled. But explaining how he did it was another matter.

Not surprisingly, Marshall was as interested in Baugh's marketing powers as his passing skills. The Washington owner had a vision of Baugh striding across the TCU campus wearing spurs and a full-length duster just like Wyatt Earp. He told Baugh over the phone, "Look, I want you to go out and buy a ten-gallon hat. Get yourself a new pair of cowboy boots. We're going to have some fun when I fly you up to Washington."

When Baugh deplaned for the contract-signing ceremonies, he was outfitted in a wide Stetson, a checkered shirt, whipcord pants, and high-heeled riding boots. The boots were too narrow, and he limped all the way to the Occidental Hotel for his welcoming luncheon. He signed the $8,000 first-year contract, and Marshall handed over five hundred bucks to cover the costume.

"I guess I'm dressing more for him than I am for me," Baugh told the sportswriters.

The demands that Marshall made on Baugh did not preclude him from pursuing a career in baseball. Baugh had also signed a contract with the St. Louis Cardinals organization, and a scout named Rogers Hornsby and an owner named Branch Rickey were set on developing him into a major-league talent. Baugh had also been a consensus All-America baseball player at TCU, where the major-league scouts often turned out in droves for his games.

In the spring before that first season with the Redskins, Baugh reported to the Pampa Roadrunners. He was disappointed that the manager moved him to shortstop to make room for a third baseman who had been sent down by the big club.

That season, the Roadrunners played in a national tournament in Denver that featured virtually every team in baseball outside of the major leagues. It was a single-elimination tournament. Tampa won its first two games and faced a team from the East Coast that boasted names like Cool Papa Bell, Josh Gibson, and Satchel Paige—it was the ultimate all-star team straight out of the Negro Leagues.

"Golly," Baugh told his manager. "I've never seen ballplayers this good."

In the third inning, Cool Papa Bell, the fastest man in baseball, singled up the middle and decided to stretch it into a double. When the center-fielder bobbled the ball, Cool Papa tore around second and headed for third. The ball and the runner arrived at the same time. Cool Papa had his spikes high and they tore into the third baseman's face, knocking him three feet backward. As the third baseman lay bleeding and unconscious, Baugh thought to himself, *His face looks like an an oil gusher*.

Both benches cleared, and players sprinted onto the field swinging bats. Skulls were bashed and bones broken. Josh Gibson decided to grab the biggest player on the white team, who happened to be Baugh. But the two merely held onto each other's jerseys as the melee swirled around him.

When the cops finally broke it up, Sammy said to his manager, "It's about time for me to go play some football. I hope it's not as rough as this."

• • •

George Halas was spitting mad. The 1937 season would start in one week and Nagurski was halfway across the country on the wrestling circuit.

"Who the hell does Nagurski think he is?" Halas said.

"Just the greatest player ever," Carl Brumbaugh responded.

A healthy Nagurski had carried Chicago to within two games of a championship the previous season. Halas knew the Bears would finish in the middle of the pack without him in '37. These Monsters of the Midway were talented but far too young to survive a championship run if the Bronk was off in Des Moines wrestling "Strangler" Lewis or in Seattle slamming "Leering Lou" Plummer into the turnbuckle.

Nagurski had grabbed the wrestling world by the throat by winning his first world championship belt two months earlier. He had defeated fabled grappler Dean Detton on June 29 at the Minneapolis Fieldhouse for the title. Nagurski had been packing arenas and pulling down large paychecks for two years. The top wrestlers in the world were Lou Thesz, Detton, Plummer, and Nagurski. But the Bronk was the biggest drawing card of them all and the bout against Detton had drawn ten thousand.

His manager, Tony Stecher, decided during the summer of '37 that it was time for Nagurski to make the leap into the major leagues of professional wrestling. For four years he had been knocking around the smaller arenas, learning the game and establishing himself as a viable force. If Nagurski was to move into a higher income bracket and start preparing himself for life after football, the time had come to shoot for the stars.

Nagurski was a fan favorite because of his football fame and because he was regarded as one of the few good guys in the sport. Pro wrestling was a dirty game littered with arm-breakers. "Hooking," a technique derived from carnival fighting, was popular in the thirties. It was not uncommon to see arms and legs broken by the hooking method.

"There are dirty people in our sport, and they are out there to hurt people," Thesz told the press. "They learned some of their stuff from the carnival fighters. At the carnival, they always had one knockout fighter and one wrestler who really knew how to take care of himself. If a tough guy came out of the audience, you could make sure he wasn't going to win the money. An arm or a leg might get broken. Wrestling has some of the same kind of guys."

Nagurski injured his share of opponents and tossed more than a few over the ropes. But most of the damage that he inflicted was caused by brute strength. Oddly, in this make-believe world where most of the bouts were rigged, the Bronk was a kind of shining knight. Promoters hyped him as the man in the white hat fighting against the forces of evil.

The Bronk was mostly a straight-ahead brawler who wrestled with the same muscle and fortitude he showed on the playing field. His favorite move was the "flying block." He would grab the upper rope in one hand and then slingshot himself across the ring like an arrow. He would slam into his opponent with an arm, a hip, a shoulder, or a leg, often plowing him under. He used the flying block on Detton, who went down like a sack of dirt and was out cold for three minutes. When Detton woke up, he asked the referee, "Who the hell hit me? No, what the hell hit me?"

That September Halas was getting worried about his prized player. He had been reading newspaper accounts about Nagurski's wrestling success and knew he was getting hooked on the sport.

Halas had dropped dozens of hints that Nagurski should quit the wrestling game. But the Bronk was not buying it. Until Halas could see the light, Nagurski was going to maximize his opportunities in the wrestling world. The Bears had done nothing but decrease his salary since 1930, and he was still going home each off-season with money still owed to him. There were financial obligations to be met. Eileen was anxious to start a family, and he was still making payments on the farm.

For the moment, at least, wrestling was fun. There was more fan adulation than he could possibly expect. An editorial in the *Minneapolis Star* that summer typified the public's feeling for him: "Who shall embody the spirit of virtue triumphant? Only Bronko, of course. For all of his horsepower, he is a nice young feller with a pleasant voice and an engaging smile. He happens to have acquired talents as a bone-crusher and dropkicker that belie his innocent looks, and that is all the better for the show.

In fact, our Bronko is a top-notch wrestler. He is the world's champion. But fame and high rating bring their burdens. Bronko must do his bit to help the mat game. He must come to take care of the emergency. The third act in the drama is coming on—'Leering Lou' must get his just desserts. Two bucks on the Bronk."

When the two met that night in Minneapolis, the name BRONKO NAGURSKI appeared in bold letters on the marquee. Lou Plummer's name was barely large enough to be read. The crowd reveled in the sight of the Bronk driving "Leering Lou" into the mat, slamming him into the turn-buckle, and flattening him with the flying block. Somewhere an editorial writer was collecting his two bucks.

Thanks to this hectic schedule, the Bronk missed all of the Bears' pre-season practices and games. But he was at the Northland Hotel when Halas and the Bears arrived the night before the season opener at City Stadium against Green Bay. Halas expected to find the Bronk limping with a cane. Instead he looked fit and years younger.

"How's the hip?" Halas asked.

"Hip's fine, George. I can play the whole game tomorrow. But I won't be going back to Chicago with you guys after the Duluth game."

"Why not?"

"I've got some wrestling to do."

Halas shook his head and walked off.

The Bronk was masterful in the first game of the season, blasting through the Green Bay line and dropping ball carriers in the backfield. He seemed refreshed, like a man just off vacation. He carried seven straight times on the first touchdown drive. This time, Ray Nolting got the honors, a two-yard touchdown run behind Musso.

In the second half, Bernie Masterson tossed a forty-four-yard touchdown pass to Jack Manders. The Monsters breezed past the defending league champions 14–2.

Halas was all smiles until Monday morning when he read a newspaper account of the Redskins' opening game against the Giants. Tailback Cliff Battles had been injured, forcing a rookie into the starting lineup. That rookie, Sammy Baugh, had completed 11 of 16 passes for 116 yards as the Redskins defeated the Giants 13–3.

It would be a hard road back to glory. Halas prayed that Nagurski's damaged hip would hold up at least until the championship game could be played in December. The Bronk's upcoming schedule might have been enough to kill another man:

Sunday, Sept. 19: Game with Bears at Green Bay.
Tuesday, Sept. 21: Game with Bears at Duluth (exhibition).
Wednesday, Sept. 22: Wrestling match in Portland.
Thursday, Sept. 23: Wrestling match in Vancouver, B.C.
Friday, Sept. 24: Wrestling match in Seattle.
Monday, Sept. 27: Wrestling match in Phoenix.
Wednesday, Sept. 29: Wrestling match in Los Angeles.
Thursday, Sept. 30: Wrestling match in Oakland.
Friday, Oct. 1: Wrestling match in Salt Lake City.
Monday, Oct. 4: Game with Bears in Pittsburgh.
Wednesday, Oct. 6: Exhibition with Bears in Philadelphia.
Friday, Oct. 8: Wrestling match in Philadelphia.
Sunday, Oct. 10: Game with Bears in Cleveland.

In a period of twenty-one days, he would wrestle in nine cities and play football in four others. He would travel by plane, train, and automobile a distance of almost eleven thousand miles. This was long before the advent of jet airliners. Nagurski would either be wrestling, buckling his chinstrap, or traveling a great distance on each of those twenty-one days.

Perhaps the most amazing aspect of this whirlwind journey is that Nagurski was playing some of his best football. The Bears reeled off five straight victories.

On October, 4, Nagurski came off the wrestling circuit and arrived at Forbes Field about an hour before kickoff. He had yet to practice with the Bears all season. Halas was angered to the point of benching his star. But his better judgment told him not to. The Bears desperately needed Nagurski to keep pace with the Packers and Lions in the Western Division.

While Nagurski was away, Halas had been tinkering with the T-formation, changing the entire numbering system. With the aid of University Chicago coach Clark Shaughnessy, hired by Halas as a consultant, the Bears were making better use of the man in motion. The Bronk was given a crash course on the new play-calling system for about thirty minutes before kickoff. Given his performance that day, no one would have thought he had been away. He carried fifteen straight times on one drive that led to a touchdown pass from Bernie Masterson to Stinky Hewitt. He played all sixty minutes and dominated the Pirates on both sides of the ball. Halas could not believe his eyes. He was now convinced that his warhorse was better than ever. Maybe the man was invincible after all.

The home opener of the 1937 season would be against a Cardinals team that finally was making the NFL pay attention. The rookie passing combination of Pat Coffee to Gus Tinsley had brought some excitement to the South Side. The duo from LSU inspired Halas to stay up late every night watching extra film. Tinsley had caused a stir in the College All-Star game when he caught a forty-seven-yard touchdown pass from Sammy Baugh as the amateurs beat the pros for the first time. The Packers were still suffering from the public humiliation of losing that game to the college boys.

Wrigley Field had a new look thanks to the green thumb of Cubs president Bill Veeck. He had planted 350 bittersweet plants and 200 Boston ivy plants at the base of the outfield wall. The ivy had started to climb, covering the spot on the left-field wall where Nagurski had once cracked a brick. Veeck also planted eight Chinese elms on the bleacher steps in the outfield, but the winds off Lake Michigan were tearing off the leaves. Veeck was already seeking advice about replacing them.

To beat the Cardinals, the Bears would need to contain Tinsley, who reminded Halas a lot of Don Hutson. Tinsley had overshadowed Hutson during a game in Green Bay by catching eight passes for 148 yards. The Chicago sporting press already was speculating on Tinsley's chances of breaking Hutson's mark of thirty-four receptions, set in the previous season when the Alabama Antelope was a rookie.

It was Halas's decision to play keep-away with the Cardinals and to hope for a low-scoring game. The Bears consumed the clock with Nagurski and Nolting pounding the middle of the line on long drives. Both Nagurski and Gene Ronzani scored touchdowns on short plunges, and Automatic Jack Manders added a field goal as the Bears beat their crosstown rivals 16–7.

Though pro football was becoming more sophisticated by the year, the lateral was still such an important component that the league kept stats on the backward tosses. Teams lateraled the ball 204 times during the 1936 season, and the Detroit Lions led the NFL in that category with 95. The Bears were second with 38.

With the biggest game of the year coming up on Halloween at the Polo Grounds, the Bears were 5–0. New York had recovered nicely from an opening-day loss to Baugh and the Redskins, winning four straight and saving Steve Owen's job. One thing was certain about a Giants-Bears confrontation. A game at the Polo Grounds would be like a heavyweight title fight even if both teams happened to be playing for last place.

"You still owe these sonsabitches from three years ago," Halas told the Bears in the pregame speech. "They cheated us out of the championship. They'll cheat you again."

In truth, this Giants team barely resembled the one that had pulled off the fabled Sneakers comeback in 1934. Gone were players like Harry Newman and Ken Strong, both defectors to the new American Football League, and Ray Flaherty, now tutoring Baugh. New York's 1936 season had been a disaster. But instead of firing the coach, owner Tim Mara had basically fired the team. His son, nineteen-year-old Wellington Mara, had convinced him to sign Alphonse Emil "Tuffy" Leemans, a little-known halfback from George Washington University. The son of a Belgian miner who had immigrated to the iron hills of Superior, Wisconsin, Tuffy had built muscles as a youth by juggling iron ore. He had grown up on tales of Ernie Nevers, also a native of Superior, and Nagurski, who grew up two hundred miles farther north in International Falls.

Owen and the Maras had scouted the entire country for talent and believed their roster was of championship caliber once more in '37. So pleased was Owen that he decided to divide the Giants into two distinct teams, with each playing two quarters. Like Halas, Owen loved to tinker with both offensive and defensive strategy. The Giants would use the five-man line and the 5–3–3 alignment to counter the passing-oriented teams of the era. For offense Owen reached back and dusted off the "fan" shift that had been used by Pop Warner twenty-five years earlier at Carlisle.

It would not have mattered if Owen had tried a swinging gate against Chicago. All hell broke loose in the first five minutes of the game, and there was nothing to slow this free-for-all. On the opening kickoff Moose Musso punched quick-tempered Johnny Dell Isola in the face. Three Giants were carted off the field in the first quarter alone—two after hits by the Bronk. Dell Isola, with his bruised face and bloodied nose, braced to tackle Nagurski in the first quarter and felt pride swelling inside him when the big man went down. Then Dell Isola heard the official say, "Second down and two." Nagurksi had gained eight yards.

Both teams were satisfied to run the ball and play for field position in the first half. The results were field goals by the Giants and the Bears. Ward Cuff, a rookie fullback from Marquette who had replaced Strong, nailed one from forty-two yards in the first quarter. Automatic Jack tied the score with a twenty-yarder in the second quarter, so it was 3–3 at halftime.

With Nagurski moving the offense down the field in short, powerful bursts, the Bears reached the Giants thirteen-yard line in the third quarter. But Masterson's pass on third down was intercepted in the end zone by Leemans.

The Giants had their chance to win the game in the fourth quarter when Tilly Manton shanked a twenty-one-yard field goal. Manton got a shot at redemption when officials ruled that Stinky "The Offsides Kid" Hewitt was offsides. It didn't matter, as Manton missed again, this time from sixteen yards.

The 3–3 final score was solid proof that the Bears and the Giants were still the two most physical teams in the NFL. Halas told the press after the game, "That was the roughest, toughest game that our boys have ever played."

Halas was not at all happy to see Nagurski limping around the locker room with a sore hip. He looked at the Bronk and said, "It's the god-damned wrestling, isn't it?"

"No, George," said Nagurski, who rarely cursed. "It's the goddamned football."

• • •

Just when it appeared the Bears' dynasty was up and rolling again, the Green Bay Packers came to Wrigley Field. Packer Backers jammed the club cars on the train to Chicago and then descended on the Cubs Grille two hours before kickoff. A crowd of 40,000 fans filled every seat at Wrigley Field on the first Sunday in November that yielded perfect foot-ball weather—temperatures in the forties, with little wind.

Preach as he might about the speed of Don Hutson, Halas could only watch helplessly from the sideline in the second quarter as the Antelope sprinted clear of the Chicago secondary and ran under a fifty-yard strike from Arnie Herber at the Bears twenty-eight. There would be no catching him. The touchdown play covered seventy-eight yards, boosting the Packers' halftime lead to 17–0.

Chicago rumbled back on the legs of Nagurski in the second half and cut the lead to 17–14. But as the Bears tried to rally for the winning touchdown, Masterson's sideline pass was intercepted and returned fifty-eight yards for a touchdown. The Bears lost 24–14.

Over the next few weeks, Nagurski continued to wrestle throughout the Midwest and along the East Coast but managed to arrive at the stadium on game day in time to play for the Bears. Night after night the Big Nag was battling some of the top names in the business, beating them all.

Chicago defeated Brooklyn at Wrigley Field 29–7 and then played their best defensive game of the season on Thanksgiving in Detroit, stifling Dutch Clark on "Dutch Clark Day." Nagurski scored one touchdown, and Automatic Jack kicked two field goals as the Bears won 13–0.

Three days later Chicago beat the expansion Cleveland Rams 15–7 to clinch the Western Division title once more. The Bears would close out the season with a meaningless game against the crosstown Cardinals. The outcome would not figure in the championship race, as the Bears, 8–1–1, had already clinched the title. The 5–4–1 Cardinals were merely playing for fourth place. But the game at Comiskey Park was one that would never be forgotten.

The storm hit Chicago Friday afternoon, and it was as relentless as Nagurski. A thick, gnarly rime of ice covered the field from the outfield wall at the north end zone all the way to the opposite thirty-yard line, a distance of eighty yards.

Needless to say, Bears equipment manager Rennie Wykowski had an ample supply of sneakers. From early November until the end of the season, the Bears never left town without them. The Cardinals were familiar with the fate suffered by Halas's team at the 1934 championship game. There was a pair of sneakers waiting in every locker when the Cardinals players arrived for the game.

But neither ice skates nor snowshoes would have helped this day. The mere act of running on and off the field caused players to slip and fall.

Hands and faces were bleeding. Nagurski, with his low center of gravity, rumbled up and down the field as if powered by malamutes. But the lighter backs were hitting the ice every other step. Heavy and out-of-shape linemen who lacked athleticism often rolled around on the frozen ground.

It was amazing that any fans showed up at all. The ones who did converted Comiskey Park into a devil's playground. Practically everyone who passed through the turnstiles was packing a flask. Before the first quarter was over, they were breaking the wooden bleacher seats apart and setting them on fire. Bonfires sprang up across Comiskey.

"Those damn Cardinal fans," George Halas yelled from the sideline, shaking his fist.

"Uh, coach," said Carl Brumbaugh, "I think those are our fans starting the fires."

Halas had counted on a good gate and a solid payday for the regular season finale. He desperately needed it. He knew that Nagurski was going to demand a healthy raise and that he might bolt if he didn't get it. *Ring Magazine* had already speculated that Nagurski was bound to seek riches as a full-time wrestler.

Halas was in a foul mood from the opening kickoff. Though he respected Cardinals owner Charles Bidwell, who had loaned him money to save the franchise in 1933, he hated coach Milan Creighton, whom he considered a punk. Now Creighton was arguing call after call with referee Bobie Cahn, and Halas was getting fed up. Without warning, Papa Bear charged across the field and engaged Creighton in a nose-to-nose argument. Then Halas threw a punch that grazed Creighton's cheek and set off the kind of flailing normally reserved for the schoolground. Neither coach landed a blow. But Halas did uncork a haymaker that missed Creighton and floored Cahn. The little referee was lying on his backside when he grabbed his flag and threw it at Halas, smacking him on the nose.

"You are out of the game this time, George," Cahn shouted.

"You couldn't get me out of here with the Third Army," Halas shot back.

"I'll call the cops."

"No, you won't. They're on my payroll."

It took Halas ten minutes to persuade Cahn to let him stay.

When things settled down, the game developed into a scoring fest that no one ever could have predicted. As it turned out, every advantage belonged to the offensive players. They at least knew where they were trying to go.

Both teams racked up passing yards as if the sky were blue and the field as solid as a paved highway. Either Masterson or Nagurski was completing a pass on every down, and the Cardinals' rookie combination of Coffee-to-Tinsley was lighting up the other side of the scoreboard. The Bears led 42–21 when darkness fell like a black curtain over the South Side. All that could be seen from the grandstand or the press box were the white pants belonging to the Cardinals. In the reflection of the bonfires, a white fleck streaked from one end zone to the other. It was Tinsley going ninety-five yards for a touchdown. Even the officials were not certain what had happened until Tinsley handed Cahn the ball and told him that he had crossed the goal line with it. Cahn awarded the Cardinals an automatic extra point and ended the game with two minutes and fifty-one seconds remaining. No one complained. The players were lucky the game had been played at all, and even more fortunate that they had set NFL records for total points scored (70), passes attempted (64) and completed (30), and total passing yards (501). It was a freakish way for the Western Division schedule to end. But it could not compete with what was going down in New York City.

On the eve of the Giants-Redskins regular season finale, which would determine the Eastern Division champion, thousands of fans boarded a specially chartered zephyr and roared north from Washington into Pennsylvania Station. Also aboard was the hundred-piece Redskins marching band and, quite naturally, leading the entire brigade was none other than George Preston Marshall.

Upon arrival, the Redskins band led the charge up Broadway behind Marshall in his trademark raccoon coat. They were followed by ten thousand screaming fans. Bill Corum of the *New York Journal-American* wrote, "George Preston Marshall slipped unobtrusively into New York today at the head of a hundred-piece band."

Marshall had finally found an audience that appreciated his antics. Just two weeks earlier, he had arranged for Santa Claus to parachute into Griffith Stadium in Washington. All the children in the stadium were quite disappointed when a gust of wind snatched Santa's chute and lifted the big, bearded cherub over the right-field wall and out of sight.

For years, the Giants and their fans had castigated Marshall. Owen had said during the '36 season that he welcomed any coaching Marshall might do from the sideline because "it's worth at least a couple of touchdowns for us."

But Owen really hit a nerve with comments made before the game that would decide the Eastern Division championship of '37: "I don't think the Redskins are in the same league with us," he said. Owen also revealed to the press that he had failed to include a single Washington player on his All-Pro ballot—snubbing Cliff Battles, Sammy Baugh, and Turk Edwards. That was a mistake. Even as a rookie, Baugh was the greatest quarterback ever to grace the NFL. His confidence knew no bounds. During practice one afternoon Ray Flaherty was explaining a certain pass play: "After you fake to the fullback, you wheel and throw and hit the receiver squarely in the eye. You get it?"

"Yeah," Baugh said. "But which eye?"

The Redskins held a 21–14 lead in the third quarter when Baugh started threading the eye of the needle. In a stretch of ten minutes, he completed eleven of fifteen passes for 128 yards, and Battles returned an interception seventy-five yards for a touchdown. Four quick touchdowns routed the Giants. The 49–21 final was a stinging reminder that Washington had its share of All-Pros. Stanley Woodward wrote in the *Herald Tribune,* "The Giants used a 5–3–2–1 defense. They should have used a 12–7–5–4." For all the Giants knew, the Indians had come back to claim Manhattan Island.

George Halas read the game stories in all six Chicago dailies that Monday morning and prayed for another ice storm.

• • •

As the Bears and Redskins prepared to play for the '37 championship, Halas decided that the easiest route to victory would be to knock Baugh out of the game.

The rules at the time stated that the quarterback was fair game until the play ended and the whistle blew. Just because the quarterback had released the ball did not mean the defense could no longer hit him. It meant that if Baugh unloaded a ninety-nine-yard touchdown pass, enemy defenders could whale on him until the receiver crossed the goal.

Halas planned to take advantage of those rules.

"I want you to hit that sonofabitch until blood is coming out of his ears," Halas told the Bears when they gathered for practice Tuesday morning.

But Baugh was a pretty tough cookie. A sixty-minute man himself, Baugh never ducked or dodged when he lined up on defense at safety in spite of weighing only 185 pounds. He was known for hammering ball carriers and had led the league in interceptions with six. A popular tactic against Washington was for the lead blocker to set his sights on Baugh and no one else. Knock him out of the game and the Redskins were through. But Baugh, in spite of a tender knee, was as resilient as West Texas cactus.

The secret to staying healthy as an NFL quarterback was to remain kinetic. Baugh's passing style allowed him to throw the ball from any posture, and he was also the master of passing on the run. This would come in handy, since the Bears planned to harass him to hell and back. They would hurt him if the opportunity arose. And they would have plenty of chances. Because Baugh played tailback in the single-wing offense, he was often called upon to run the ball and, on other plays, to block the defensive end. He had grown all too accustomed to the "bootsie" play in which the defense would gang up on one man. That one man wore thirty-three—Baugh's number.

But Baugh was no quitter. Instead of "Slingin' Sam" his Redskins teammates called him "Fighting Legs," because he was always fighting to the end of the game and was the maestro of the fourth-quarter comeback.

More ice and snow fell upon Chicago three days before the championship game. The mercury was dipping below zero at night, meaning the winter precipitation was sticking and holding like glue. Asphalt burners that were used in road construction were brought to Wrigley Field. The fire-spreading machines were driven up and down the field to thaw the ice. Then a thick coat of hay was spread over the field to soak up the water. Workers spent the better part of the day covering the entire playing surface with a tarpaulin. No one was sure these methods would work because field maintenance in 1937 was still undeveloped. But the field was greatly improved by Sunday, with only a few splotches of ice.

Halas's pregame pep talk was to the point: "You can have a session with your girlfriend, and how long does that last? Twenty minutes? But a win in the National Football League is a thrill that lasts a whole week. And what a thrill!"

The Redskins would receive the kickoff at the north end of the field, which abutted the outfield wall. Baugh surveyed that end of the field and noted there was more ice than at the south end. His receivers would be able to avoid the ice patches but perhaps the defensive backs who were backpedaling would not.

Jack Manders's opening kickoff was a line drive that slipped through the fingers of Cliff Battles and bounded between the legs of Ernie Pinckert. It was finally fielded by Max Krause at the one-yard line, where he was smothered by a pack of Bears. Baugh smiled. The Redskins had the Bears exactly where they wanted them.

It was Baugh's job at tailback to take the snap from center and to be the triggerman of the offense. But it was not his job to call the plays. That responsibility belonged to Riley Smith, who held the title of quarterback but was really nothing more than a blocking back. So it was not uncommon for Baugh to offer an opinion on the play calling or to take over the show altogether.

In the huddle Baugh said, "We're gonna trick 'em. I'm dropping into punt formation. But I ain't punting. Cliff, see that chunk of ice right over there. Run straight to it, cut to the sideline, and look for the ball."

Baugh was the first quarterback in the history of pro football not afraid to pass on any down. Now he was standing in punt formation in his own end zone, though, and the Bears never figured his intent was to pass. Battles ran his appointed route past Bears halfback Gene Ronzani, who slipped on the slick spot and fell. Battles caught the pass over his right shoulder and roared up the sideline for a forty-three-yard gain.

Halas almost had a conniption on the sideline, throwing his fedora ten feet onto the field.

"That's a goddamned rookie pulling that crap," he yelled at the defense. "You're not playing like the Chicago *Bears!*"

On their next possession, the Redskins breezed down the field as Baugh completed four straight passes. From the Chicago ten-yard line, Battles took the handoff on the reverse around right end and scored easily.

The Bears responded in typical fashion. Nagurski carried the ball six straight times, all the way to the Washington forty-yard line. Then he tore through a large hole opened by Musso. One man stood in his path, and he was wearing number thirty-three. Nagurski lowered his shoulder and exploded into the rail-thin Baugh, sending him head over heels. The trainers came running with smelling salts.

"That sonofabitch ran plumb over me," Baugh said. "And he didn't even need no blocker in front of him." Baugh pledged to himself that he would simply try to slow Nagurski the next time while waiting for reinforcements. Jack Manders rushed for a ten-yard score and made the point-after as the Bears tied it up.

The woozy Washington passer was unable to muster a drive on the next possession and was intercepted by end George Wilson at the Redskins forty-nine. On the next play, Masterson hit a streaking Manders over the middle at the twenty, and a block by Wilson on Battles provided clear sailing. Manders's touchdown and point-after made it 14–7, a score that stood at halftime.

In the second half, the Bears could not control Baugh and were having even more trouble with end Wayne Millner. The former Notre Dame star thrived on clutch catches. He had single-handedly won the 1935 Ohio State game with a leaping one-handed grab at the back of the end zone. Now, on the fourth play of the third quarter, Baugh sent Millner on a pattern past a patch of ice. Ray Nolting slipped as he was making the cut, and Millner grabbed the pass at the sideline and sprinted fifty-five yards to the end zone.

The Bears came fighting back. Manske scored on a four-yard reception. Chicago led 21–14 after Manders's PAT.

That lead stood up less than twenty seconds. After the kickoff was returned to the twenty-two-yard line, Baugh lofted a rainbow for Millner, who was ten yards behind the Bears secondary and off to the races. The score was tied again.

As might be expected, all eyes were on Millner as the Redskins drove deeper and deeper into Chicago territory late in the third quarter. Baugh jumped high in the air and pump-faked to Millner. With his feet back on the ground, Baugh pivoted and fired to a wide-open Ed "Chug" Justice in the left corner of the end zone. The Redskins led 28–21.

The Bears had tried every means at their disposal to put Baugh out of commission. He was limping with a bad knee and hip, and blood was trickling from his nose; his jersey was turning crimson. But there was no stopping him. When Dick Plasman caught a pass from Masterson and took off down the sideline, Baugh caught up with the Bears end and blasted him out of bounds. Plasman, who did not wear a helmet, landed on top of his head. He whirled and punched Baugh in the face. That was a mistake. It happened in front of the Washington bench, and the Redskins swarmed Plasman. As the players piled on Plasman, fans came pouring out of the stands. It appeared the riot was on. Washington guard Eddie "King Kong" Kahn found himself at the bottom of the pile with cleats in his face. Nagurski ran into the melee and started pulling bodies off the stack. It took Nagurski, the cops, and a bevy of Wrigley Field ushers about three minutes to stop the fight.

Plasman left the fracas with a bloody nose, gashed eye, and split lip. Much to the Bears' chagrin, Baugh came away unscathed—at least, he had suffered no further damage.

With only seconds remaining in the game, the Bears seemed saved when Masterson spotted a wide-open Les McDonald at the Washington thirty-two-yard line. No one stood between the Bears backup end and the goal. But McDonald became tangled with back judge Ed Cochrane, a sportswriter with the *Chicago Tribune* who moonlighted as an official. Cochrane was limping on a sprained knee and lost his balance as his cleats found an icy area of the field. By the time McDonald freed himself of Cochrane, Battles and Baugh were rushing up from behind. They caught McDonald just as the final gun sounded. The Redskins slipped out of Wrigley Field with a 28–21 victory.

Baugh had completed seventeen of thirty-four passes for 358 yards in the greatest passing performance in the history of the game. But the play he would never forget was being leveled by Nagurski.

As the players left the field, the Bronk extended his hand to Slingin' Sam. "You're a fine fella and a great quarterback," Nagurski said.

"May I ask you a question?" Baugh said.

"Sure."

"Why don't they put a blocker out in front of you?"

"I don't need one. Besides, George told me to run over your ass."

"You dang sure did that."

• • •

Nagurski and Halas scheduled a meeting for the next morning to discuss a new contract. Rumors were flying that Nagurski was finished with football. Tony Stecher had promised "millions" if the Bronk would hang up his cleats and take to the mat full time.

"How much will it take, Bronko?" Halas asked

"Sixty-five hundred."

"I'm offering six."

"I want sixty-five hundred."

"You'll walk over five hundred and go stinking wrestle?"

"Yes."

Halas tried to control his temper, but his voice was rising.

"You're the best football player I've ever seen. And you're stupid if you walk away." It was the first time Halas had ever raised his voice to this man. He was already regretting it.

Nagurski, in his heart, loved Halas. He appreciated him as a great coach and a leader of men. He was certain that no greater mentor existed in the game of football. But enough was enough.

"I'm through, George," he said.

He picked up his suitcase and walked through the door. Halas's eyes locked on the back of his powerful shoulders as Nagurski strode down the sidewalk toward Michigan Avenue, where he would turn right and head for the Illinois Central Station. Halas wondered if he would ever see the Bronk again.

He told himself no.

• • •

When the news arrived in Detroit, Lions owner George Richards jumped from his chair and banged the top of the desk.

"By God, the king is dead!" he yelled. "We're going to win us another championship."

George Preston Marshall was apprised of Nagurski's decision when he arrived at Union Station in the District of Columbia. The Redskins band was coming off the train and starting to assemble when the wild-eyed owner started waving his arms. "Play something!" he demanded. "Anything! Nagurski has just retired!"

The banner headline in the *Chicago Tribune* read, NAGURSKI RETIRES AT PEAK OF CAREER.

Red Grange opened his daily radio show in Chicago by saying, "Bronko Nagurski was the greatest football player who ever lived. He was the best I have ever seen. Football will never be the same without him."

# 17

# Hunk

George Halas flew into a rage on the opening day of the 1940 season.
"Dammit," he yelled from the sideline. "This wouldn't be happening if Nagurski were here."

Assistant coach Hunk Anderson, standing behind Halas, cleared his throat.

"Uh, George," he said. "I don't know if you've checked the scoreboard lately. But we're winning by twenty points."

"Yeah, and if Nagurski were here, we'd be winning by forty!"

Halas had never fully recovered from the break-up with his favorite player. There had been no word from Nagurski in three years—not even a postcard from the road. He had recently won his second world championship belt by defeating Lou Thesz, and no one figured he would ever come back.

Without Nagurski, the Bears had fallen to 6–5 in 1938 and completed the '39 season with an 8–3 record. New York and Green Bay now were the dominant teams in the NFL, having met in the championship game both years, with the Giants winning the first title and Green Bay taking the rematch.

Replacing Nagurski, a man who could carry an entire team on his broad shoulders, had been the toughest task imaginable. Halas had tried two fullbacks—Joe Maniaci, a hot-tempered midseason trade from the Brooklyn (football) Dodgers, and second-year player Sam Francis. Neither panned out.

The Bears had also dumped Beattie Feathers, trading him to the Brooklyn Dodgers for something akin to an air pump. After making history as the first player in pro football to gain more than a thousand yards in a single season, Feathers would need another six seasons to gain nine hundred more. He was never the same without Nagurski.

Bill Osmanski, drafted in the first round from Holy Cross in 1939, was now the Bears' fullback. He was not a Nagurski-like bruiser, but he possessed decent speed along with a penchant for breaking long runs. He gained 699 yards as a rookie with an impressive average gain of 5.8 yards.

The retirement of Nagurski had sent the Bears into a tailspin. But Halas's efforts to reconstruct the Bears had recently taken an upward turn. There were hints of a new dynasty on the rise. The Bears had drafted a little-known tailback from Columbia named Sid Luckman, who would be shifted to quarterback. Their top choice in 1940 had come from a distant place that few people in pro football circles had ever heard of— Hardin-Simmons College in Abilene, Texas. It didn't matter that Clyde "Bulldog" Turner was not exactly a household name, either. He was the center-linebacker that Halas had been praying for.

Halas had been loading up on rookie stars. But the most formidable addition of recent years was not a young stud from Alma Mater U. It was Heartley William "Hunk" Anderson, a forty-two-year-old jack-of-all-trades who was now the best line and defensive coach in the game. Here was a man whose résumé was so rich with football history that it was hard to imagine anyone covering so much ground in so little time.

Anderson's early football lessons had been learned from the legendary Knute Rockne back at Notre Dame, where Hunk was a guard on the Rock's first two undefeated teams in 1919 and '20. He was the Fighting Irish's second All-America behind George Gipp, and it was the Gipper himself who had recommended that Rockne recruit Anderson.

Hunk was Rockne's lone assistant coach through the fabled seasons of the twenties when the Four Horsemen rode across the American consciousness and the Fighting Irish won four national championships. Rockne, one of the game's greatest innovators and thinkers, depended on

Hunk to instill mettle in his players. Practice would start each day with Rockne giving preliminary instructions to the backs and ends while Hunk whipped the linemen into shape. Finally, the Rock would call out, "Ah, Heartley, would you be kind enough to bring the behemoths over here?"

"Hell, Rock," Hunk would say, "they ain't even bleeding yet."

Anderson had grown up leather tough on the Copper Peninsula of northern Michigan, where his parents stuck him with a given name that hardly inspired manliness—Heartley. Copper Peninsula is a rocky spur thrust into the icy water of Lake Superior, with villages like South Range and Trimountain carving out rugged images. Just up the road was the small town of Laurium, the birthplace of George Gipp, the name that would become the holiest of all in South Bend.

Gipp learned to play football in Calumet, where, each Saturday, the kids gathered for a bruising game on a cobblestone road. Gipp was the captain of his team and Anderson the captain of the other. Because the kids were too poor to afford a football, a pig's bladder would have to do. The boys were lucky if the start of the football season happened to coincide with a pig slaughtering or two.

After graduating from high school, Gipp took off for Notre Dame, and the boys living on the peninsula figured they would never see him again. Of course, they heard plenty about his exploits in sold-out stadiums from South Bend to Ann Arbor to West Point. After Gipp led Notre Dame to victory over Army, coach Charles Daly said, "Gipp is no football player. He's a runaway sonofabitch."

Hunk finished high school a year after Gipp left the Copper Peninsula. With no money and zero options for an education, he went to work first as a streetcar conductor and then as a chauffeur for a prominent mining executive. He somehow kept his athletic dreams alive by playing semipro baseball and football and boxing all over the state and was becoming known as the best amateur fighter in Michigan with an eye toward the pro game. That is when Gipp came home during the summer break and said that Rockne wanted to see him. Hunk packed a trunk and caught the electric train into downtown Calumet and got his teeth fixed. Then he rode the train all night to South Bend. George Gipp met him at the station. They strolled down Michigan Street with hopes of bumping into Rockne. They found him standing outside of Hullie and Mike's, a favorite watering hole.

"George here tells me you want to play football for us," said Rockne, sizing up the muscled boy. "We need some tough boys to play in the line."

"Mister Rockne, I am your man," Hunk said.

Rockne was not initially sold on this eighteen-year-old who stood but five-ten and weighed 170 pounds. Notre Dame had halfbacks that big. But there was a fire in the boy's eye that impressed the coach. Hunk was both a likable and a happy fellow. And he had a constant expression that said, "One wrong move and I'll knock your teeth out."

As they prepared for the first day of practice, Gipp provided some priceless advice to his friend: "Hunk, you will make a lot of friends here at Notre Dame. But once you get inside that green fence at Cartier Stadium, you've got to knock their asses off—and I'm talking about everybody."

That first practice, Rockne tried to demonstrate blocking techniques to Hunk, who knocked his coach down a total of six times. His scholarship was won that first day as the Rock started making plans for this boy with the razor's edge.

Anderson's most celebrated confrontation was with a Notre Dame center by the name of George "Brute" Trafton. They battled like baby bulls on the practice field, so Rockne asked them to fight on a charity boxing card for the South Bend Elks Club.

Hunk pounded Trafton mercilessly until his knees wobbled and he fell flat on his face. Blood was smeared all over the canvas. The other Irish players stood in awe of their new teammate. Trafton was considered the toughest man on the Notre Dame team and one of the meanest hombres anywhere. But Hunk pounded him into a piece of rubber. This freshman had iron deposits where most men had only muscle. He also possessed a thundering right hand that landed with the force of a slaughterhouse sledgehammer.

At a time when freshmen were eligible for the varsity, Anderson was a dead solid choice for the starting lineup. With Anderson blocking and Gipp running, the Irish sprinted to their first two national titles in 1919 and '20, making Notre Dame an overnight sensation. Oddly, baseball was the sport that had initially put Notre Dame on the map. But that would change as rapidly as the turning of the leaves in early October on the northern Indiana plains.

Rockne was obsessed with the teaching of sound fundamentals and the executing of plays. No man would make a greater impression on Hunk's life. So preoccupied was the Rock with teaching blocking techniques that his voice could be heard all the way across the Notre Dame campus on practice days. "Knock the bastards into the nickel seats," he bellowed. At the time, Rockne was also making a lasting impression on a halfback who played alongside Gipp. His name was Curly Lambeau.

Rockne did not suffer fools gladly, but it seemed he was always looking the other way as George Gipp drifted into a life of gambling, drinking, and womanizing. In truth, the Gipper was both an aloof and a troubled young man, and he bet on the very games he played. When Rockne once berated him at halftime for a lack of effort, the Gipper replied, "Look, Rock, I got four hundred bet on this game. I'm not about to blow it."

Downtown South Bend was filled with gambling halls and saloons. Gipp often vanished into that life for days without returning to campus. He sought out bookmakers and was not afraid to pull a wad of bills from his pocket and bet on the Irish games in broad daylight with a crowd watching. Gipp was an accomplished poker player who won hundreds of dollars in the all-night gambling orgies. At Christmas break in 1919 he filled two suitcases with bottles of booze that he planned to sell back in Calumet. He put the suitcases under the seat of the train. Two railroad inspectors boarded the train and one asked, "What's in those suitcases?"

"Just our clothes," Anderson said. The inspectors moved along without checking the trunks. The boys were lucky. Otherwise they might have spent a few nights in the local jail. Gipp took his bootleg booze to Calumet and made a nice profit over the holidays.

Hunk kept his nose clean at Notre Dame and worked diligently toward his degree in engineering. Though the cabs and trolleys ran constantly from the campus to the devil's dens around South Bend, Hunk never made the trip. His sights were set on becoming the next Rockne. Meanwhile, the Gipper sank deeper into his secret world. Soon his health would decline to the point where he had to be hospitalized. Two days before Thanksgiving in 1920, he was admitted to St. Joseph's Hospital in South Bend complaining of a tender throat and chills. Fans in East Lansing were sorely disappointed that he missed the final game of the season against Michigan State. At first his illness was not considered serious. But his condition would change within hours. Newspapers across the country carried daily updates on his pneumonia as cards and telegrams flooded into the hospital. Businesses came to a standstill in South Bend as crowds gathered on street corners waiting for the next bulletin from the hospital. For the next two weeks, Gipp's medical status was like a roller coaster. Doctors managed to gain control of his pneumonia and the raging fever. But two days later he relapsed. Rockne paid one of his several visits to the hospital on the night of December 14. Supposedly, Gipp told his coach, "Rock, when the team's up against it, when things are wrong and the breaks are beating the boys—tell them to go in there with all they've got and win one for the Gipper."

Hours after making that dramatic plea, Gipp died. Rockne would save his famous "Gipper speech" for several years until the 1928 Notre Dame–Army game when he told the team about the deathbed scene. After hearing Rockne holler, "Go out there and win one for the Gipper!" the Irish stormed onto the field and whipped the Cadets 12–6. Somewhere, George Gipp must have been smiling.

Hunk would become Notre Dame's next All-America the year after Gipp's death. Then he was off to the National Football League. George Halas liked him from the moment he saw him. Hunk, with his hard-fisted style, was a perfect fit for the Bears. During the Red Grange tour in 1925, he was the only player on the roster who remained injury-free throughout the grueling eighteen-game marathon and played every position on the field. Hunk possessed the constitution of an ox. He would work for ten hours a day at Edwards Iron Works in South Bend and then hustle out to the campus to assist Rockne. On Saturdays Anderson stood on the sideline with Rockne during the Notre Dame games. Then he would catch a train to Chicago to play for the Bears on Sunday.

The Rock, in spite of not paying Anderson a penny, insisted that he quit the Bears, citing the poor moral standards of the pro league. The Notre Dame coach crusaded against the NFL at every turn. He railed against the practice of signing collegiate players before graduation. The Rock failed to mention, however, that he had played and coached professional football under several aliases back in 1915 and 1916 while still a member of the Notre Dame team.

Rockne would surprise Anderson by calling him into his office in 1928 and informing him that he had been hired as the head coach of St. Louis University for the princely sum of $8,500 a year.

When Rockne's plane went down in the spring of 1931, Hunk was regarded as the natural successor. He took over a program that had not lost a home game in twenty-seven years but was now on the brink of change. With Rockne no longer around, the priests were able to regain control of the program. They began to slash scholarships, saying that football did nothing to promote academics, and they further cut Anderson's resources. But that did not stop the priests from coming around to watch practice. Most wore earmuffs, even in the heat of September, to muffle the expletives that flew from the mouth of their colorful coach.

As money was subtracted from the football budget, Hunk found himself operating with far less clout than Rockne had enjoyed. When the Irish compiled a .640 winning percentage over the next four years, he was forced to take the fall. The firing came after the 1934 season.

He would be the head coach at North Carolina State the next five years before serving a stint as the line coach at Michigan. In the college ranks, he had been tinkering with a defensive maneuver known as the "red dog." "Red" meant "be alert" and "dog" meant "hound the quarterback."

The Detroit Lions came calling in 1939. The timing of Anderson's return to the NFL could not have been better, as more teams were embracing the passing game. That season, Anderson introduced the red dog to the NFL, and it soon became known as the "blitz." It changed the game forever. Rushing a linebacker to red dog the quarterback was an instant success. The offense was suddenly forced to block seven rushers with six blockers. It was not long before Hunk introduced the safety blitz.

Anderson revolutionized defensive philosophy, too. He allowed Lions linebackers and safeties to initiate the action. Previously, they were merely reactors. Now, under his tutelage, they were forcing the action and pressing the game. Much of his philosophy had been developed while watching Nagurski patrol the field at linebacker, wrecking everything in sight.

That season of 1939, using Anderson's defense, the Lions held Halas's modernized T-formation to an all-time low of fifty-six yards. Anderson's creative defensive concepts contributed greatly to the 10–0 victory, but his fighting spirit went a long way toward producing the shutout.

Minutes before kickoff, he gathered the Lions around him and said, "I want seven men to line up against the Bears line. And when the ball is snapped, I want every man to slug the man in front of him. The worst we can get is a fifteen-yard penalty. Whether one slugs, or seven slugs, the most we can get is fifteen yards."

Of course, if Nagurski had been in that line, the Lions would have had a fight on their hands.

On the first play of the game, all you could hear was bang, bang, bang, all the way down the line of scrimmage. At a time when face masks still were not in use, the Bears front line was left with bloodied lips and noses. George Musso, in fact, did not wear a helmet at all in 1939. "Jumbo" Joe Stydahar had to leave the game as blood was pouring from his mouth and nose.

The Lions were penalized fifteen yards, moving the ball to the Chicago thirty-five-yard line. Then, to the amazement of everyone, including the Lions, Anderson ordered more punches to be thrown. Blood was spilled once more, and another fifteen-yard penalty was marked off. With the ball now at midfield, Anderson yelled, "Do it again!" By now the Bears were fighting back. But the referee still penalized Detroit for unnecessary roughness. The fighting finally stopped at the thirty-five-yard line, which also happened to represent the deepest offensive penetration of the day for the Chicago Bears.

After being whipped and held scoreless by the Lions, Halas was left scratching his head. That is when he decided to employ one of his oldest tricks: "When you can't beat them, hire them," he always said. Halas then proceeded to outbid Detroit for Anderson's services for the 1940 season.

Early in the season, Hunk was around Detroit for the heavyweight title fight between Joe Louis and Bob Pastor. Louis had avenged his 1936 loss to Max Schmeling in 1938 by bludgeoning the big German to the canvas in the first minute of the opening round and winning the fight in slightly over two minutes.

During the week before the big boxing match in Detroit, Hunk was invited by his good friend Grantland Rice to a cocktail party that would be attended by both fighters and several members of the sporting press. He seemed to be having a good time until Henry McLemore, a noted writer, said something that provoked him. Punches flew. As Rice described the scene, "McLemore was bouncing off the floor like a tennis ball." After disposing of the writer, Hunk decided to take on the entire room. He challenged Louis, and then invited both Louis and Pastor for a two-on-one. Rice managed to calm down his friend before he busted up the place.

The Anderson spirit is what Halas wanted to bottle. Then he wanted to inoculate his Bears with it. Paddy Driscoll once said, "Hunk Anderson would have been in his element in the Roman Colosseum—and God help the lions!"

• • •

It was all coming together even without Nagurski. The Bears led the Packers 20–0 in the opening game of the 1940 season and rookie halfback George McAfee had already accounted for three touchdowns. Anderson had the defense performing at its highest level since Nagurski's departure. The T-formation had been revamped with an emphasis on the man in motion. Luckman was rapidly making the transition from a single-wing college tailback to the man under center, thanks to the tutoring of quarterbacks coach Carl Brumbaugh, the first man to master the position back in the early thirties.

On the opening kickoff against Green Bay, McAfee had galloped ninety-three yards for a touchdown. The defending world champions were not ready for the swift rookie from Duke, who also passed for a second touchdown to Ken Kavanaugh and ran nine yards for a third. After seeing McAfee's debut with the Bears, former Bears great Red Grange would say, "He's the most dangerous man with a football under his arm in the game today."

McAfee was merely one of many stars from the rookie class of '40. Kavanaugh, the Louisiana State All-America end, would soon make his mark as one of the best receivers in the game. Bulldog Turner, the center from West Texas, was inspiring comparisons to Mel Hein, the Giants' All-Pro.

Halfback Ray Nolting was not to be outdone by the rookies. He returned the second-half kickoff against Green Bay ninety-seven yards for a touchdown. The Bears swamped the Packers 41–10 in the most lopsided game in the history of the rivalry. One of Anderson's first assignments when he was hired back by the Bears was to write a report on precisely how he had shut down the offense the previous season. Halas admitted that he learned a lot from that evaluation, and it was now apparent that he had made good use of it.

It would be written in virtually every newspaper in the country that the Monsters of the Midway were back. Without Nagurski, though, Halas still had his doubts.

After Green Bay, the Bears would play an oddly scheduled game the following Wednesday night under the lights at Comiskey Park. They would meet a Cardinals team that had been the dregs of the NFL the last fifteen years. It was surprising that Charlie Bidwell's team had even survived the Depression. They had enjoyed just two winning seasons since 1925, finishing the previous season with a 1–10 record under the guidance of former playing great Ernie Nevers.

When Nevers bailed out, Bidwell hired a man who had turned him down twice—a man once described by George Strickler of the *Chicago Tribune* as "an actor who writes and coaches." Jimmy Conzelman was both eccentric and unpredictable. He did not seem to be the right fit for pro football. He seemed more interested in directing civic operas. He warmed up for the '40 season by playing a supporting role in *Good News,* a production of the St. Louis Civic Theatre.

For years the Cardinals had been labeled lazy and disorganized. The public suspected that owner Bidwell actually loved the Bears more than his own team because of his longtime friendship with Halas. And there was no reason to suspect that Conzelman would improve the situation. The Cardinals' best player, Marshall Goldberg, almost quit the game when he learned that a part-time actor had been hired to lead the ragtag Cardinals. Team morale continued to slide when summer training camp was moved from the cool, crisp air of Duluth, Minnesota, to the hot and steamy South Side of Chicago. Times were so tough that the Cardinals could barely afford enough footballs to conduct a decent camp.

But the players quickly bonded with the likable Conzelman. He won them over with his quick wit. He turned out to be a disciplinarian and a stickler for detail. But he also knew how to lighten the atmosphere with a wink or a joke.

After winning but one game against the Bears the last decade, the Cardinals were established as the 5–1 underdog by local bookies. Then came the shock. The Cardinals won the game 21–7. Hugh McCullough opened the game with a touchdown pass to John Hall, and the scrappy little Goldberg ran seven yards for another to make it 14–0. The Bears cut the lead to 14–7 on a ten-yard touchdown run by fullback Bill Osmanski. But the Cardinals were fortunate to have receiver Gus Tinsley back in the lineup. Tinsley, after setting five NFL records in his first two seasons, had taken off for his native Louisiana to coach high school football. He came back at the behest of Conzelman. His ten-yard touchdown reception in the fourth quarter sealed the victory.

The Superman image of the Bears had been shattered.

Halas had work to do. The Bears would not play another game for eleven days, and Papa Bear spent the time trying to motivate his players. He would begin pep talks by saying, "Let me tell you about the old days with Nagurski . . ."

The Bears would defeat the Cleveland Rams 21–14 and reel off four more victories over Detroit, Brooklyn, New York, and Green Bay.

Chicago was 6–1 and atop the Western Division standings. But coming up next was the annual blood-and-guts game in Detroit. This one was not played on Thanksgiving, but it still drew a capacity crowd to Detroit University Stadium, along with a national radio audience.

In spite of this resurgence, luck did not favor the Bears in 1940—at least not during the regular season. They blew a touchdown against the Lions in the fleeting seconds of the first half when they were unable to get off one final play. Harry Clark had carried the ball to within inches of the goal and was tackled by an alert Les McDonald, who pinned the Chicago end to the ground as precious time ticked away. Eggs Manske tried to pry McDonald off his teammate and was flagged for a fifteen-yard penalty. Luckman's last pass before halftime fell incomplete in the end zone.

Still, the Bears were leading the game 14–10 late in the fourth quarter when Cotton Price heaved a desperation pass to Lloyd Cardwell, who broke through four tackles and covered seventy yards as time expired. Detroit 17, Chicago 14.

The upcoming game between the Bears and the Redskins in the nation's capital was billed as a preview of the 1940 championship game, and rightly so. The Redskins were 7–1 and Chicago stood at 6–2. The sellout crowd of thirty-six thousand fans at Griffith Stadium expected a high-scoring game from the two leading offensive units in the NFL. Instead, they saw Baugh twice boom punts of more than seventy yards. They saw the defensive units control the game. Hunk Anderson's red-dog rushes befuddled Baugh, who spent most of the afternoon scrambling for his life.

The only touchdown pass of the day was thrown, not by Luckman or Baugh, but by Frank Filchock. The halfback was sweeping right end when he hesitated and tossed eighteen yards to Dick Todd at the back of the end zone. The Redskins led 7–3 with forty seconds to play. That is when Bears backup quarterback Bob Snyder stepped into the huddle and told George McAfee, "Head for the goal line and I will hit you with the ball."

Simple as that, Snyder took the snap at midfield and looped the pass to McAfee at the fifteen-yard line. It appeared that nothing could stop the fastest man in the NFL. But Redskins halfback Dick Todd tripped him from behind at the three-yard line and he fell inches short of the goal. Then the referee assessed the Bears a five-yard penalty for faking an injury. In fact, McAfee had badly sprained his ankle and had to be helped off the field before another play could be run. Snyder's final pass of the game for Osmanski was perfect, but Filchock pinioned the receiver's arms from behind and the pass fell incomplete.

It was obvious to most people in the stadium, including the sportswriters, that the Redskins were guilty of blatant pass interference. The Bears vehemently protested the fact that no flags were thrown, and Halas dashed onto the field and stomped about like a mad bantam rooster. It did no good. The game was lost. Chicago had fallen.

The Bears were devastated. Some of the players cried as they walked down the ramp toward the locker room. Bulldog Turner approached Baugh and said, "Just remember, we will be seeing you bastards in three weeks. Don't forget that."

Baugh knew better than to rub it in. Chicago was the team that he respected more than any other. The Bears had battered and bruised him black and blue. It would take days to recover from the soreness inflicted by the likes of Joe Stydahar, George Musso, and Turner.

Washington owner George Preston Marshall couldn't care less. Marshall never thought twice about the things he said. When Halas and the

Chicago players complained to the press about the controversial no-call on pass interference, Marshall went ballistic.

"They are nothing but a bunch of goddamned crybabies," he said. "Crybabies, crybabies, crybabies."

Pressed further by reporters, Marshall said, "They are a bunch of quitters. They fold up when the going gets tough. Just look at what they did today. They quit. They don't know how to win a close game."

Baugh and his teammates cringed when they read those quotes in the Monday morning newspapers. They knew the Bears would expend every ounce of energy to win the final two games against Cleveland and the Cardinals. Predictably, the Bears breezed through the final two weeks, and the Washington-Chicago championship game was set for December 8 at Griffith Park. The grudge match was on.

As if Marshall had not inflicted enough damage, he fired off a telegram to Halas that read: CONGRATULATIONS. YOU GOT ME IN THIS THING AND I HOPE I HAVE THE PLEASURE OF BEATING YOUR EARS OFF NEXT SUNDAY AND EVERY YEAR TO COME. JUSTICE IS TRIUMPHANT. WE SHOULD PLAY FOR THE CHAMPIONSHIP EVERY YEAR. GAME WILL BE SOLD OUT BY TUESDAY. RIGHT REGARDS, GEORGE.

Halas was in a rage. He would not rest until the Redskins had been buried. Ten hours a day, the Bears were either locked in meetings or out on the practice field. Halas was the first coach in the history to use game film as a teaching tool, and in the week leading to the title game he almost wore out the projector. Players were given written examinations on every assignment. Clark Shaughnessy worked around the clock culling plays from the playbook and adding others that would take advantage of Ray Flaherty's defense.

The two-day train ride from Chicago to Washington was eerily quiet. Players studied their playbooks. Not a single hand of cards was played.

Halas was the first one to the stadium Sunday morning, and he spent more than an hour pasting newspaper clippings to the locker-room walls. All of the quotes uttered by Marshall in the last three weeks were in plain view. Marshall's latest offering concerned the 7–5 betting line that favored the Bears: "That is ridiculous," he said. "We already beat them. The bookmakers must be crazy."

In the final minutes leading to kickoff, Chicago's locker room was library-quiet. Then Halas stood up and addressed the team.

"Gentlemen, that is what George Preston Marshall thinks of you," he said, pointing to the walls. "That is what the people of Washington think of you. Now go out there and show the world that you are not a bunch of quitters. But before you do that, listen to what Shaughnessy has to say."

Normally, the assistant coach consultant was not called upon for pregame speeches. Shaughnessy was a cold and distant man with virtually no personality. He often locked himself in his office for entire days to study film and to plan strategy. He rarely spoke to the players unless it was during a meeting. His lectures were so boring that many fell asleep during the meetings only to be awakened by a well-aimed piece of chalk.

But when Shaughnessy stepped to the chalkboard in the minutes leading to kickoff, something was different about him. The players could see a glint in his eye.

As he drew up the first play of the game, he said, "Men, I promise you this one will go for a touchdown. And if it doesn't work, I've got another one coming up that will." Just like that, Shaughnessy introduced the modern pro set with two backs and two ends split.

On the first play of the game, George Wilson, the left end, was flex to the left, and left halfback Ray Nolting went into motion to his right and settled into his stance as the right flanker. Right halfback George McAfee carried eight yards to the Chicago thirty-two-yard line.

In truth, it was the second play of the game that had Shaughnessy excited. From the same formation, Osmanski took the handoff at left tackle and cut outside the block of end George Wilson. Showing a typical burst of speed, Osmanski shot up the field behind a block by pulling guard George Musso and was sprinting down the sideline before the Redskins could react. At the Washington thirty-five-yard line, two defenders were closing in. Remarkably, Wilson caught up with the play and slammed into defensive back Ed "Chug" Justice, who then rolled like a bowling ball into teammate Jimmy Johnston. Both Redskins were knocked flat, and Osmanski continued his merry course down the sideline to the end zone. The Bears led 7–0.

It seemed that Baugh would match the score two minutes later when he threw a perfect pass to a wide-open Charlie Malone at the five-yard line. But Malone dropped the ball.

Reminiscent of the Nagurski days, the Bears rolled eighty yards to the end zone on seventeen plays without throwing a pass. Luckman churned the final yard on a quarterback sneak behind Bulldog Turner's block, and the Bears had a 14–0 lead. Minutes later, the lead increased to 21–0 when fullback Joe Maniaci rumbled forty-two yards on the exact play used by Osmanski for the opening touchdown. Before the half ended, Kavanaugh caught a thirty-yard touchdown pass from Luckman. The score was 28–zip at intermission.

The snowball was just beginning to roll. Hampton Pool intercepted a Baugh pass and returned it fifteen yards for a touchdown to start the second half. Ray Nolting scored on a twenty-three-yard run, and McAfee returned an interception thirty-five yards for a touchdown. Then Turner also returned an interception, galloping twenty yards for the score. At the end of the third quarter the score was 54–0.

But the Bears weren't done yet. Less than five minutes into the fourth quarter, Harry Clark scored on a forty-four-yard double reverse and the lead was 60–0. Just then came an announcement over the public address system: "Hey, fans," came the brassy voice, "it's time to start thinking about purchasing those season tickets for next year––" The rest was drowned out by the boos and catcalls.

Not only were the fans flooding toward the gates but the officials were running out of footballs. Nine had sailed into the stands on extra points, and none was returned.

Bob Snyder, the holder on place kicks, reported from the sideline and stepped into the huddle. He said to Turner, "George says make a bad snap. We're running out of footballs."

Turner barked back, "Tell George Halas to go to hell. I ain't ever made a bad snap in my life and never will. It's coming straight back to you. If you don't want the dang ball kicked up in the stands, then just drop the dang thing."

Snyder did, and the extra point failed. The Bears would throw the ball for PATs after the last two touchdowns. The final score was 73–0. Nothing would ever compare to it. Fans from coast to coast were astounded to hear the news.

Marshall stormed into the locker room after the game and shouted to the press, "My players quit. They are yellow. There'll be plenty of new faces around here next year."

A reporter asked Baugh what he thought would have happened if Malone had caught the early touchdown pass. "The score would have been 73–7," he said.

Halas and the Bears danced in the other locker room.

"Thank God for George Marshall and his big mouth," Halas told reporters.

Red Smith wrote the next day in the *Philadelphia Record,* "George Preston Marshall, the meddlesome laundryman who owned the Redskins, looked on from the stands—except when he turned his back to charge up the aisle and throw a punch at a dissatisfied customer—and when his ordeal was over, every hair in his raccoon coat had turned white."

It was the Bears' first NFL title in the post-Nagurski era.

# 18

# The Return

Life in America in 1943 was changing by the minute as World War II raged in Europe and the South Pacific. This was especially evident with the National Football League, an institution built on muscle, grit, and testosterone. Nowhere could you find better-qualified citizen-soldiers than the NFL.

League owners initially considered suspending the games for the '43 season as the war escalated and players started trading their helmets and shoulder pads for rifles and hand grenades. Even George Halas had sailed off to the South Pacific on the troop transport *Robert L. Howze*. At half-time of the '41 Bears-Cardinals game at Wrigley Field an announcement had come over the public address system: "Ladies and gentlemen. The Japanese have bombed Pearl Harbor."

"Looks like I'll be going to war," Halas mumbled to himself. He said it just loud enough to reach the ears of Hunk Anderson.

"What the hell?" Hunk said.

Halas wheeled and said, "By God, I promised myself a long time ago that I wasn't going to miss another war. And by God, I'm *not*."

He had enlisted as a volunteer during World War I in 1918 and asked for sea duty. But he was assigned to the sports program at the Great Lakes

Naval Training Station. Among other accomplishments, the Great Lakes football team won the 1919 Rose Bowl, but that did little to satisfy that empty feeling inside Halas. Missing out on a good fight was not his nature. Almost a year would pass after the attack on Pearl Harbor before a navy punch-card sorter seeking a former officer turned up Halas's card. At age forty-seven, he was really going to war this time. But not before having a skirmish with George Preston Marshall at the 1942 NFL spring meetings that was inspired by these fighting words: "George, you're too old to fight. Why don't you leave the fighting to the younger guys?" Halas jumped over the table and bopped Marshall on the top of the head with his right fist. This middle-aged man was not about to leave the fighting to anyone else.

The Bears won their second straight NFL title in 1941, this time beating the New York Giants 37–9. They were well on their way to number three in '42 when Halas took off for military action in the South Pacific. He was presented with his sword at halftime during the Detroit game on the sixth Sunday of the season. Before leaving, he named Luke Johnsos and Anderson as co-head coaches with Paddy Driscoll and Carl Brumbaugh as the assistants.

The Bears finished the regular season with an 11–0 record. It was the second perfect season in the history of the NFL, the other a 13–0 finish by the Bears in '34.

But Redskins coach Ray Flaherty was planning an ambush when it came time to play the NFL championship game. He managed to take advantage of Halas's absence and capitalize on some reverse psychology. Instead of delivering a hellfire pregame pep talk, he slowly walked to the front of the room minutes before kickoff and wrote "73–0" on the chalkboard. Then he circled it. Reminded of that painful 73–0 beating back in 1940, the Redskins stormed onto the field with so much rage inside them that nothing short of eleven Nagurskis could have slowed them down.

Chicago's offense was held to virtually no yardage in the first half, and tackle Lee Artoe scored the only touchdown by scooping up a fumble and running fifty-two yards to the end zone. Then he proceeded to miss the extra point. The Bears led 6–0 but the Redskins offense kicked into gear as Sammy Baugh passed thirty-nine yards to Wilbur Moore for a touchdown.

The score at halftime was 7–6 Washington. The Redskins' next drive almost died at the Bears twenty-one when Andy Farkas tried to dive over the pile of bodies on fourth-and-one. He somehow managed to land on top of the pile and was suspended there for two full seconds. Luckily for Farkas, the pile toppled forward, depositing him at the twenty-yard line for a first down. He then carried four straight times to the one. On the next attempt, Farkas fumbled as he crossed the goal line, but officials ruled that the ball had broken the plane of the goal. Washington scored the touchdown that sealed the victory 14–6. The Chicago dynasty had been sidetracked once more.

The '42 title game was the end of the NFL as America had come to know it. By the start of the '43 season, 376 players who had been listed on NFL rosters the last three years were serving somewhere. Two had already been killed in action—Brooklyn's Don Wemple and Washington's Keith Birlem. A total of forty-eight Bears, including Ken Kavanaugh, George McAfee, Joe Stydahar, and Bill Osmanski, were already gone. Halas had been sailing the Pacific Ocean for several months.

At the '43 owners meetings, it was agreed that the Cleveland Rams would cease operations for at least one season as their owners Fred Levy and Dan Reeves served in the military. The Pittsburgh and Philadelphia franchises were folded into one team with a new nickname—Steagles. To fill out the rosters, old stars like Mel Hein, Ken Strong, and Bronko Nagurski came back.

Along with the reclamation of Nagurski, the Bears had caught yet another break in picking up halfback Dante Magnani and end Jim Benton from the Rams. Magnani and Benton had finished third and fourth respectively in receptions the previous season. On paper, it appeared that the Redskins, Giants, and Bears would be the teams to beat.

Chicago's biggest worry was the military status of quarterback Sid Luckman, who was planning to enlist in the merchant marine. Everyone in the Bears organization held their breath and hoped that Luckman would not be called to duty before the '43 season ended. The departure of the twenty-seven-year-old Luckman would leave Johnsos and Anderson with no choice but to activate Carl Brumbaugh, now the Chicago quarterbacks coach. Brummy, who was thirty-five, had once been a great T-formation signal caller. But he had not taken a snap in five years, and his time had passed.

The return of Nagurski had all of America talking. Only the comeback of Babe Ruth would have created a bigger buzz. Every coach and player in the NFL wondered if all of the pistons were firing in those powerful legs. Players like Sammy Baugh still boasted of scars from the Nagurski train wrecks.

"Bronko is the one man that I never wanted to see again," Baugh said. "I still have nightmares about that big monster."

When Mel Hein heard about Nagurski's comeback, he said, "God save us all."

Both Tim Mara of the Giants and George Preston Marshall sought rulings from the commissioner's office to halt Nagurski's return. But commissioner Elmer Layden, one of the Notre Dame Four Horsemen, could find nothing in the rules that forbade Nagurski from playing again.

The realists knew that the old Bronk could not possibly replicate the young and powerful Nagurski. Bronko himself was skeptical about his weathered talents. He was not nearly as well proportioned as the monster who burst onto the pro scene in 1930. The hip, knee, back, and rib injuries had left him in constant pain. There was rust all over him.

"My joints are barking," he told Hunk Anderson. "You'd need a sundial to time me in the hundred."

Thirteen years earlier, he had run the hundred-yard dash in 10.2 seconds as a senior at the University of Minnesota. No one could ever remember the young Nagurski being caught from behind on the football field.

The Bronk knew that wrestling had also taken its toll on his body. He had been bounced around pretty hard. Though the matches were rigged, and Nagurski was normally cast as the good guy, his body had been battered and bruised by some rough characters. The degenerative condition in his left hip had left him virtually unable to run. His ribs and lower back ached every waking minute. His left knee often popped out of joint, thanks to the torn cartilage that had never been repaired. Traveling great distances from city to city by automobile and by the slow, clattering trains had sucked vitality from his being. Bronko might have been the toughest player ever to suit up. But his youth had faded.

If Nagurski had his druthers, he would have been storming though Italy with the Fifth Army. The day after the Pearl Harbor attack, he caught the train from International Falls to an enlistment station in Minneapolis. He had already kissed Eileen and his two boys good-bye and figured he would not be coming back for at least two years. That was before the doctor who examined him cocked an eyebrow and said, "Mr. Nagurski, I have already found six reasons to flunk you from military duty. I think it's time to stop counting."

As the doctor inspected Bronko from head to toe, he said, "I still don't know how you played pro football all those years. You're a physical wreck. And how'd you get those big knots on your back, anyway? An axe?"

Nagurski grunted and said, "Football is a rough sport. Yah. You've got to be tough to play."

At first, the Bronk had tackled the wrestling circuit with the same zeal that had driven him to the pinnacle of the pro football world. He might be in Provo, Utah, on Thursday and Philadelphia on Sunday. Wrestling was cheap entertainment throughout the Depression years, and promoters were prospering with the big names: Lou Thesz, Whipper Billy Watson, Dean Detton, Ali Baba, Ed "Strangler" Lewis, "Leering Lou" Plummer, and Nagurski.

The Bronk had trouble turning down matches. When Tony Stecher called to say that Lou Thesz was ready to rumble in Montreal, Nagurski was normally on the next train to Canada.

By the summer of 1943, though, Nagurski had seen enough of the slimy sport to know he could stomach it no more. He had been ripped off by promoters, hucksters, and arena managers from Los Angeles to Bangor, Maine. Plus he was growing homesick for his wife and two young boys back in International Falls. Bronko Jr. was now five years old, and Anthony had just turned three. He missed his wife every day he was on the road.

When Hunk Anderson called to plead for his return to football, Nagurski said, "I will come back under one condition. You tell George Halas that this is my last season. Period."

Nagurski knew the glory days were over. At best, he would play two to three quarters each Sunday and never touch the ball. But it excited Anderson to know this legend would be around the team for one full season, to know that that the players could reach out and touch him. Nagurski walking into the locker room and strapping on the gear would be a powerful emotional lift for everyone. If the Bronk could bang with the young studs, no one could ever complain about their bumps or bruises.

236

Anderson also knew that Nagurski would still be able to control his side of the line. Great speed was not required to become an impenetrable human wall. Nagurski would be that brick fortress for the Bears in the '43 season.

When he arrived at training camp on that sweaty August afternoon, Nagurski could feel the eyes of every Bear player tracking him. It was like a ghost emerging from the mist. No one spoke, and it seemed that everyone was holding his breath until Clyde "Bulldog" Turner tilted his ball cap onto the back of his head, wiped his right hand on the side of his pants, and extended it to Bronko.

"Gol' dog, Mr. Nagurski," he said. "I feel like I'm shaking the right hand of God. Shit, George Halas has been talking about you since the day I got to Chicago. I was beginning to wonder if a superman such as you really existed. It's a pleasure to see you with my own eyeballs."

Bronko grinned. "Bulldog," he said, "I've had my leg pulled before. But never that hard."

It was true that Halas had talked endlessly about the football legend. Whether tutoring his players or trying to inspire them, Halas would say, "If that goddamned Nagurski were here, he'd be doing it this way . . ."

It was amazing how many familiar faces had gone away in the last six years. Nagurski knew just five players on the thirty-man roster—guard Danny Fortmann, tackle George Musso, halfback Ray Nolting, backup quarterback Bob Snyder, and end George "Ducky" Wilson. Musso was still his best friend. But he had never really hung around the other four.

Musso bear-hugged the man who had saved his pro career back in 1933. Nagurski had intervened when Halas wanted to send the 257-pounder to the minor leagues. It would have been a mistake. Musso now had seven All-Pro seasons under his substantial belt, along with five trips to the NFL title game and three world championships. Halas could thank the Bronk for it all.

Musso was the last of a breed of players who did not use a helmet. He had a crooked beak, thanks to having his nose broken eleven times. But he never seemed to stop smiling. Musso devoured life just like the steak and potatoes served to him each night. Nagurski loved to be around the funnyman.

Nagurski was introduced to the young players. After the first few he held up an open palm and said, "If one more of you guys calls me Mr. Nagurski, I'm going to lay you out."

The practice field fell silent. Most did not know that the Big Nag was really a pretty easygoing fellow when a game was not on the line.

"The Bronk is only joking, guys," Musso said. "But if he does decide to lay you out, run for the hills!"

Bulldog Turner could not take his eyes off this football legend. The Chicago center could scarcely wait for the first game against Green Bay when he could line up with the Bronk. Turner was in the process of building quite a reputation for himself. At six foot one and 235 pounds, he was a rugged package of muscle and thick bone that could block any man on the planet. He could also run like a halfback. Turner had set an NFL record during the 1942 season with eight interceptions, this from a man playing linebacker. When the Bears ran out of halfbacks late in one game in '42, Halas simply switched his center to the backfield. On his first play, Turner carried the ball forty-eight yards around end for a touchdown.

They liked to say in pro football that a lineman was really a "back with his brains knocked out." That was not the case with Bulldog. He religiously studied the playbook and had come to know the responsibilities of every player on the field. That was quite an accomplishment in the Halas system, which included more than four hundred plays. No other playbook in the league could approach the Bears'.

There were times that Turner seemed like a second quarterback in the huddle. He didn't mind sharing his thinking with Luckman and never was short of opinions. Once, when the Bears were stuck deep in their own territory, Luckman paused momentarily as his brain tried to find the right play. Bulldog said, "Sid, just throw the damn ball deep." Sid did. The result was a ninety-yard touchdown pass.

When asked about the pass, Luckman told the press, "I didn't know which play to call. So I just left it up to Bulldog."

Turner was full of ideas. He noticed during the '42 season that Green Bay linebacker Buckets Goldenberg was practically reading Luckman's mind. Goldenberg seemed to know instinctively when Luckman was going to pass. He was already backpedaling into the secondary, clogging the passing lanes, before Luckman could get the pass off. During the game, Bulldog pulled Luckman to the side and said, "Why don't you fake the pass and hand off to the fullback? Then he can run up to where I am because there's nobody there but me."

This play averaged about thirty yards every time the Bears tried it that day. The draw would become a staple of every offense.

That Turner had attained so much success in just three seasons seemed beyond comprehension. Football had almost never entered his life. He had grown up so far out in West Texas that cattle outnumbered humans there fifty to one. The playing of organized sports was never an option. The first football he had ever set eyes on was in a Sears, Roebuck catalog.

Turner was born and raised in a ranch shack on the high plains about fifteen miles from the New Mexico border. Thanks to the drought and the Dust Bowl, his father was forced to sell the property and to move the family into Plaines, the only town in Yoakum County that had two stores and two gas stations. One building housed the first grade through the twelfth grade, and, of course, there was no football team.

It would be a life-changing experience when the family moved two hundred miles east to Sweetwater as the big, muscled-up boy was about to enter the eleventh grade. The first thing he noticed at the new school were the boys wearing slip-on knit sweaters with a big S sewn on the front. He had never seen a football letter sweater.

"I want to get me one of those sweaters," Turner told his mother. "Seems those boys are getting all the gravy around here."

The Sweetwater football team was the centerpiece of the town's social structure. There were pep rallies every Friday morning, and it seemed that everybody was at the train station to see the team off that afternoon. Adding to the legend of Sweetwater football were the memorable Friday nights that had been produced by one Sammy Baugh, the former Sweetwater Mustang star who had taken off for Texas Christian University, where he was slinging the ball.

Turner had to wait for his sweater. To help the family make ends meet, he picked cotton after school that first fall in Sweetwater, making about thirty-five cents a day. But he was determined not to miss his senior season. He quickly blossomed into one of the best linemen in West Texas, but, thanks to his limited experience, the college recruiters knew little about him. So he stuck out his thumb and started hitchhiking for hundreds of miles across parts of Texas and Oklahoma, looking for a college team that needed a rawboned lineman they had never heard of. To raise money for the journey and to buy a new coat and gloves, he sold his cow for eight bucks. Then he hit the highway and started chasing his dream.

Turner showed up at places like SMU in Dallas and TCU in Fort Worth, where he would say, "I want to be a football player." The answer was always the same: "We've got enough players. We don't need any more." He left Fort Worth with a dime and a candy bar in his pocket. But he managed to make it all the way to Cameron State Agriculural College in Lawton, Oklahoma, where, after not eating for two days, the coaches invited him to the cafeteria. He had never heard of a cafeteria, and the word scared him. So rather than expose his ignorance, he passed on the free lunch.

When he was turned down at Cameron State, he spent the next three days hitchhiking back to Sweetwater, where he practically fell through the front door of the family's ranch house. He was broke and hungry and gaunt. He had not eaten in five days. His mother nurtured him back to health.

Two months later, some good news finally arrived. The coach at Hardin-Simmons College in nearby Abilene invited Turner and his friend A. J. Roy for a tryout. That is when they invented nicknames for each other. If Turner happened to be having a bad practice, Roy would say, "Hey, Bulldog, you ain't cracking these boys like you did back home." Or Turner might say, "Tiger, you need to get your butt in gear."

Both players made the team and, yes, the nicknames stuck. So much so, in fact, that the only time Turner was ever again called Clyde was by his wife, Gladys, or by his drinking buddies when he got too drunk.

In spite of being a small country college, Hardin-Simmons's football program boasted a creative publicist by the name of Hershell Schooley, who also taught journalism and wrote sports stories for the local newspaper. Schooley hired Dallas photographer Jimmy Laughhead to shoot publicity shots of Bulldog holding a calf over his head and running toward the camera. Bulldog was also photographed dressed in full cowboy garb—chaps, boots, and hat—while riding high in the saddle of a bucking white stallion.

Thanks, in part, to the hype generated by Schooley, Turner was selected to the All-America team as a senior. Still, not many folks outside of Texas had ever heard of Bulldog Turner when Halas drafted him in the first round. Unlike many of the other coaches and owners, Halas was not afraid to seek out players from distant outposts. As late as 1940, seventy percent of the NFL players were still produced by the eastern or midwestern powers. Of course, the eight NFL franchises were also limited to those sections of the country. The farthest team to the south was Washington, and the farthest west was Chicago.

Halas did not mind that his players were not all alike. He worked to create a diverse team and wanted tough guys mingling with the smart guys. That is why a cowboy from West Texas was snapping the ball to an Ivy Leaguer from New York.

Clyde Turner and Sid Luckman were as different as Franklin D. Roosevelt and Huey P. Long. Roosevelt was everything that haughty New York stood for, and Long, also known as the "Kingfish," was the epitome of backwater Louisiana. Luckman was Columbia University through and through. Turner was Hardin-Simmons College to the bone.

Bulldog looked like he had been chiseled from a block of granite. Luckman was a chubby man with soft features, a high forehead, and wavy black hair.

Unlike Bulldog, Luckman had several offers from colleges up and down the East Coast and as far away as Stanford. He was one of the most publicized football players in New York, playing tailback at Erasmus High School in Brooklyn. Luckman's team won the city championship playing before twenty-five thousand fans at Ebbets Field, home of the Dodgers, in 1934.

Luckman later would reveal that several of the college football powers had offered him money under the table. But he chose instead to play at Columbia, where not even a scholarship was made available. Luckman said he planned to place a greater emphasis on academics than athletics, and therefore the campus at Morningside Heights was the place for him.

While Turner was posing with a calf over his head, Luckman was making the dean's list and leading the Columbia Lions to wins over Army and Yale, two of the leading teams in college football, in 1938. Luckman was the toast of New York. Turner was the best cowhand playing football this side of Abilene.

Luckman was determined to enter the business world straight out of Columbia, with his sights set on Wall Street. A headline in the *New York Herald-Tribune* read, LUCKMAN TURNS DEAF EAR TO PRO OFFERS. Luckman even wrote a letter to his former college coach Little and asked, "Is this Halas guy on the up and up?" It took Halas three months and two trips to New York to convince Luckman to join the Bears. Luckman finally accepted the richest contract offer in the history of the NFL, worth $10,000 that first season.

Bulldog couldn't have cared less about riches, fame, or the stock market. He had never heard of Wall Street. He signed a contract for $200 a game and was just happy to have a home in professional football.

Luckman arrived in Chicago a month before his rookie training camp, and the Chicago coaches prepared him for the transition from the single wing to the T-formation. It would not be an easy adjustment. At Columbia Luckman had taken the deep snap from the tailback position and was the team's leading passer and runner. After several days of watching Bears film, he turned to assistant coach Carl Brumbaugh and said, "I'm just wondering how your running backs don't get killed. You send them into the line with nobody in front of them."

"Don't worry," Brumbaugh said. "You won't be tearing through the line anymore."

"What do you mean?" said Luckman.

"You're going to be throwing the danged ball now. You ain't going to be running it much."

Luckman shook his head in disbelief. He had never set eyes on the T-formation, much less played it. There were so many new responsibilities. On running plays the quarterback was required to perform fakes, twists, spins, and off-balance tosses. On passing plays, he would throw to a wide variety of receivers, including split ends and halfbacks going in motion. Dropping back to pass was yet another trick to be mastered. In the single wing, the tailback simply caught the long snap from center and let it fly.

Mostly, Luckman would need the hands of a cardsharp, the feet of Fred Astaire, and the eyesight of a peregrine falcon. And that was before he was tackled by a blindsiding behemoth determined to separate his head from his body.

"Sid, my, boy, you can do this," Halas said one day. "I have all the confidence in the world in you."

Halas, of course, had never seen Luckman take a single snap from under center. He had traveled to the Columbia games on three occasions to see him make pinpoint passes, dart through the line, return a punt eighty-five yards, and make jarring tackles in the defensive backfield. But never had Sid stepped under center.

But thanks to Luckman's toughness, Halas was assured the boy could make the adjustment. Never had he seen him flinch under the pressure of an onrushing lineman. Sid always had the dirtiest uniform on the field. The Ivy League before the war played a rugged brand of football that resembled the NFL to a degree. Of Luckman's resiliency, referee Red Freisell said, "I saw him get knocked out of his britches by onrushing opponents. I saw him get creamed. But never once did I see him in fright, nor did I see him wince when he got his lumps."

College rules were similar to the NFL's at the time. You could whale on the quarterback until the whistle blew. The mere act of releasing a pass did not take you out of harm's way. It was a cinch that Luckman would be hit and hit hard long after delivering the pass.

As a senior, Luckman completed ten of seventeen passes to beat Yale. Eli coach "Ducky" Pond later confessed that he had nightmares for months about Luckman. "It was the greatest one-man show that I've ever seen at the Yale Bowl," Pond said.

That same season, Columbia trailed number-one-ranked Army 18–6 when Luckman returned a punt eighty-five yards for a touchdown. He then completed a late touchdown pass for the 20–18 upset.

Little did anyone know that Halas was tracking Luckman's every move all the way back to his days at Erasmus High School in Brooklyn. All of the Luckman data was kept inside the Burgundy Room on Wabash Avenue in Chicago, so named because of the burgundy carpet inside the Bears' offices. Every time Luckman passed the ball, ran the ball, returned a punt, or punted, the information went into his file. It had been accepted by the rest of the NFL that Luckman would be a Bear, come hell or high water. Halas already had a deal with Steelers owner Art Rooney to obtain the first choice of the 1939 draft.

As might be expected, the Giants' Tim Mara made overtures to Luckman, and Brooklyn Dodgers coach Dan Topping said, "I'll give every man on my ball club for Luckman and be glad to start from scratch." But Halas would not have traded Luckman for every player on the All-Pro team.

Almost nothing went right during that first training camp. Handoffs were fumbled and passes intercepted. But Luckman never stopped working or studying. At night he would stand in front of the full-length mirror of his hotel room and work on his feints, pivots, and ball-handling skills. Then he would call Brumbaugh at home and the two would talk for hours about the playbook.

That first season went better than anyone could expect. Luckman not only dazzled the Giants in his first game of the season, he tricked them twice. He noticed that the Giants were slow in breaking their defensive huddle. So he called two quick plays to open the game. Before the Giants had a chance to line up, Luckman was twenty yards up the field en route to a thirty-five-yard gain. Luckman did it again on the next play and gained thirty yards. It would be the final time that Steve Owen's Giants used a defensive huddle.

The Green Bay game that season was one of the most exciting in the history of Wrigley Field as the lead changed six times. The Bears trailed Green Bay 27–24 with under a minute to play. Luckman completed a forty-five-yard pass to end Bob MacLeod all the way to the four-yard line. Bill Osmanski scored the winning touchdown on the next play, and Chicago won 30–27.

The Ivy Leaguer's first season was an unqualified success. The Bears finished with an 8–3 record, one game behind a Green Bay team that would defeat the Giants in the NFL championship game.

Luckman was the perfect quarterback for the time, as the Bears were light-years ahead of the competition in terms of strategy and preparation. Halas was the first coach to have team meetings, film sessions, and a playbook. He also introduced, just as Luckman was arriving, the press-box phone for help in play calling.

Halas initially put Johnsos in a seat near the press box for a game against the Brooklyn Dodgers. When Johnsos noticed a weakness in the Dodgers' defense, he would whistle for a messenger who would catch the note down at ground level and run it to Halas. Soon, though, the Brooklyn fans picked up on the scheme. Late in the game, he dropped the note to the messenger just as the fans unleashed a blizzard of paper. The note was lost, and so was the opportunity to exploit a hole in the Brooklyn defense.

After the game Halas and Johnsos mapped a plan to hook up a telephone in an upper box. It would create a tremendous advantage until the 1942 championship game in Washington, when George Preston Marshall devised a plan to mute Johnsos. He stationed the Redskins band close to the Chicago box. Every time Johnsos picked up the phone, the band would play a loud number. No wonder the Bears lost 14–6.

That defeat by the Redskins would stop the Bears shy of three straight titles. It would motivate Halas, now five thousand miles away on the South Pacific, to chart a route to redemption. And it would inspire the return of Bronko Nagurski.

The 1943 season would be like none other in the history of pro football.

# 19

# Season of Change

A soft breeze blew off Lake Michigan that September afternoon in 1943 as the sailboats bobbed in the blue water and the first chill of autumn tinged the air. It would have been a light and carefree day on the North Side of Chicago if not for the reality of a world conflict raging from Salerno to the Solomons.

Though the world was turned upside down, Hunk Anderson and Luke Johnsos could not help but feel the promise of a new season pulsing through their veins. As people liked to say at the time, the Bears were "as sound as a Roosevelt dollar." The sporting press was predicting another NFL championship. Surely, the lieutenant commander now stationed in New Guinea and eagerly awaiting the early results of the 1943 season would have been proud of his interim coaches. George Halas could not have done a better job of retooling the Chicago Bears.

Anderson and Johnsos had kept their eyes focused on Bronko Nagurski the past three weeks. Training camp would be the tale of the tape for the man six years removed from football. They were not surprised to learn that his speed had diminished and that the battered knee and hip had produced stiffness in his gait. Nagurski had not lied when he said to Anderson a month earlier, "I couldn't run from here to the bathroom if my bladder was bursting." But the Chicago coaches were not asking for miracles, just some balls-out play in the line.

"This is a different Bronko than we used to see around here," Anderson told the *Chicago Tribune*. "But believe me, I wouldn't want to be lining up against him."

George Musso chuckled and said, "The Bronk is still a scary sumbitch. That man'd make a freight train take a dirt road."

They learned during training camp that the Bronk was still as strong as a bull. More than a dozen years had passed since he had played in the line. But it seemed he had never left. It took two strong men to move him, much less block him out of the play. A quality that would never fade within Nagurski was his all-consuming desire to make the next play his best. No one had ever been more devoted to winning football games. But Anderson wanted to make certain before the start of the season that the Bronk was back in hitting shape. Everyone in pro football knew there was a wide margin between hitting shape and merely being in condition. Muscle and bone had to be pounded. Only then would the body become resilient enough to absorb the hard knocks that the pros meted out each Sunday.

The heavy hitting of training camp did not wear down Nagurski, but it sent several of his teammates to the training room with everything from broken noses to a fractured clavicle. The Bronk was at the root of each injury. One afternoon, as Musso was about to line up against the Bronk, he said, "Hey, Hunk, can you find somebody else to block this big bastard? I'm too old for this shit."

Hunk pushed Musso aside and dropped into a three-point stance in front of the Bronk. At age forty-five he wanted to prove to his players that he was still tough enough to handle all comers. It was a big mistake. Bronko was not about to allow himself even the slightest embarrassment. He bolted out of his stance and slammed a powerful right forearm into Hunk's breastbone and rocked him backward. The coach landed hard on his backside. When the back of his head slammed into the rocky ground it sounded like a sledgehammer crashing into concrete. Hunk was out like a light. Trainer Andy Lotshaw sprinted toward the fallen coach with smelling salts ready. He snapped the capsules under his nostrils and he jerked awake. Hunk snorted loudly and yelled, "Tell that sonofabitch that I can still whip his ass. But not today."

Nagurski was like an aging boxer still packing a powerful right cross. He could knock out the heavyweight champion in the first round. But asking him to endure twelve grueling rounds might be too much. He no longer had the stamina to play four quarters at full tilt.

Nagurski had been a sixty-minute man for eight straight seasons. Under the rules of the NFL's one-platoon system, a player who left the game could not return until the next quarter. But thanks to the shortage of bodies caused by the war, those rules had been changed for the '43 season. Coaches would now have the freedom to substitute on every play, and that suited the Bears just fine. Nagurski could stay in the game until he got tired and then take a breather.

"I can play in the line all year long," Nagurski told Anderson two days before the season opener. "I just don't think I can cut the buck at fullback anymore."

Nowhere would you find a better lineup than the one the Bears were about to put on the field in 1943. Johnny Siegal and George "Ducky" Wilson were the ends. Rounding out the line were George Musso, Danny Fortmann, Bulldog Turner, Al Hoptowit, Bill Steinkemper, and Nagurski. The backfield was reminiscent of the great Chicago seasons with Sid Luckman at quarterback, Harry Clark and Bill Geyer as the halfbacks, and Gary Famiglietti at fullback. Halfback Dante Magnani and end Jim Benton, players on loan from the Cleveland Rams, would be two of the best substitutes in pro football.

"What a pleasure," Magnani said. "I now get to play with the Bears instead of against them. I don't get beat up anymore."

No one could be sure, however, if all of these studs would be around at the end of the season. Draft boards were busier than a munitions factory. The good news was that Allied forces on all fronts were starting to turn the tide of war. Japanese positions in the South Pacific had been weakened, and Adolf Hitler's army had been forced to retreat in Sicily, Italy, and the Ukraine. Italy was under siege. Fascist dictator Benito Mussolini had been overthrown and exiled by his fellow countrymen to Ponza. He would be rescued weeks later by German forces and returned to Italy, where a phantom government called the Salò Republic was set up. But it was only a matter of time before Mussolini was ousted once more and Rome captured.

The war was far from over. But the upper hand belonged to the Allied forces. Nine million Americans were serving in the military—6.9 million in the army, 1.7 million in the navy, and more than three hundred thousand in the marines. Seventy-three percent of the men were fighting overseas and spending an average of sixteen months away from the homeland.

No wonder Bette Davis was singing the blues back in America.

The number one movie of the year was the musical *Thank Your Lucky Stars*. Davis, the hottest box-office attraction of the forties, performed a song that captured that lonely feeling back home—"They're Either Too Young or Too Old." With sad eyes, she sang, "You marched away and knew so well our love would stay alive / I'm stuck here with sweet sixteen and kids of sixty-five."

It was a typical sun-splashed afternoon on the final Sunday of September when the Bears and Packers opened the season for the twelfth straight year. The crowd of 23,649 was the largest in the history of Green Bay's City Stadium, and it was apparent that the war had been placed on the back burner—at least for three hours. Given the amount of alcohol imbibed before kickoff and the rowdiness in the stands, you could be sure that the Chicago Bears were in town.

The Packers had been severely depleted by the war, having lost quarterback Cecil Isbell, the NFL's leading passer of the last two seasons and the first ever to surpass the two-thousand yard mark in '42. Rookie Irv Comp from Benedictine College replaced Isbell. Comp could barely throw a spiral. The Packers still had Don Hutson, who at age thirty-three could win any game single-handedly, along with Buckets Goldenberg, one of the best guards in football. Clarke Hinkle had retired two years earlier, but unlike retirees Nagurski and Mel Hein of the Giants, he chose not to come back, saying he was sick and tired of negotiating contracts with the miserly Curly Lambeau.

Chicago clearly held the advantage in overall talent. But the best team did not always win when the Bears and Packers played. This was never more evident than in the opening game of the season just three years earlier. Green Bay, coming off a championship season, had lost the opener to Chicago 41–10.

Anderson and Johnsos agreed that their duties would remain the same on game day. Johnsos, the offensive guru, would carry on his work from the press box, where he had a better view of the field and could spot weaknesses in the opposition. He would stay in phone contact with Paddy

Driscoll on the sideline. Anderson, the more outgoing of the two, would run the team from the sideline while overseeing the defense. Anderson and Johnsos rarely argued, in spite of Anderson's high-strung personality.

On the opening possession of the game, the Bears mixed the run with the pass, and the methodical eighty-yard drive was proof that a strong lineup had been properly prepared by the Chicago coaches. Bill Osmanski and Bill Geyer did most of the damage on the ground and Luckman completed a twenty-eight-yard pass to Connie Mack Berry, a fine receiver who ironically had been released by the Packers just two weeks before the season began. He stood six foot three and turned out to be an excellent target for Luckman, who loved the short passing game. Berry's reception moved the ball to the Green Bay two. Geyer then scored the opening touchdown of the season around left end, giving the Bears a 7–0 lead.

The Packers would answer with an eighteen-yard touchdown run by Tony Canadeo. But when Nagurski entered the game on the next series of downs, the Packers running was stymied for the rest of the first half. It was time for Lambeau to dust off one of his famous fire-and-brimstone speeches during the halftime break.

"Those sonsabitches have always thought they were better than you," he yelled. "But the Packers have always had the bigger heart. Teach those boys a lesson in the second half."

The Bears defense in the third quarter was reminiscent of the old days when helmetless Bill Hewitt forged a steel curtain in the defensive front and Nagurski rattled bones at linebacker. Now it was Nagurski playing tackle and Bulldog Turner patrolling the field at linebacker. It was clear from the moment they lined up together that the Nagurski-Turner tandem would be hell on wheels.

The Bronk never left the field in the second half, and it was evident that he was in far better condition after a six-year layoff than some had expected. He delivered the crunching block that cleared the way for Geyer's second touchdown run of eight yards, and the Bears led 14–7.

When Luckman passed thirty yards to Jim Benton for a third touchdown, the game seemed all but decided. Chicago had overcome three fumbles and still led the game 21–7.

Green Bay was going nowhere on the ground, or through the air for that matter. Comp's passes fluttered everywhere but into the hands of his receivers. Hutson could not be expected to pull off a miracle comeback if he could not get his hands on the ball. That is when Lambeau reverted to trickery. With the ball at the Green Bay forty, Comp handed off to full-back Ted Fritsch, who then gave the ball to Canadeo running the other way. But instead of a double reverse around left end, Canadeo stopped and fired a sixty-yard touchdown pass to Hutson, who had outsprinted the Bears secondary by ten yards.

Midway in the fourth quarter, the Packers ran the exact same play around the other end, with Canadeo passing forty yards to Hutson for the tying touchdown. Hutson also kicked the extra point, his third of the day, and the Bears were a frustrated mess as they tried to mount a late drive to win the game.

Penalties and fumbles had caused the offense to backfire a good part of the day. Now Luckman managed to complete passes to Berry and Benton that moved the ball to the Green Bay thirty-five-yard line with thirty seconds to play. The Bears rushed to the line for a last-ditch forty-two-yard field goal attempt by Bob Snyder. The ball was tipped at the line by Green Bay's Goldenberg, and it rolled benignly to the ten-yard line where everyone but Packers halfback Andy Uram ignored it. Realizing that the ball was still in play, Uram scooped it up and sprinted in the other direction. At midfield, one Bears player stood between him and the winning touchdown. It was Nagurski.

Uram tried to elude Nagurski by cutting toward the sideline. But the Bronk managed to kick his legs into gear for a short sprint and grabbed Uram around the waist, dragging him down at the forty-five.

"The sonofabitch can still run when he has to," an elated Hunk Anderson yelled. The game had been saved. Chicago players and coaches took off running for the buses parked at the north end of City Stadium. They felt lucky to escape with a tie.

• • •

The hero of Sid Luckman's life was Hank Greenberg. It was easy to idolize a fellow Jew who had also grown up in Brooklyn and then battled prejudice all the way to greatness in the major leagues.

There would be no stopping Greenberg once he got a spike-hold in the batter's box of America's pastime. In 1934, his second year in the major leagues, Greenberg's .339 batting average led the Detroit Tigers to the

World Series, where they lost in seven games to the Dizzy Dean–led St. Louis Cardinals. But the next season Greenberg hit thirty-six home runs, drove in 170 runs, and helped the Tigers into the 1935 World Series against the Chicago Cubs.

Never had a Jewish athlete accomplished so much in so little time. But Greenberg was just getting started. The final game of the '37 season found him needing two RBIs to break Lou Gehrig's all-time record of 184 RBIs. He plated only one run that day and fell one RBI short of the record. But he created even a greater stir the following season when he blasted fifty-eight home runs in 149 games. He had five more days to break Babe Ruth's record of sixty, set eleven years earlier, and he seemed certain to do it. Then came the bases on balls. No one would pitch to him. Greenberg got no more than three decent swings in his final twenty at-bats. He hit no more shots out of the park and finished with fifty-eight home runs, two short of the record. Speculation was rampant that a baseball conspiracy had stopped Greenberg from breaking the grandest record in the grand old game.

Greenberg was a bona fide superstar in a game where the great ones were forever worshipped. But instead of living the glory, Greenberg faced an ancient enemy everywhere he turned—anti-Semitism.

Less than two months after Greenberg's attempt to better Ruth's record was foiled, there was a massive coordinated attack on Jews throughout the German Reich. The night of November 9, 1938, is remembered today as *Kristallnacht,* or "The Night of the Broken Glass." Nazi storm troopers, along with Hitler Youth and ordinary citizens beat and murdered Jews and wrecked Jewish businesses. Hundreds of synagogues were systematically burned. The destruction of the European Jews was beginning.

Meanwhile, Greenberg found himself fighting his own war against prejudice in ballparks all over America. "I now feel that if I hit a home run, I am hitting that home run against Adolf Hitler," Greenberg said.

It seemed that everyone else was hitting back. One afternoon at Comiskey Park, Greenberg could no longer tolerate the verbal abuse. For nine innings he had been showered with epithets from the Chicago dugout. He marched into the White Sox clubhouse after the game and shouted, "If you have a gut in your body, stand up!"

At six foot four and 210 pounds, Greenberg was a large and intimidating man. No one stood up.

The persecution of Hank Greenberg was not limited to ballparks outside of Detroit. The Tigers had not been to the World Series for twenty-five years before Greenberg came along, and Detroit fans should have sung his praises. Instead, they hurled racial slurs with the best of them.

"When I strike out, I am not just a bum," Greenberg said. "I am a Jewish bum."

Detroit also happened to be the hometown of one of America's leading industrialists and leading Jew haters. Henry Ford, who invented the automobile assembly line and created the Ford Motor Company, was not a fan of Hank Greenberg, or of any Jew for that matter. He promoted a virulent brand of anti-Semitism and disseminated his point of view through the privately owned *Dearborn Independent*. Among his more bizarre statements: "Jews are not sportsmen. Never will be."

It was not comforting to Luckman that the Bears were now on their way to the Motor City on the second weekend of the 1943 season.

Like his hero, Luckman was forced to turn a deaf ear to opposing players and fans. The verbal abuse had begun with the first game of his rookie season. If the games were not being played at Wrigley Field or the stadiums in New York, Luckman could count on a tongue-lashing wherever he went.

Only two other Jews had ever played in the NFL—Benny Friedman, a quarterback from 1927 through '34, and Marshall Goldberg, a running back with the Chicago Cardinals now sitting out the '43 season with a broken arm. Friedman had spent most of his pro days with the New York Giants and Brooklyn Dodgers. Those teams drew a large Jewish following. Friedman, in spite of his high profile, never faced the anti-Jewish sentiment that Luckman would endure.

It had been stunning at first to hear the barrage of cruel insults. Luckman had barely been west of the Hudson River before he signed that first contract with the Bears in 1939. Most of his college games had been played in New York, an area populated by millions of Jews. Places like Princeton, New Jersey, and New Haven, Connecticut, the home of Yale University, were not known for anti-Semitism.

Halas was worried at first about the reception that Luckman would receive among the NFL crowds, who were far more hardened and cynical than those in the Ivy League. Places like Franklin Field in Philadelphia and even Comiskey Park in Chicago could be brutal to opposing players—

especially if they were Jewish. The NFL had banished blacks from the league ten years earlier. It had been one of the most open-minded institutions in America before that.

But the manner in which Luckman handled the ethnic slurs often disarmed his enemies. This was a typical give-and-take between a Luckman tormentor and the Chicago quarterback:

"Hey, Luckman, you're a Jewish bastard!"

"Oh, yeah! Well, why don't you take a look at the scoreboard, pal?"

It was rare that the Bears were not ahead. With Luckman they had captured two of the last three NFL championships while winning thirty-three regular-season games and losing only five.

Luckman had a lot of fighter in him, just like Nagurski. This might have seemed surprising, since Luckman looked more like a CPA from midtown Manhattan than a quarterback for the most rugged team in football. His athleticism was nothing to brag about. He still toted around some baby fat and moved about the pocket like an old man on stiff legs. His passes fluttered. There was nothing artistic about his passing style. Instead of releasing the ball over the top of his shoulder, he slung it sidearm. His follow-through looked like an old pug throwing a short right cross.

Chicago receivers were often chided by opposing defensive backs when they ran pass patterns of more than thirty yards.

"Better slow down, buddy," they would say tauntingly. "Luckman can't throw it that far."

Luckman hardly ever hummed one more than thirty yards. But he was the master of hitting a receiver on a short timing pattern. Thanks to the three-step drop, he was able to release the ball quickly, before the defensive back could react. His favorite was the fade route, especially close to the goal. The Chicago receiver would break quickly to the right sideline, cut upfield, and find the ball floating perfectly over his left shoulder. Luckman worked on that pass every day after practice until his hand almost bled. If the pass was on target, it could not be defended. Most were squarely on the mark.

In spite of his lack of athleticism, Luckman actually seemed at his best in the midst of chaos. Only Sammy Baugh could be compared to Luckman when it came to courage under fire. He was amazingly accurate with a defender right in his face. And to the utter amazement of all who played against him, Luckman was not a bad ball carrier. Thanks to his experience as a running and passing tailback at Columbia University, he was quick to locate the open space and run to daylight. Though Halas frowned on using Luckman as a ball carrier, he had grudgingly agreed to an addition to the playbook called "Bingo keep-it." It was a quarterback draw, a play that routinely gained twenty or thirty yards. The defense never seemed ready for it.

The Lions team that the Bears would play on October 3 in Detroit had fallen on hard times. They hardly resembled the team that had vied for the league title practically every season in the thirties. Gone were Glenn Presnell and Dutch Clark. Perhaps the greatest loss was owner George Richards, the radio magnate who had sold the team at the end of the 1939 season. They had won but nine games the last three years and finished the 1942 season with an 0-11 record.

But things would be different with the Chicago Bears coming to town.

Briggs Stadium, constructed five years earlier, could not squeeze in another body. Fans were standing in the aisles, and they stood four deep around the field. A few were actually sitting on the Bears bench when the players trotted onto the field for the start of the game. They started chanting "Jew, Jew, Jew!" as soon as they spotted Luckman.

Nagurski decided to take on the job of clearing the area.

"Now why don't you boys get on out of here before somebody gets hurt," he said to the belligerent fans.

They were gone in a matter of seconds.

The crowd was announced at 48,118. For the second straight week, the Bears would be playing to a record crowd on the road. The largest gathering the last two years for a Lions game at Briggs Stadium had been less than twenty thousand.

Nagurski was still a big draw in spite of his having been away from the game for six years. He would be in the starting lineup, and a surprising cheer went up when he trotted onto the field for the first play.

The Lions had struggled to assemble a roster, thanks to the war. They had borrowed from high school coaching staffs around the city and then begged players like Frank "Fireball" Sinkwich, guard Riley Matheson, and center Alex Wojciechowicz to play the '43 season. Those were the only familiar names on the roster.

Sinkwich had become the first Heisman Trophy winner at the University of Georgia in 1942. He had led the Bulldogs to an 11–1 record and a Rose Bowl victory over UCLA. He had volunteered for the U.S. Marine Corps but flunked the physical because of high blood pressure and flat feet. That was great news for the Lions. The bad news was that Sinkwich had heard too many horror stories the last few days about the monster known as Nagurski. The first time he carried the ball that afternoon he froze in his tracks as the Bronk drove him into the dirt. Sinkwich lay on the field for several seconds before getting up.

"Jesus Christ!" Musso bellowed. "You done scared this Detroit rookie to death."

Sinkwich would be pulled from the game.

The Bears scored the first two touchdowns of the game with Luckman passing thirty-eight yards to Berry and Benton. They led 14–0 midway in the second quarter and were in total control of the game when Detroit's Lloyd Cardwell stepped in front of a Luckman pass and returned the interception fifty yards for a touchdown. The Lions were suddenly charged up and so was the capacity crowd. When Detroit recovered a fumble at the Chicago ten-yard line late in the second quarter, the momentum of the game had completely shifted to Detroit.

"Smack 'em in the faces," Anderson bellowed from the sideline.

Musso took him literally. He slugged guard Riley Matheson in the mouth before the ball was snapped and drew a penalty to the five-yard line. The Lions scored on the next play as Bob Keene sprinted around left end to tie the score.

The Bears were showered with beer bottles as they ran through the end zone tunnel toward the locker room at halftime, and Luckman was besieged with anti-Semitic epithets.

When Detroit coach Gus Dorais noticed that Nagurski was not starting the second half, he sent Sinkwich back into the lineup.

"Don't freeze up, kid," Dorais hollered.

Sinkwich broke the ice on the first play of the third quarter, sprinting seventy-eight yards around right end to the end zone. The Bears were stunned. This was supposed to be a cakewalk against a team that had not won a game since the 1941 season. Now they were trailing the Lions 21–14.

Nagurski returned to the game late in the third quarter, and to no one's surprise Luckman started calling running plays over his right tackle position. The Bears moved down the field and managed to consume eight minutes from the clock on an eighty-yard drive. Bill Geyer scored the touchdown from the two-yard line behind a devastating block by Nagurski. Bob Snyder's PAT kick sailed right of the upright, and the Bears still trailed 21–20 midway in the fourth quarter.

The Bears offense went nowhere on their next possession, and all hopes for a comeback were fading until Nagurski recovered a fumble at the thirty-yard line with a minute to play. Luckman stepped into the huddle and said with great conviction, "Bingo keep-it." With the words barely out of his mouth, Bulldog Turner said, "You're one crazy Jew, Sid."

"Run the play, dammit," Luckman said.

"Which way?" Bulldog spat.

"Right off Nagurski's ass!"

From the moment he had set eyes on Nagurski, Luckman had the utmost respect for the big bruiser. He was quick to notice the fear the Bronk struck in opposing players. The young ones could hardly fathom that they were lining up against a man their fathers had told them about. They looked across the line to see an overweight thirty-five-year-old man who tipped the scales at 235 pounds. But through those eyes, Nagurski really looked ten feet tall.

The play was a quarterback draw. Luckman dropped three steps, faked a pass, and waited for the linemen to converge upon him. Then he took off upfield, following the human shield known as Nagurski. The Bronk was driving defenders out of the way. There was not a Detroit Lion in sight when Luckman trundled over the goal line for the winning touchdown.

Breathing heavily, Luckman walked over to Nagurski and slapped him on the hip pads.

"Damn proud to have you around," he said. "Thanks for saving our asses today."

Detroit fans were throwing everything but the scoreboard at Luckman. Bottles, cans, seat cushions, and flasks flew down from the grandstand.

"Looks like we'd better get out of here," Nagurski said.

•  •  •

George Halas, aboard a battleship in the South Pacific, was smiling. His Bears were on a roll. He had already received a series of dispatches from a proud Hunk Anderson. After dispatching Detroit 27–21, the Bears defeated the Chicago Cardinals, Philly-Pitt Steagles, Brooklyn Dodgers, and Detroit once more by the combined score of 136–56.

In terms of success, little had changed with the Bears since Nagurski's departure back in 1937. No team was more organized or efficient. Halas had built the Bears into a machine back in the thirties. Though they had lost some of the great talent that had lifted the teams of 1932, '33, and '40 to the championship, this team was clearly capable of winning yet another title—the sixth in the history of the franchise. The team had a solid nucleus of players, and it had been a stroke of genius to bring back Nagurski.

Bronko was having a fun final ride. But he still missed the old days and the old guys. This was not a close-knit unit like the old Monsters of the Midway who had gathered almost every night at the Cottage Lounge at the corner of Diversey and Clark. There were no colorful hard-nosed characters like George Trafton, or battlers like Carl Brumbaugh, or genuine leaders like Red Grange.

The thirties produced a brand of player that was blue collar and bereft of ego. Nagurski and Grange were the biggest stars in the early part of the decade, and they were about as pretentious as a grain elevator. It would have been hard to separate Brumbaugh from a bar filled with ironworkers. He could outdrink any sailor in Chicago.

In the thirties the players generally lived in the same hotel, normally the Wellington Arms. They ate at the same restaurants and drank at one bar. They wore the same clothes and lived the same lives.

The '43 Bears seemed to go thirty different directions at the end of the day. Of course, the Bronk went straight home anyway. He was sore from head to toe and limped most of the way. He was lucky to have Musso as his best friend. The big guard rubbed his buddy's legs every afternoon, and that helped alleviate some of the pain. Musso's massages kept Nagurski on the field.

Away from the game, the Moose was a big teddy bear of a man who loved nothing better than mashed potatoes and ice cream. He also liked to cook for his roommate, who loved to eat. The Bronk and the Moose were the perfect couple, on and off the field.

Musso might have seemed a soft touch out of uniform, but he was a terror on the field. It was nothing to see his nose broken and bleeding and lying over to the side while the big man kept pounding away at the other team. Just like Nagurski, he feared nothing and no one, and, thanks to quick feet, he could still throw his 270 pounds around with the best of them. Thanks to Musso, Nagurski, and Turner, the Bears had the best line in football. Rarely did defenders get a clean shot at Luckman.

Nagurski liked Luckman and appreciated the professionalism and toughness he displayed on the playing field. But he could not understand why Sid always seemed so detached from his teammates. No one could be sure where he was staying during the season because no one had ever been invited there. Players still gathered at the Cottage Lounge on occasion, but Luckman never joined them. One night as Bulldog got deep in his cups, he said, "I just don't think ol' Sid loves us. Hell, we never see the boy."

"Why is it?" the Bronk said.

"It's Halas," Bulldog said. "He tells Sid to stay away from the other players. He doesn't want him acting like us jackasses."

It was true that Halas had asked Luckman to distance himself from his teammates for the purpose of maintaining an objective view of them all. But Luckman carried Halas's wishes to an extreme. He was like an investment banker in the midst of leather-skinned longshoremen. He drove a brand-new Chrysler convertible and was a fashion plate in his tweed and gabardine suits. He drank wine.

Luckman did not hide the fact that he fashioned himself to be a businessman as well as a football star. He had become a partner in a Chicago Chrysler dealership and was willing to give his name to the company. He was also part owner of a candy company.

Sid wore his success on his sleeve, and it came to annoy most of the players.

"It's a danged good thing that you're a Jew," Bulldog would say. "Otherwise, you wouldn't have a pot to piss in."

Luckman was always the last player to arrive for the team bus. One morning, he straggled out of the hotel lobby five minutes late and seemed in no hurry to board as he signed some autographs. As he finally walked onto the bus, Bulldog's voice blared from the back of the bus: "You are a goddamned prima donna. Why don't you just grab a cab next time."

Laughter filled the bus.

It might have worried Halas to hear Bulldog's rants against the Chicago quarterback. But Anderson and Johnsos couldn't have cared less.

"If Bulldog keeps blocking the way he's blocking, Sid will be the best damned quarterback in the league," Anderson said. "Screw the rest."

Anderson was fully confident that first week in November that the Bears would take the Packers in the rematch at Wrigley Field. The night before, he had dispatched Connie Mack Berry to the Packers' hotel on a fact-finding mission. Berry had played briefly for the Packers and still had friends on the roster.

Berry was instructed to stroll into the hotel lobby that Saturday evening, mingle with the players, and keep his ears open.

"I know that ballplayers like to brag," Anderson said. "Stick around long enough and they'll tell you something we can use."

Berry telephoned Anderson just before midnight. The coach was eager for the news.

"I didn't learn anything about their plans," Berry said with an apologetic tone. "But I did find out how Buckets Goldenberg knows when Sid is going to pass."

"Tell me," Anderson said.

"Well, if Sid is standing upright under center, Buckets knows that it's a pass. But if Sid is down in a crouch, he knows it'll be a run."

The Chicago coaches had been baffled for years as to why Goldenberg dropped into pass coverage even before the ball was snapped. This sixth sense had disrupted the Bears' passing game and caused great confusion for Luckman. So right after the team bus arrived at Wrigley Field, Anderson pulled his quarterback aside and delivered his scouting report on Goldenberg. On the first play of the game, Luckman was told, he was not to bend his knees but to stand as upright as possible. He would take the snap from Bulldog and drop three steps to pass. Then he would stuff the ball into the belly of fullback Gary Famiglietti, who would rumble up the middle into the space left open by Goldenberg. The play was called thirty-one draw. Famiglietti gained fifty yards on the play. Halfback Scooter McLean then tore around for twenty yards and the first touchdown of the day. Later in the half, McLean sprinted sixty-six yards for a touchdown, and Luckman passed thirty-eight yards to Harry Clark for a third touchdown in the fourth quarter. Chicago cruised to victory 21–7.

The Bears were 6–0–1 and leading the Western Division with a trip to the Polo Grounds next on the schedule. The Giants were in a nip-and-tuck race with Washington for the Eastern Division title. With Halas away, Giants coach Steve Owen decided to try a little psychology on the Bears. Owen knew that a few timely comments to the New York writers might stir self-doubts within the Bears.

"The Chicago T-formation is not what it used to be," Owen told the press. "Just look at it. It stinks. Besides, I don't think the Bears could beat Notre Dame with this lineup."

The quotes appeared on every New York sports page the next day, and Hunk Anderson had his hands on each one. Just like Halas, he plastered the walls with that newsprint. The Bears players were romping, stomping mad when they got off the train at Penn Station the day before the game. Anderson knew that Papa Bear would be proud.

At the moment, Luckman was the leading passer in the NFL. But there was a reason for worry in the Bears camp. Luckman had injured his right shoulder in the previous game against Green Bay, and he could barely raise his arm above his shoulder. Anderson and Johnsos were considering a switch to Bob Snyder when Luckman approached them both at the team's hotel Saturday night.

"I really want to play tomorrow," he said. "In fact, I have to play. Tomorrow is a special day, and I have to be in the lineup."

Sunday was indeed one of the most important days in his professional life. It was "Sid Luckman Day" at the Polo Grounds. They planned to honor the former New Yorker and former Columbia star during pregame ceremonies. There was no way he was going to miss this game.

Before kickoff, officials from the borough of Brooklyn presented Luckman with a $1,000 war bond and Mayor Fiorello La Guardia was photographed with him on the sideline. After the crowd of 56,681 fans gave Luckman a standing ovation, Bulldog Turner cupped his hands and yelled, "The rich just get richer, Sid!"

In truth, the biggest thing on Luckman's mind was the sore shoulder. Trainer Andy Lotshaw had rubbed it with hot liniment before the game, but it barely worked to loosen the joint. Novocaine was becoming a popular painkiller at the time, and Lotshaw recommended it to Luckman.

"It might be the only way I can play," the quarterback said. "Let's give it a try."

Lotshaw drove the needle deep into the shoulder joint and Luckman felt a hot sensation shooting all the way to his fingers. Sweat broke out on his forehead and his breathing and heart rate began to rise. This worried Lotshaw, who knew little about the side effects of the drug. He thought about summoning a doctor or even an ambulance, but Luckman was breathing normally again in less than a minute. A warm, relaxing feeling washed over his body.

"Wow, that is pretty strong stuff, Andy," he said. "I'm feeling pretty good."

Luckman was able to raise his arm over his head for the first time all week. In a matter of minutes he would be on the field firing crisp warm-up tosses to the Bears receivers. The shoulder was now loose and pain free, and even Luckman could not believe the velocity of his passes as the game began. His first touchdown pass of thirty-eight yards was to end Jim Benton, and the second of twenty-four yards was to Hampton Pool, Harry Clark caught the third one, and Dante Magnani the fourth. When Luckman tossed the fifth touchdown pass to Benton, the Bears led 35–0. Anderson quickly pulled his quarterback from the game to rest his sore shoulder.

Up in the press box, Luke Johnsos felt a tap on his shoulder and turned around to find Associated Press sportswriter Sid Feder standing behind him.

"Luckman needs just one more touchdown pass to tie the all-time record," Feder told Johnsos. "He needs two to break it."

A week earlier, Baugh had set the record with six touchdown tosses. Johnsos hurriedly called the sideline and relayed the message to Anderson, who passed it along to Luckman.

"Want to go for the record?" Anderson asked the quarterback.

Luckman said nothing. He simply picked up his helmet and walked back onto the field.

A few plays later, after the Bears moved into Giants territory, Johnsos sent a play down to the field and then walked over to Feder.

"OK, here comes number six," he told the sportswriter. On the next play, Luckman passed thirty yards to George Wilson for yet another touchdown. The Bears got the ball back with three minutes to play and, up in the press box, Johnsos held up seven fingers to Feder. Johnsos mouthed the words, "Here it comes."

Luckman's twenty-yard pass found Pool at the five-yard line. So determined was the Bears end to set the record for Luckman that he dragged three Giants into the end zone.

That day, Luckman set two records that would have the NFL talking for decades. Seven touchdown passes and 433 passing yards seemed beyond comprehension at a time when the NFL was still a running league and the value of the forward pass remained a matter of great debate.

After the 56–7 victory over New York, the Bears were but two games from an unbeaten season, and the Washington Redskins and Chicago Cardinals were still on the schedule.

There was a train ride to the nation's capital for their next game. It was their bad luck that Luckman and Benton came down with the flu the night before the Redskins game. Bob Snyder had to play most of the game at quarterback, and the Chicago offense had no punch. Baugh and the Redskins beat the Bears 21–7.

Anderson said afterward, "The Bears, I regret to say, were outcharged, outmaneuvered, and outthunk. We had one advantage. We outstunk them."

There was more bad news. Green Bay had defeated Brooklyn, leaving the Packers one game behind Chicago in the Western Conference race. The ailing Bears would need a victory over the Cardinals the following Sunday to assure themselves of a spot in the NFL championship game.

Chi Town was getting nervous.

# 20

# Rock of Ages

Hunk Anderson could not believe his ears.

"Our fullbacks can't block," Bronko Nagurski said flatly. "No wonder the offense didn't do squat against Washington."

Anderson looked him squarely in the eye.

"What are you telling me, Bronk?" he said. "You want to play some fullback?"

"Why not?" he said. "I can still cut the buck."

Nagurski's attitude had taken a radical turn. Playing fullback never would have crossed his mind just three months earlier. The bowed legs and the bum knee were not sturdy enough to carry an aging man and his aching body into the teeth of an NFL defense. But the Bronk's confidence had grown with each passing week, and an old flame was burning.

Anderson shoved the ballcap to the back of his head. "You think you can still lug the leather?" he asked.

"Is George Patton a tough bastard?"

Anderson never expected to hear this kind of talk. The original deal with Nagurski was a simple plan: He would bang heads in the line for one final season, help the Monsters of the Midway win one more championship, and then retreat to the Big North Woods for good. The Bears needed big, strong, and able bodies in the line. Despite the long layoff, the Bronk had provided some serious muscle up front. It had helped Chicago stay in first place in the Western Division for an entire season. But running the football again?

Hunk had never been able to read the Bronk's mind. No one could, really. But he knew in his heart that the aging warhorse was ready to answer the call for a team beset by injuries and by a flu bug working its way through the locker room.

Anderson was not one to make alibis. As the Bears prepped for the regular-season finale against the Cardinals, he told the Chicago writers, "Our tackles are still barely breathing. We're patching our backs so they don't need crutches anymore. If we don't win the football championship, we'll surely win some kind of title over at the Illinois Masonic Hospital."

Neither Sid Luckman nor end Jim Benton had been able to practice more than thirty minutes all week, thanks to their urgent dashes to the rest room. The "grippe" had hung on longer than trainer Andy Lotshaw had ever expected, and both Benton and Luckman were suffering from acute dehydration. There was no telling how many others would miss the game on Sunday. Regular fullback Gary Famiglietti was recovering from a deeply bruised thigh, and his backup, Bob Masters, could barely walk because of a severe ankle sprain. The Bears had re-signed Ray Nolting three weeks earlier to take up some slack in the ailing backfield, but he was better suited to playing halfback.

Despite the team's record of 7–1–1, a black cloud had been hovering over the Bears for two weeks. They had the locker-room blues. Losing a crucial game to the hated Redskins in such a pathetic manner had created enormous doubts.

Nagurski lined up at fullback for the first time all season during the Thursday practice at Wrigley Field. Neither Anderson nor Luke Johnsos could believe their eyes. In spite of the stiff legs and the round belly, the Bronk bolted out of the three-point stance and tore through tacklers like the bruiser of old. On consecutive carries, he gained six yards, eight yards, nine yards, twelve yards, and seven yards. After ten straight carries, the Bronk was still pounding away at the defense and growing stronger by the minute. Players on defense labored to fill their lungs. They dreaded the thought of Nagurski roaring out of the backfield once more with elbows and knees pumping.

Anderson wondered what George Halas would have done in this situation. Papa Bear was a master at keeping a secret under his hat. That is why practices were always closed to the press and the public and why guards were stationed at every gate around Wrigley Field. Halas's paranoia knew no bounds, especially in the days leading to make-or-break games. Anderson wondered whether anyone could be spying on the practice at that very moment. His eyes surveyed the west grandstand and he saw no one. Then his eyes carefully scanned the east grandstand. Nothing or no one seemed to be stirring. But darkness was starting to fall on the North Side, and shadows were forming beneath the upper deck, where a spy could tuck in behind one of the pillars and keep watch on the field. Anderson squinted into the setting sun and tried to detect movement in the dark and distant corners of the ballpark.

Halas had dispatched Anderson on several occasions to Comiskey Park to spy on the Cardinals. Hunk had dressed like a maintenance man replete with toolbelt and ballcap pulled low. He managed to diagram several of the plays. Predictably, the Cardinals were always adding new formations and plays specifically for the Bears, and thanks to Anderson's undercover work, adjustments were made in advance to stop them. Now Anderson wondered whether it was payback time.

He blew his whistle. "Nagurski, get back to tackle," he snapped.

Everyone on the field turned at once to see whether Hunk had lost his mind. Johnsos held up open palms, as if to say, "Are you crazy?"

The Bears ran three more plays, and Anderson halted the practice, telling the players to take a knee.

"Look guys," he said. "Just forget what you saw from the Bronk here today. We can't ask this man to save our bacon. He's been playing in the line all season. For God's sake, we've got to stick with what got us here. Now go get dressed. We're going with our regular lineup on Sunday."

What he wanted to say was "Keep your mouths shut." But that would have never worked with so many young players on the team. News traveled fast in Chicago, especially when that news concerned Bronko Nagurski.

As the players trudged toward the locker room, Anderson caught Nagurski's eye and winked. It was not necessary. Nagurski had the horse sense to know what the coach was up to.

Johnsos, on the other hand, could not have been more confused. As the players showered and dressed, Anderson called Johnsos and Paddy Driscoll into his office and closed the door.

"Look, I know you think I'm nuts," Anderson said. "But if word leaks out that we're going with Nagurski at fullback, the Cardinals'll stack the line of scrimmage. Besides, there's no way the Bronk can play four quarters at fullback. We've got to pace the man. We've got to surprise them."

"So when do we put him in at fullback?" Johnsos said.

"When we need him. And you can be damned sure we will."

Anderson was not surprised the next day when three writers approached him with questions about Nagurski. He knew that somebody from the Cardinals had tipped them.

"We hear you're moving the Big Nag to fullback?" asked Harry Sheer of the *Chicago Daily News.*

"Nah," Anderson said. "Hell, Nagurski's older than dirt. He's slower than Grandma."

"But you used him at fullback yesterday at practice," said Dick MacMillan of the *Tribune.*

"We did," Hunk said. "But we got so many boys hurt that we just needed a body out there. Hell, he almost needed oxygen when practice was over. The Bronk ain't no ball carrier any more."

The writers were not buying it. Their stories the next day would be filled with speculation about Nagurski's comeback at fullback.

• • •

Sid Luckman awoke Sunday morning at Chicago Memorial Hospital with a nurse standing over him.

"Mr. Luckman," she said. "Are you planning to play football today?"

Luckman's eyes widened as if he had seen a ghost.

"Oh, my God," he blurted. "Have I missed kickoff? What time is it? Why didn't you wake me up earlier?"

"It's only seven o'clock," the nurse said. "You've got plenty of time to make it to the stadium."

Luckman suddenly remembered his roiling stomach. He had been unable to hold down food for over a week, and an intravenous needle was sticking out of his right arm. He settled back into the mattress and wondered if he would have the energy to quarterback the Bears this day.

An hour later, Bulldog Turner was awakened at the Wellington Arms Hotel by the sound of a jackhammer on the street. He wondered if the steel bit had worked its way into his brain. Hung over from a long night of drinking beer at the Cottage Lounge, he stumbled across his hotel room and turned on the shower and drank heavily from the faucet. Then he stepped beneath the cold spray and prayed that it would deliver him from his grogginess.

Hunk Anderson had slept on the couch in his office at Wrigley Field. His restless sleep had been filled with dreams about George Halas. Hunk dreamt that he was adrift on a rubber raft in the middle of the South Pacific with an aircraft carrier steaming toward him. Halas stood on the deck of the carrier, flailing his arms and yelling. Hunk could make out only a few words and phrases: "Nagurski . . . kill the bastards . . . give him the goddamned ball."

At their apartment on the North Side, George Musso and the Bronk drank coffee and contemplated the biggest game of the year—perhaps the biggest of their careers. Musso pulled out the rubbing liniment and went to work on Nagurski's sore and aching legs.

"I'll get you ready for fullback today," Musso said.

"What makes you think I'm playing fullback?"

"Because Hunk was just jacking around. He knows we've got to have you. Shit, Bronk, he's got no choice."

"I can handle it," Nagurski said. "Just block for me, big man. I'll need some room to run."

"Hell, Bronk, you know I'll block for you. But please . . . don't run over my big ass."

Musso took stock of the bowed legs and the swollen left knee and said, "How you feeling, my friend?"

"I feel like a mule that pulled a plow too long," the Bronk said. "Otherwise, I feel pretty good."

Most Chicagoans would have spent the frigid morning of November 28 by their warm fires if not for the word on the wind that Nagurski was going back to fullback. Heavy moisture portended snow, and lots of it. A mist hung over downtown Chicago, obscuring the upper floors of the great towers as the elevated train carrying Nagurski and Musso rattled and clacked over Lake Street en route to the South Side. Neither man spoke a word. The game occupied their thoughts.

A few miles away, Luckman shuffled across the shiny, cold linoleum of the hospital lobby toward a waiting cab.

"Mr. Luckman," the cabbie said, "you don't look so good today."

"I feel worse than I look," said Luckman, chuckling. "Get me to Comiskey. There's a man there who knows how to fix me."

Turner grabbed a taxi at his hotel that he would share with Ray Nolting. As they headed for the stadium, Nolting turned to the Bears center and said, "Well, Clyde, you certainly outdid yourself last night."

"People only call me Clyde when I'm drunk."

"Well."

An hour later, Anderson did not know what to make of the Bears' eerily quiet locker room as he passed through it. Had the Monsters' morale sunk even lower, or were they quietly focusing on the game ahead? Anderson was on his way to the training room, where he planned to check on Luckman and to see if the grippe had finally passed. He was surprised to find Luckman and Turner sitting side by side on a taping table, both men looking as if they had not slept in a week.

"What's wrong with you, Bulldog?" Anderson said.

"Sid here gave me the flu."

"Yeah," Luckman said. "The Jim Beam flu."

"Nah, it was just beer. Just a few too many Old Styles."

"Both of you guys are playing, right?" Anderson said. "No bullshittin'."

"Yeah," they said in unison.

Trainer Andy Lotshaw was fetching aspirin from the medicine cabinet. He handed both players three apiece and said, "That's about all we got to offer. I'd give you novocaine if you had a sprained ankle. But novocaine can't cure the flu. And it sure as hell can't cure Bulldog's hangover."

Anderson's next stop would be Nagurski's locker. He found the big man stretched out on the floor and snoring. This did nothing to quell the coach's anxiety.

Sitting next to the adjoining locker, Musso said, "Don't worry, Hunk. The old man's fine. You know how these geezers are. He just needs to rest up for the big game."

Anderson knew that Halas would be bouncing off the wall by now. Kickoff was less than two hours away, and the locker room looked like a hospital ward. Blind, crippled, or hung over, the Bears still had the talent and the resources to steamroll the Chicago Cardinals, the NFL's most pathetic team of the last decade. Marshall Goldberg, Chicago's best player and leading rusher, was on the sideline with a broken leg. No team had suffered greater losses to the war. Coach Jimmy Conzelman had taken one look at the roster back in September and quit on the spot. He was so frustrated with pro football that he decided to give baseball a try and signed on as an assistant to the president of the St. Louis Browns.

The Cardinals had limped through the season using players under assumed names from the Great Lakes Naval Training Station. Anderson knew the navy did not approve of enlisted men playing in the NFL. So he made a phone call and complained to one of the local navy commanders, who shut off the pipeline to the Cardinals. Now they would be suiting up only eighteen players for the regular-season finale compared to thirty for the Bears.

So shorthanded were the Cardinals that local bookmakers had made the Bears 23½-point favorites. Pro sports had recently entered the era of point spreads. No longer would games be bet strictly according to odds. The point spread, also known as "the line," had been invented in 1940 by a University of Chicago mathematics graduate named Charles McNeil.

Local bookies stationed at taverns around Comiskey Park were shocked at the amount of money being wagered on the Bears. The South Side might have been the home turf of the Cardinals, but the North Siders had come bearing money.

It was little wonder that the public had so little faith in the Cardinals. They had not won a game in 1943, and could boast of only three victories the last two seasons. Phil Handler, chosen as the emergency replacement for Conzelman, had been an assistant coach for eleven seasons but never a head coach.

The best the Cardinals had to offer was a dynamic duo from Texas that had helped tiny Centenary College of Shreveport pull off the biggest upset of the college football season back in 1934. Conway Baker from Marlin, Texas, and Buddy Parker from Kemp had teamed up to lead Centenary over the powerful Texas Longhorns by the score of 9–6. Parker, one of the nation's leading rushers, had kicked an eighteen-yard field goal in the final minute of the game. Most of his yards that day were gained behind the bone-crushing blocks of Baker. Texas, having defeated Notre

Dame 7–6 and Oklahoma 19–0 the previous two weeks, was the top-ranked team in the country before running into tiny Centenary.

The only other player of note on the Cardinals roster was fullback Johnny Grigas, a rookie fullback from Holy Cross who had gained three hundred yards rushing. Ed Prell's season preview of the Cardinals in the *Tribune* had been hardly flattering: "Through eleven dreary seasons with the Cardinals, Phil Handler has learned to persevere in the face of hardships. There is no indication the script will be changed this season."

Handler's team faced the damning prospect of having only seven substitutes. The players on the Cardinals sideline were mostly out-of-work high school coaches who had never played pro ball. Most were merely killing grass. The line of Chet Bulger, Gil Duggan, Marshall Robnett, Vaughn Stewart, and Baker would be expected to play the entire sixty minutes. Meanwhile, Anderson would exploit the new rules of free substitution and rotate two or three players after every change of possession.

But the Cardinals had one large factor in their favor—pure unadulterated hate of the Bears. It was said that if crowbars were issued to the Cardinals during pregame warmups, all the Bears would be dead after the opening kickoff.

Nagurski was on the sideline at the start of the game, and this confused the crowd of forty thousand fans no end. They had come to see the old man play fullback, and now he was wrapped in a full-length black cape with "Chicago Bears" stenciled on the back. There was an uneasy feeling in the Bear-dominated crowd as the game began.

Even more perplexing were the events of the first quarter. Clearly the team with the crack in its whip was the Cardinals. The Bears seemed to be sleepwalking. Danny Fortmann, George Wilson, and Harry Clark had been suffering from flu symptoms the last few days, and the entire line already seemed dead-legged. Anderson's concerns about the stillness of the pregame locker room were now justified. It seemed the Cardinals and Bears had switched uniforms. Cardinals fullback Bob Morrow and Grigas ripped off big gains behind some resounding blocks that were heard high in the stands. Practically the only voice that could be heard around the stadium belonged to Anderson, who cursed and raged like a boot-camp drill sergeant. He could barely believe what he was seeing. The Cardinals marched eighty yards without throwing a single pass, and Grigas scored the opening touchdown on a one-yard cross buck. Not a single Bear laid a hand on him. Conway Baker added the extra point. Comiskey Park was library-quiet.

Anderson still was not ready to make his move.

The Bears' first offensive possession stalled after only three plays. Luckman was forced to punt. Chicago got the ball back at its forty-yard line following a punt by the Cardinals. Two plays later, Luckman's pass over the middle for Hampton Pool was intercepted by Grigas.

As the second quarter began, Nagurski shed the coat, picked up his helmet, and trotted onto the field. Fans held their collective breath and prayed. They were disappointed when he lined up at right tackle but happy when the offense finally started moving, thanks to his bulldozing blocks.

At the Cardinals' twenty-yard line, though, Baker broke through the line and sacked Luckman for a seven-yard loss. He stood over the quarterback and shook his fist: "I'm going to kill you, you sonofabitch."

"Over my dead body!" Turner shot back. He spun Baker around and pushed him backward across the line of scrimmage.

Luckman was struggling to get to his feet when Turner put his arm around the quarterback's shoulders and lifted him.

"Everything's going to be all right," the big center said. "I know you ain't feeling good, Sid. But, son, we got to get going."

Luckman was out of breath and could not call the next play.

"Just throw the damn thing to Harry," Turner growled.

The Bears broke the huddle. Luckman dropped three steps in the pocket and fired a perfect strike over the middle that hit Harry Clark in stride at the two-yard line. Clark split two tacklers and shot into the end zone. Bob Snyder's extra-point kick tied the score midway into the second quarter. Still, there was little cheering inside Comiskey Park—just a long sigh of relief.

The Cardinals were hardly intimidated. They marched down the field as if they were the ones fighting for the NFL championship. Not one substitute had entered the game, and they were still pushing the Bears around. At the Bears' ten-yard line, though, Nagurski tackled Grigas twice for no gain. Baker kicked a seventeen-yard field goal for a 10–7 Cardinals lead. Five minutes remained until halftime.

Luckman was suddenly a new man. Either Baker's remark or Turner's pep talk had lit a fire under the Bears' quarterback. He uncorked a fifty-yard completion to Ray Nolting down the right sideline that moved the Bears to the twenty-seven-yard line. Luckman, hoping to keep the pressure on the Cardinals, heaved a pass into the end zone on the next play, and Hampton Pool came up with the catch. But the Bears were called for backfield in motion— Nolting had jumped before the snap.

"Shit," Luckman yelled in the huddle. "Pull your head out of your ass."

No one could ever remember Sid cursing.

"You got it," Turner said with a grin.

Luckman unloaded one for the corner of the end zone, and Pool once more leaped between defenders and hauled it in. Snyder kicked the extra point and the Bears had a 14–10 lead. A nervous tension filled the air as the teams trotted to their locker rooms for the intermission.

Anderson had planned a fiery halftime speech until Luckman's late touchdown pass put the Bears ahead. Instead, he set up the chalkboard and began to make some defensive adjustments while Johnsos discussed second-half strategy with Luckman. That is when they could hear all hell breaking loose in the Cardinals' locker room next door. Only a thin wall separated the teams. Cardinal players were banging on that wall and yelling at the top of their lungs.

"You're dead meat, Luckman," somebody shouted.

"Nagurski, you're an old sonofabitch," came another voice.

Luckman quickly strode to the front of the room.

"Those guys are a bunch of bastards," he said, pointing toward the Cardinals. "And they're standing between us and our dreams. We've got one half left to go. Let's fight!"

Both teams ran out of their respective locker rooms and managed to reach the narrow tunnel leading back to the field at the same time. Players from both sides were bumping into each other as skirmishes broke out. Baker took a swing at Luckman and missed. Nagurski grabbed the big Cardinals guard by the jersey and slung him to the ground.

"Somebody's going to get you in the second half," Bronko yelled at Baker. "You just wait."

Nagurski and the Bears might have been riled, but it was the Cardinals with the fire in their bellies at the start of the second half. Anderson decided to put Nagurski back on the bench to keep his legs fresh. It was a mistake. The Cardinals' offense rolled down the field and did not stop until it reached the end zone. To cap the eighty-yard drive, Morrow plowed three yards behind a block by Baker, who also kicked the extra point. The Cardinals led once more, 17–14. Comiskey Park was silent.

Nagurski was still on the bench, and the crowd was getting antsy, when Luckman tried to jump-start the Bears' offense. He completed quick passes to Clark and Pool and seemed to be settling into a groove when he got greedy. He called for a deep sideline route by Pool. It was the kind of pass that defensive backs licked their chops for—especially when Luckman was throwing it. The high arcing pass looked more like a punt, and Cardinals linebacker Buddy Parker broke toward the sideline like a bullet and plucked it from the air at the Cardinals thirty. The crowd groaned. Flasks went bottoms-up and the smell of whiskey wafted across the grandstand. Fans were trying everything to soothe their anxiety.

The wind was starting to kick up as the Cardinals' eleven switched over to defense. Not a single substitute had entered the game. Anderson made his lineup changes, but still no Nagurski. The Bronk was sitting on the bench, and it seemed that every eyeball in the stadium was keeping track of him.

After a change of possession, Grigas punted back to the Bears, and Clark fielded it. He faked two tacklers and was hit head-on by Parker as the ball squirted loose. Gil Duggan recovered the free ball at the thirty-five-yard line. On the sideline, Anderson fell to his knees and pounded the ground. A cold burst of wind roared over the rim of Comiskey Park as a canopy of thick, gray clouds settled over the South Side.

Grigas carried over right tackle for a gain of two yards, and the crowd suddenly came awake. They were now on their feet, exhorting the defense to halt these pesky Cardinals. One more touchdown might kill the Bears. With forty thousand fans still in full throat, Grigas burst through a hole at right guard. Baker blocked Turner out of the play, and Parker's flying block swept Luckman off his feet. Grigas sprinted twenty-eight yards straight as an arrow to the end zone. Bulger's conversion kick increased the lead to 24–14. The place grew deathly quiet.

One minute remained in the third quarter. Anderson thought about Nagurski, but still he was not ready to play his hand.

Luckman looked tired and defeated as he trotted back into the huddle. The ball was at the Bears thirty.

"Get it together, Sid," Bulldog said. "We still got time."

The Bears quarterback dropped back to pass and felt the pocket collapsing around him. Baker broke through two blockers and grabbed Luckman by the helmet, wrenching his neck and wrestling him to the ground. As they lay side by side, Baker punched Luckman in the gut and said, "Serves you right, Jew!"

Luckman, a peaceful man who handled every situation in a professional manner, jumped to his feet and kicked Baker in the teeth.

Baker rose up and slugged the Bears quarterback with a powerful right cross, knocking him over two bodies. Turner reared back to throw a haymaker but his arms were pinned by Musso from behind. Musso could see that referee Tom Marshall was about to make the right call; he had seen the punch by Baker but not the kick by Luckman. Marshall ran toward Baker and pointed at the big man: "You're out of the game, mister! Fifteen-yard penalty on the red team!"

Now the Cardinals players were yelling, cursing, and stomping, and Phil Handler ran to the middle of the field. He grabbed Marshall by the shirt.

"Get out of my face," the referee yelled, "or I'll throw you all out."

Baker, who had never been ejected from a game, would spend the rest of the day watching from the sideline and dabbing blood from his face.

Hunk Anderson had seen enough. As the teams changed ends of the field for the fourth quarter, he turned and called for Nagurski. The big man rose slowly and let the cape slide from his shoulders. As he reached for his helmet, a low rumble rose up from the stands. A woman behind the Bears bench screamed. A man sitting on the forty-yard line turned to his twelve-year-old nephew and said, "He's coming in! I told you he would!"

The kid, Bill Goldman, had heard about Nagurski for years. He covered his eyes with his hands. "I can't watch," he said.

Nagurski was the Bears' last hope. If he failed, the Bears would face certain defeat. More important, it would mean sudden death to the legend. Those who revered the man would depart Comiskey Park with the wrong memory. A twelve-year-old boy who had never seen Nagurski play would feel betrayed.

That is why forty thousand people rose up and chanted, "Bronko! Bronko! Bronko!" They wanted to believe.

Snow began to fall as Bronko trotted toward the huddle. The Bears

MONSTER OF THE MIDWAY

players turned to watch him coming toward them as if they were witnessing history. The bedraggled Cardinals players barked at him as if a fat black cat had just been spotted crossing the street.

"You're nothing but a goddamned old man," Chet Bulger yelled. His broken nose had been shoved an inch to the left. But Bulger had yet to miss a single play. In fact, the Cardinals had made only one substitution all day—Clarence Booth for Baker.

"Bronko *who?*" shouted Vaughn Stewart. The Cardinals' center and middle guard had never left the field. His jersey was soaked with blood and his white pants were spattered with red.

Luckman stepped into the huddle and, above the din of the stadium, yelled, "Thirty-one on two. Ready, break!"

Nagurski, the "three" back, would carry the ball through the "one" hole, which was over center. Turner had already been warned, "Block or get out of my way or I will break your spine."

The Bronk hit the line with the force of a locomotive, but the stubborn Cardinals were not giving an inch. Eleven red jerseys converged on number three, and his feet were suddenly off the ground—he was being lifted! Bill Goldman turned his face away from the field as thousands of others felt the same impulse. Then came some startling news from the public address announcer: "Second and six at the thirty-seven," boomed the voice over the loudspeakers.

Nagurski had gained four yards.

Ernest Hemingway once wrote, "Nobody lives their lives all the way up except bullfighters." Perhaps he had never seen Nagurski. A man on his last legs trotted back to the huddle and said, "Sid, give me the ball again."

Then the Bronk remembered what his mother often said in her native Ukrainian when times were tough: *Ty moz'esz robyty tse.* "You can make it."

This time Musso managed to pry open some daylight. Nagurski stormed into the secondary and was met by defensive back Johnny Martin and Parker. Both hit Nagurski with a flying tackle. He fell to his knees, but since he had not been pinned to the ground, he could keep going. The Bronk was now crawling and the crowd was screaming. He managed to gain five more yards on his knees, for a total gain of eleven yards, to the Bears forty-eight.

Before the game Luckman and Johnsos had discussed the strategy of faking to Nagurski and sending Pool on a sideline-and-go pattern. Turner anticipated that Luckman was about to call a pass when he said, "Just give the goddamned ball to the old man." Luckman changed his mind and called thirty-four-counter. Nagurski gained four yards at right tackle. Then he took four Cardinals on a piggyback ride for five yards. Now he was like an axe hitting a tree. It does not matter how big the tree is when the axe starts working. Nagurski slammed into the line for an eleven-yard gain, and the ball rested at the Cardinals thirty-two.

Luckman stepped into the huddle and before Turner could interrupt said, "Shut up, Bulldog. Eighty-eight cross." It was a post pattern for Pool after a fake to Nagurski. Luckman pulled the ball out of Bronko's belly, retreated three steps, and flicked a quick pass over the middle to Pool. The lean tight end broke two tackles before being knocked down at the twenty.

The snow was picking up when Luckman called for Nagurski straight up the middle behind Turner. The Bronk found an opening between the center and right guard Danny Fortmann and rumbled through it. He was hit by three defenders at the twelve-yard line and put his right hand down on the ground to keep his balance. Now he was like a bear walking on three legs—the ball cradled in his left hand. Two Cardinals jumped on his back at the eight-yard line, and somehow he kept going. Two more hopped aboard at the five, and it did not stop him. The Comiskey Park partisans were howling and pulling their hair. Nagurski, a walking human tripod, had six men on his back when he reached the three-yard line. He managed to stumble two more yards before collapsing on his stomach. It was first-and-goal at the one.

Luckman called the same play, and as the Bears broke the huddle, Nagurski muttered to himself, *"Ty moz'esz robyty tse."* The Cardinals linemen pounded each other on the butt and shook their fists at the Bears. They were covered with mud and blood.

"Ain't no way, old man," Stewart bellowed.

"Better throw it," Bulger yelled.

Luckman felt the force of a freight train blow past when he handed Nagurski the ball. Eleven red jerseys were welded together at the goal—the defense had sold out to stop him. A fake to Nagurski, and Luckman could have strolled around either end for a touchdown.

Nagurski slammed into the line and vanished into the wall of humanity, popping out on the other side, his piston legs still churning. The heartbroken Cardinals crumbled to their knees as hats flew out of the stands. Nagurski had carried the ball seven times for fifty-four yards. The Bears now trailed only 24–21 with eight minutes to play. It was snowing harder.

The Bronk would rest as the defense took the field. Wrapped in the black cape, he was bouncing up and down to keep warm when the chant began again: "Bronko! Bronko! Bronko!"

The Cardinals were not a beaten team—not yet, anyway. Runs by Grigas and Parker netted three first downs. It was solid proof of their enduring spirit. Anderson yelled his lungs out on the sidelines: "Stop the sonsabitches." The Bears defense finally did, and a great sense of relief washed over Comiskey Park.

A booming punt by Grigas pinned the Bears at their thirteen-yard line. Only five minutes remained on the scoreboard clock, which glowed in the gathering darkness.

"Here's something the bastards in red don't want," Luckman spat. "Thirty-four cross buck."

Nagurski blasted up the middle for seventeen yards, and the defense's backbone started to break. Then Anderson did something the crowd could not fathom. He sent Nolting in for Nagurski.

Nolting carried twice for six yards, and Luckman's pass on third down for Hampton fell incomplete. It was fourth-and-four from the Bears thirty-six-yard line. The crowd was riled. Whiskey bottles were about to fly toward Anderson's head until he sent Nagurski back into the game just in time.

"Thirty-one fold," Luckman shouted above the din. Nagurski would carry the ball behind Turner as Fortmann folded the linebacker to the inside.

Nagurski read the blocks perfectly and angled to the right, scraping off Fortmann's backside and rumbling for twelve yards. Then he looked up to see Nolting trotting back onto the field. The crowd booed lustily.

Three plays later, the Bears were in the same predicament. It was fourth-and-one at the Cardinals forty-three as Nagurski trotted in. The Cardinals felt a sudden rush of energy. Nagurski was stopped cold by a great red wall, but he kept his feet moving. It was like battling upriver against the rapids. The powerful body of Nagurski leaning forward finally moved the pile until he had gained three yards. It was first down at the forty with two minutes to play. The thought of subbing for Nagurski never crossed Anderson's mind again.

On the next two plays Bronko rumbled for gains of seven and eight yards. The clock was winding down. Luckman peered across the line at the battered and bloodied Cardinals, who had given every ounce of sweat and energy their worn-out bodies could muster. He called thirty-four cross buck once more but left himself with an option to audible. The active color was "blue."

All eleven Cardinals were stacked at the line of scrimmage. Luckman had no choice. He shouted, "Blue eighty-four!" He was checking off. It was the hitch-and-go pattern for Harry Clark, now at wingback. Luckman faked the handoff to Nagurski and the Cardinals defense took the bait. Eleven men tackled Nagurski. The quarterback dropped three steps and looped a perfect spiral to Clark at the ten-yard line. There was no one within twenty-five yards of the little wingback as he caught the pass and danced into the end zone. Comiskey Park erupted with a sound that could be heard halfway to St. Louis. Several thousand fans jumped over the retaining wall and ran down to the sideline but were quickly halted by a phalanx of cops on horseback. Snyder kicked the extra point for a 28–24 lead. There were fifty-nine seconds left to play.

It was almost pitch-dark. You could not see from one end zone to the other. But the Cardinals would have one last shot at a comeback. Grigas dropped back and prayed he could find a receiver. As he set up to throw, Turner hit his arm and the ball fluttered high into the air. Luckman ran under the errant pass and caught it. He quickly fell to the ground and cradled the ball.

Luckman had planned to take a knee to end the game. But Turner said, "Let's stick it up their asses one more time."

Luckman nodded and smiled. He could barely see five feet in front of him. But he told end George "Ducky" Wilson to head for the right corner of the end zone. No one but the back judge could see Wilson catching the pass. In truth, this little stunt almost gave Anderson a heart attack. If the Cardinals had somehow intercepted and returned it for a touchdown, the Bears would have lost. Instead, they won 35–24.

Fans poured onto the field and hats flew everywhere. Turner put his arm around Luckman and said, "You're one tough bird, Sidney."

Nagurski resisted, but a horde of fans managed to hoist him onto their shoulders. The Bronk smiled and actually pumped his fist in celebration. The old man had gained eighty-four yards on sixteen carries in the fourth quarter alone. Forty thousand voices were now chanting, "Bronko! Bronko! Bronko!"

High in the stands, Bill Goldman covered his face with his hands and cried.

Up in the press box, Harry Sheer of the *Daily News* wrote, "This is a story of what men are made of. Fighting-mad, desperate men of football. The right words in the right place might even make it a saga. A saga of an 'old man' of thirty-five, of a couple of kids in their twenties, of raw courage and of a little blood. It's too easy just to sit down and say the unruly Chicago Bears rallied yesterday from an upset. How the Monsters turned their backs to fate and in a bitter hand-to-hand duel wrecked the ambitions of the crosstown Cardinal rivals and won 35–24."

They would never forget the day Bronko Nagurski came back.

# 21

# Champions Again

The Chicago Bears locker room that day was a snapshot of history. They had come home from around the globe—George Halas, George Trafton, Red Grange, Carl Brumbaugh, and Ken Kavanaugh. More than two decades of Bears tradition was walking around the bowels of Wrigley Field.

Lieutenant Commander Halas had taken a Christmas leave from the navy, as had Kavanaugh from the Eighth Air Force. Trafton, Grange, and Brumbaugh could not resist the temptation to live vicariously once more. It would be the Bears and the Redskins on the day after Christmas for the 1943 NFL championship at sold-out Wrigley Field. It was cold and windy and sunny on the North Side, and the smell of cigar smoke and roasting peanuts filled the air. At a time when America agonized over the bloody images emanating from Europe and the South Pacific, it was a time to put aside the newspaper, to don the warmest woolens, and to catch the El up to Addison and Clark. It was a day that made the heart beat faster.

Nothing cured the blues like Chicago versus Washington. These were the titans of professional football, and everyone knew the names by heart—Bronko Nagurski, Sid Luckman, Sammy Baugh, Bulldog Turner, and Andy Farkas. The war had crippled the NFL and taken away some of the biggest headliners, but the Bears and the Redskins, thanks to progressive management and solid coaching, had survived and actually flourished in these tough times. They would be playing in the championship game for the fourth time since '37, with the Redskins holding a 2–1 edge. For Halas, the aroma of vindication was in the air, and it did not smell like George Preston Marshall's cigar.

Halas was decked out in his dress blues and seaman's cap, and he prowled the Bears locker room like a man ready to rumble. He strutted up to Nagurski and said, "You're tougher than a five-cent steak, mister, and meaner'n a junkyard dog. And I know, by God, you'll be back next year."

"Hold on, George," Bronko said with a chuckle. "Let me get through this game first."

Trafton had been drinking beer and hustling bets since seven that morning at the Cubs Grille across Addison Street. His face was flushed and wild with excitement.

"Damn, if they'd just give me a uniform," he howled, "I could lick every Redskin out there."

Nobody doubted Trafton. He had not suited up since 1932, but he still looked and acted the part of a street fighter.

An hour before kickoff the Bears locker room was like a Wild West saloon. Players laughed and joked and played cards. Halas and Trafton were slapping backs and telling stories. It seemed that everyone had a smile on his face. Even the Bronk was cutting up a little.

This bugged the hell out of Hunk Anderson.

He walked to the front of the locker room and loudly cleared his throat. The place finally drew silent.

"Gents," he said, "I don't mean to hurt nobody's feelings, but we got a football game to play today. Our guests need to skedaddle. And that means you, too, George."

Halas laughed and said, "Wouldn't have it have any other way. I'd do the same thing, Hunk. I'd kick me out, too. You've learned well, son."

Halas would someday return as the Bears' coach, but Hunk Anderson was still the boss. He wanted to make certain that the day was not spoiled. A healthy Chicago squad held the upper hand on the Redskins, a team that had struggled for three weeks just to reach the NFL title game. Washington had been ambushed by the lowly Pittsburgh-Philadelphia Steagles on the same weekend that the Bears came back to beat the Cardinals.

Washington had concluded the regular season with two games against the Giants—and lost both. A playoff game was then required to determine the Eastern Division title. The Redskins defeated the Giants 28–0 two weeks before they were to meet the Bears. Now they were dead-legged.

Meanwhile, the Monsters of the Midway had enjoyed a four-week vacation. It was more than ample time to overcome sprains and bruises and the nasty flu bug. It was little wonder the local bookmakers had installed the Bears as a ten-point favorite.

Anderson's greatest worry this day was the gunslinger named Slingin' Sammy Baugh, who in 1943 had captured the NFL's first triple crown—leading the league in three statistical categories. He led the league with 133 completions, a punting average of 45.9 yards, and 11 interceptions. Only Luckman had more touchdown passes—28 to Baugh's 23.

Baugh was the longest thorn in the side of the Chicago Bears. He had almost single-handedly defeated them in the '37 and '42 championship games. Washington had also handed the Monsters their only loss of the '43 regular season by the score of 21–7. Of course, no one would ever forget the 73–0 pasting of Washington three years earlier in the championship game. But it seemed that horrible humiliation had worked to build a fire inside the Redskins. They hated the Bears. And they were confident they could whip the Monsters a third straight time. Baugh had turned downright cocky as he talked to the writers two days before the game.

"I ain't as worried about the Bears as I am that danged cold weather in Chicago," he said. "We can handle the Bears. I just don't know whether we can handle that goddamned hurricane coming off Lake Michigan."

His teammates were infected with the same swagger. "The Bears are a bunch of old men," All-Pro fullback Andy Farkas said. "We'll outhit them and outquick them."

The Bears were known as the "Old Men of the North Side." Conversely, the 'Skins possessed the youngest roster in football. With Baugh at quarterback, they could strike from anywhere on the field, and the dry elements of Wrigley Field suggested a possible shoot-out. Luckily for the Bears, Luckman was over the flu. Anderson knew the Bears could outgun the Redskins if necessary. All week in practice, Luckman had looked like the same quarterback who had thrown seven touchdown passes in New York back in November.

But no one was prepared for what would happen in the early minutes of the game. Baugh booted a forty-four-yard punt. It sailed above the rim of the stadium in a tight spiral. Luckman fielded it at the Washington thirty. He angled for the left sideline, hoping to find a picket fence of blockers. Instead, he found Baugh steaming toward him. Baugh fell while trying to tackle Luckman and got kicked in the head. It happened in front of the Redskins bench, and Baugh's teammates could not believe their eyes. The greatest quarterback in the history of the game was down for the count. Baugh was not just a quarterback. He was one of the toughest men in a league of rough customers. The mood on the Washington bench quickly shifted from sadness to outrage. They came after Luckman with spears and daggers disguised as words.

"We will kill that Jew!" shouted wingback Wilbur Moore. Bulldog Turner hustled into the fray and rescued his quarterback. His presence had a calming effect on the angry Redskins.

Baugh's face was twisted in pain and tears rolled down his cheeks as he took a seat on the bench.

"Do you know where you are, Sam?" the team doctor asked.

"Fort Worth," he replied.

"Who do you play for?"

"The TCU Horned Frogs."

It looked like Sammy Baugh was done for the day.

In the blink of an eye, Washington had gone from a passing offense to a running offense. Backup quarterback George Cafego was content to hand the ball to fullback Andy Farkas. Washington's offensive line outweighed Chicago's defensive line, and the Redskins mowed down the Bears on an eighty-yard drive and grabbed a 7–0 lead in the opening minute of the second quarter.

Luckman answered on the next possession with four straight completions, including a thirty-one-yard touchdown pass to Harry Clark to tie the score.

Anderson had decided that Nagurski would not play tackle this day; he had become too valuable as a fullback. When he trotted on the field for the next series, the crowd erupted into "Bronko! Bronko! Bronko!"

The Bronk smashed through the line on four straight carries for nineteen yards. Then Luckman completed three straight passes to Clark and Dante Magnani, moving Chicago all the way to the three-yard line. Luckman needed no suggestions from Bulldog on what to call. It was the

Nagurski cross buck. The line delivered a huge hole as the Bronk thundered into the end zone. Forty-five thousand fans rose up with an ovation that sent chills down the big man's spine. He could not remember a greater feeling at any time in his football life. He seemed to be floating as he trotted back to the bench.

With halftime approaching, Washington owner George Preston Marshall, wearing the raccoon coat, decided to saunter down to the sideline and take a seat on the Chicago bench. Just like that. Bears players started pointing at Marshall, who barely disguised his intention to eavesdrop on the opponent's coaching strategy. Chicago general manager Ralph Brizzolara charged toward the Washington owner and grabbed him by the collar.

"What the hell you think you're doing?" he said.

"Oh, I just came down to say hello to the coaches at halftime. I just got here a little early."

Two minutes remained before the half.

"Get your ass off my bench before I have you arrested. Or I sic George Halas on you."

Marshall shrugged his shoulders and quickly removed himself.

The Bears led 14–7 at halftime. The Washington players were clacking up the tunnel toward their locker room when Baugh blurted to one in particular, "How in the hell did we get to Chicago?"

At the behest of coach Dutch Bergman, the team doctor reexamined Baugh. He determined that Baugh's head was clear enough to return for the second half. The Redskins suddenly had a pulse as Baugh was going back in.

But the Bears had almost put the game away by the midpoint of the third quarter, with Luckman throwing touchdown passes of thirty-six and sixty-six yards to Magnani for a 28–7 lead. Washington cut the deficit to fourteen points late in the quarter on Farkas's seventeen-yard touchdown catch from Baugh.

For one last hurrah, Anderson sent Nagurski back into the game. He powered the Bears down the field to set up a touchdown pass from Luckman to Benton. Facing a third down at the Washington forty-yard line, Luckman handed off to Nagurski and thought his arm had been torn off. The Bronk ran over Baugh, who was knocked groggy and had trouble rising to his feet. Luckman did the gentlemanly thing by helping Baugh up.

"That Nagurski is the toughest son-of-a-gun I've ever seen," Luckman said to Baugh.

"Shit," Sammy said. "You should've seen that sumbuck in his prime. I ain't never seen a player that big, that strong, and that fast. He's the best there ever was."

Two plays later, Luckman broke the NFL record for a postseason game with his fifth touchdown pass, this one to Clark, and the Redskins added a late touchdown run by Farkas. The Bears had defeated Washington 41–21 and captured their sixth NFL title. The game ended with the crowd on its feet chanting, "Bronko! Bronko! Bronko!"

Halas led the celebration in the locker room and was photographed with several jubilant players around him.

"This team probably was not as great as the one that beat the Redskins 73–0 four years ago," Halas said. "The '43 team was three-deep at every position, and this one is about half deep. But they had the power to win."

Anderson, too tired to celebrate, sat slumped on a trunk in the locker room. A reporter asked him about Marshall's bizarre behavior.

"I guess he just wanted to be on the winning side," Hunk said.

Halas told every reporter he could find that he expected Nagurski to return for the 1944 season. But the Bronk was not buying.

"I can't listen to George Halas's songs forever," he said.

A Chicago sportswriter said, "Bronk, there are a lot of people who thought you had no business playing this year."

He grinned. "I guess I don't know much about business."

A cab was waiting on Clark Street when Nagurski walked out into the darkness. George Musso was by his side. Tears were streaming down Musso's cheeks.

"You are the greatest player who ever lived," Musso said. "And you're the greatest friend I've ever had."

"Don't cry, big man," the Bronk said. "Just keep knocking them down."

Nagurski stepped into the cab that would take him to the Illinois Central station. Along the way, he watched the bright lights of the city roll past, and his eyes studied the skycrapers. Chicago was alive from snout to tail, as H. L. Mencken once wrote, and would celebrate far into the night. They would never stop toasting the greatest player who had ever lived.

It had been the happiest run of his life, and he would not have changed a thing. Coming out of retirement for the 1943 season turned out to be a great decision.

But Bronko Nagurski never came back.

# 22

# Beyond the Game

Bronko Nagurski arrived at Memorial Stadium that Saturday morning and was greeted at the locker-room door by Billy Bye, a former Minnesota quarterback who would be acting as player-coach for the alumni team. The annual spring game between past and current players of the Golden Gophers was scheduled for that afternoon.

"God, it's good to see you, Bronk," Bye said. "Shoot, you can sit with me on the bench today."

"The hell I can," Nagurski said. "I'm here to play."

"Jeez, Bronk, we didn't expect this. We thought you were just gonna watch. I guess we'd better scrape you up a uniform."

No wonder they didn't expect him to play. Nagurski was fifty years old. He had not suited up since December 26, 1943, when the Bears defeated Washington for the NFL championship.

Finding a uniform for the 260-pound legend was not that difficult. Locating a helmet that would fit was another matter. There was not a size eight in the house. In fact, the largest hard-shelled helmet with a face mask used in 1958 by Minnesota was a size 7½. The equipment staff had to dig deep into storage to find something that would cover his head. They finally located a leather helmet that had not been used since the forties— and it had to be stretched.

These varsity-alumni games were all the rage in the fifties and sixties at practically every major college in the country. They could be as competitive as any game in the fall. They offered a sixty-minute battle for bragging rights that drew huge crowds each year.

The Minnesota alumni team in 1958 was a virtual who's who of college and pro football. Three from the squad—Leo Nomellini, Bud Grant, and Nagurski—would be inducted into the Pro Football Hall of Fame. Nomellini and Grant had played for the Gophers in the late forties. Nomellini was an All-American tackle and Grant a two-time Big Ten choice at end. Grant would play in the NBA, NFL, and CFL before a celebrated coaching career with the Minnesota Vikings that included four Super Bowl appearances.

Another up-and-coming pro star was Gino Cappelletti, the former Gophers quarterback who would lead the AFL in scoring four times as a kicker and wide receiver. Center Clayton Tonnemaker, another All-American of the late forties, was now an All-Pro with the Green Bay Packers. Other familiar names were tackle Frank Youso, Bobby Cox, Dick Larson, Gordie and Jim Soltau, and Verne Gagne, a two-sport star who also was the reigning world heavyweight wrestling champ.

The Minnesota Golden Gophers, in spite of a down year in 1958, were still one of the most respected teams of the Big Ten. They had come within a touchdown of winning the conference title and playing in the Rose Bowl two years earlier. They would capture the national championship in 1960.

There was no greater symbol of the success of the Minnesota football program than Bronko Nagurski. That is why news spread like wildfire through Memorial Stadium that he would be making a comeback of sorts that day. The varsity players could not contain their enthusiasm.

The Bronk received a standing ovation from the home crowd when he trotted onto the field during pregame introductions. No one cheered any louder than the current Minnesota players. A kid growing up in the state of Minnesota knew every detail about the life of Bronko Nagurski.

Bye decided to insert Nagurski into the starting lineup as the alumni team would receive the kickoff. They wasted no time in putting him to work. He carried on the game's first play and plowed five yards straight up the middle. As he lay on the ground, every Gopher player ran over and put a hand on the Bronk. They wanted to be able to tell their grandchildren they had helped bring down the living legend.

The big man carried again on the second play of the game, and Frank Youso, a 260-pound tackle, swore he could feel the earth move as he rumbled through the line. Running with his left shoulder close to the ground, tunneling between defenders—it was the same running style he had made famous in the thirties. His second carry netted seven yards, and now the crowd was going wild.

"How're you feeling?" Bye asked in the huddle.

"Good enough to keep going," Nagurski said, breathing heavily. Bye could tell from the gleam in his eye that Bronko was ready for more.

He carried for a third straight time and broke two tackles on a six-yard gain. Again, each defensive player ran up and touched him as he lay on the ground. It was surprising that they did not have pens and papers ready for autographs.

When Nagurski carried the ball a fourth straight time, the stadium erupted in an ovation that was beyond anything anyone could remember for a spring game. He powered through three tacklers and gained another seven yards. The ageless wonder jumped to his feet and trotted back to the huddle with vigor in his step.

Bye decided to give Nagurksi a breather. He called for a pass to Grant and completed it for a thirteen-yard gain.

Then Nagurski carried for the fifth time and moved the ball all the way to the varsity twenty-yard line for a gain of twelve yards. Once again, every defensive player put a hand on him.

Bye called for another pass for Grant. Before breaking the huddle, he whispered to the end, "Catch it but don't score. Let's save it for the Bronk." The completion to Grant moved the ball down to the five. Everyone in the stadium knew what was coming next. The Minnesota varsity stacked eleven men near the line of scrimmage. Nomellini, Tonnemaker, and Youso opened a hole in the middle of the line and Nagurski crashed into the defense for what appeared to be a three-yard gain. He was stopped momentarily at the two-yard line by a wall of tacklers. But his aging legs had one last power surge left in them. Three tacklers fell away and Nagurski dived into the end zone for the final touchdown of his glorious football life. Everyone in the stadium was on their feet as he trotted back to the sideline.

A tired Bronko Nagurski watched the rest of the game from the sideline as the alums rolled to a 26–2 victory.

## SEPTEMBER 7, 1963

It was a sunny and warm afternoon in Canton, Ohio, when the Pro Football Hall of Fame swung open its doors for the first time and inducted seventeen charter members. From the Bears came George Halas, Red Grange, and Nagurski. Among the greatest Bear rivals were Sammy Baugh and Don Hutson.

Typically, Nagurski's induction speech was short and sweet:

"In the past, I have been asked many times if I wouldn't like to return to pro football. Well, I can tell you if I had to face the men sitting behind me right now, nothing could ever get me off the farm. I have had a lot of thrills in my life, but I can sincerely say that to be so honored here today, and with this fine group, this is the thrill of all thrills. And I want to thank all you people and all of the writers for making this possible. Thank you."

He was then presented with his Hall of Fame memento—a size 19½ ring. A spokesman for the L. G. Balfour Company said it was the largest one ever manufactured in America.

## JANUARY 2, 1960

It was Bronko's dream that he would someday open a gas station in International Falls. The doors swung open in 1960 in a downtown location not far from the bridge that connected the Falls with Ontario. Folks came from all over the Midwest and Canada—some going great distances out of their way—to have the Bronk fill their tank, whether it was ninety above or ninety below. He did all of the work—washed windshields, fixed flat tires, even handled a wrench. His fans were always happy to see him, and some wanted their pictures taken standing beside the football legend.

A woman in International Falls was asked one day why she did all of her business at the Nagurski Pure Oil Station.

"When Bronko puts the gas cap back on, nobody else can get it off," she said.

As his wrestling career was winding down in the late fifties, the Nagurskis lived a quiet and comfortable life in International Falls. Bronko took his sons on fishing and hunting excursions across the lakes and through the forests of the Big North Woods. He spent a great amount of time with all of his children and especially doted on daughters Janice and Eugenia.

One of his great loves was the hunting cabin that had been constructed during his NFL days. Just a few steps from the front door, it offered great fishing in the summer and unmatched deer hunting in the winter. Bronko loved to sit around the campfire and tell stories. He did not mind sharing his football experiences with close friends. But if the crowd ever grew too large, he would clam up. The man not once in his life was accused of bragging.

He encouraged the Nagurski kids to play sports but never overemphasized it.

"You do whatever you want," he would tell them. "But first, you have to do your homework and make up your bed."

It was the dream of Bronko and Eileen Nagurski that all six kids would graduate from college. It was a dream fullfilled. In order of diplomas there was Bronko Jr. (Notre Dame), Tony (St. John's University in Collegeville, Minnesota), Janice Carlson (St. Catherine's in St. Paul), Ron (Minnesota), Eugenia Jauma (Creighton), and Kevin (Notre Dame).

Bronko Jr. starred as a Notre Dame linebacker from 1956 through 1958 and played nine seasons in the Canadian Football League. During Junior's college career, Bronko would drive about eighty miles into Virginia, Minnesota, where he could find a hill tall enough to pick up a radio signal. Or he would visit the home of his good friend, Paul Bonicatto, to watch some of the bigger games on TV.

Bronko rarely traveled to Chicago for games or to the Pro Football Hall of Fame. After purchasing his first television set in the sixties, he remained connected to the NFL for the rest of his life. He had definite opinions about the evolution of the sport: "The game is just so doggone specialized. You have an offensive team, a defensive team, and special teams. I don't know how those boys would stand up against an old-time team that played sixty minutes."

He made one of his rare trips out of International Falls in 1963 to attend the Baseball Writer's Association dinner at the Americana Hotel in New York. Among the stars introduced that night were Mickey Mantle, Whitey Ford, and Joe DiMaggio—all received healthy applause. Then from the dais came these words: "Let's now pay a tribute to a star from another sport—Bronko Nagurski." The Bronk was the one who got the standing ovation.

## JANUARY 23, 1983

Two months earlier, NFL commissioner Pete Rozelle had been traveling back from Chicago to New York following the funeral of George Halas when he turned to his assistant, Dick Weiss, and said, "Let's try to get Bronko Nagurski to the Super Bowl. Do whatever it takes. I'd like to have him toss the coin."

At first, Nagurski balked at the offer. It had become almost impossible to lure a seventy-five-year-old man with arthritic joints and swollen ankles off the back porch of his lake house in International Falls. But if the NFL would agree to pay the expenses of his entire family—his wife, Eileen, six children, and their spouses—he would be happy to come to Tampa for Super Bowl XVIII.

The national press assembled in a hotel ballroom the week of the game to hear him reminisce about his fabled career. He entered the room listing to the right with an immense right hand gripping an aluminum crutch. An electric current seemed to be running through the room.

He peered cautiously through thick glasses at the assemblage of writers. "What am I in for?" he cracked.

In truth, the writers did not know what *they* were in for. He would take them on a magical journey of more than a half century into the past to places and people they had never seen.

"This is not the kind of stuff that I do very often," he said. "I'm not much of a speaker. But I'll do the best I can."

Someone asked about the time he ran headfirst into the wall at Wrigley Field. Did he really crack the brick?

He shifted uneasily in the chair. "Oh, they say I cracked it. I don't know. I never went back and looked." Then he paused and looked straight ahead as if searching for a light from the past. "I will say this. I hit that wall pretty doggone hard."

The next question focused on the mythical story of Minnesota coach Doc Spears seeing him lift the plow back in 1926. Nagurski chuckled and said, "Doc Spears never saw me plow. He only saw me plow through the line."

On his relationship with George Halas, he said, "I know George had a tough time for several years in that the club was losing money. He didn't have a lot of money because we just didn't have that many people in the stands. When he had money, he never was very generous. But I'm not going to hold that against him."

Then came the question he had dreaded. Somebody asked about his wrestling career and whether he had enjoyed it.

"I didn't like it at all," he said. "There was never enough money. It was a sport where you worked every night, traveled a great distance, and it never paid off. Promoters said I would make a million dollars. I didn't."

He was asked why he had always remained so attached to his hometown of International Falls.

"Well, it's beautiful country," he said. "Actually, to appreciate it, you need to be there in the summertime. They say we have seven months of winter and five months of poor sledding. But, really, our summers are pretty good."

The Bronk was getting tired after forty-five minutes of answering questions. An NFL public-relations man now looked around the room and asked if there were any more questions. No one spoke. Then all fifty writers rose in a spontaneous standing ovation. No one could ever remember the sporting press doing such a thing.

That Sunday, he would toss the coin before the game between the Redskins and Raiders. It would be the final public appearance of his life.

• • •

## JANUARY 7, 1990

Nagurski was a recluse in the final stages of his life, thanks to a body ravaged by arthritis, his eyesight growing dim. He made a trip to the Mayo Clinic, where doctors fused the degenerating bones in his ankles. One of the doctors asked him for an autograph for his son. Nagurski wrote, "To Jeremy—Do Not Play Football. Bronko Nagurski."

He spent much of the time in his later years at the lake house. In the summer months he sat on the wide back porch and watched the boats on Rainy River, wishing that he could fish some more. Not long after his wife Eileen died in 1989, he suffered a stroke. He was admitted to a nearby nursing home for the final year of his life.

He died of heart failure. The funeral was held six days later, on January 13, at St. Thomas Catholic Church, where Bronko and Eileen had been married back in 1936. The Rev. Father Dennis Deis presided over a ceremony attended by virtually every citizen of International Falls, along with several former teammates, including George Musso and George Gibson. It snowed that day as a long line of cars snaked through the narrow streets to the local cemetery. Bronko Nagurski was buried next to his wife on a hill overlooking some farmland. It was the same cemetery he used to run through on his way home from school. Nagurski fans from all over the world still visit the grave.

# Bibliography

Heartley Anderson with Emil Klosinski: *Notre Dame, Chicago Bears and "Hunk,"* Florida Sun-Gator, 1976.

Laurence Bergreen: *Capone: The Man and the Era,* Simon & Schuster, 1994.

Bob Carroll: *Total Football II,* HarperCollins, 1997.

John M. Carroll: *Red Grange and the Rise of Modern Football,* University of Illinois Press, 1999.

Cliff Christl and Gary D'Amato: *Mudbaths and Bloodbaths,* Prairie Oak Press, 1997.

Myron Cope: *The Game That Was,* World Books, 1970.

Bob Curran: *Pro Football's Rag Days,* Bonanza Books, 1953.

Dan Daly and Bob O'Donnell: *Pro Football Chronicle,* Hungry Minds, 1990.

Hiram Drache: *Taming the Wilderness,* Interstate Books, 1992.

William Goldman: *Magic,* Delacorte Press, 1976.

Peter Golenbock: *Wrigleyville,* St. Martin's Press, 1997.

Robert Goralski: *World War II Almanac,* Bonanza Books, 1984.

Barry Gottehrer: *The Giants of New York,* G.P. Putnam's Sons, 1963.

Richard C. Lindberg: *Quotable Chicago,* Loyola University Press, 1996.

John Miller and Genevieve Anderson: *Chicago Stories,* Chronicle Books, 1993.

Donald L. Miller: *City of the Century,* Simon & Schuster, 1997.

Bob Oates: *Football in America: Game of the Century,* Quality Sports, 1999.

Robert W. Peterson: *Pigskin: The Early Years of Pro Football,* Oxford University Press, 1997.

Richard Rainbolt: *Gold Glory,* Ralph Turtinen Publishing, 1972.

Howard Roberts: *The Chicago Bears,* Putnam, 1947.

Stevenson Swanson: *Chicago Days,* McGraw-Hill, 1997.

Jim Terzian: *New York Giants,* MacMillan, 1973.

Clyde "Bulldog" Turner: *Playing the Line,* Little Sports Library, 1948.

Richard Whittingham: *The Bears: A 75-year Celebration,* Taylor, 1994.

Richard Whittinghan: *What a Game They Played,* Fireside, 1984.

Joe Ziemba: *When Football Was Football,* Triumph Books, 1999.

# Index

CPSIA information can be obtained at www.ICGtesting.com
Printed in the USA
LVOW06s1123240414

383091LV00002B/337/P